The Anxious Brain

The Anxious Brain

The Neurobiological Basis of Anxiety Disorders and How to Effectively Treat Them

MARGARET WEHRENBERG, PSY.D.

STEVEN PRINZ, M.D.

W. W. Norton & Company
New York • London

All illustrations are by Jeremiah Cherwien.

All case examples used in this book are composites of actual clients for purposes of protecting confidentiality.

For information about permission to
reproduce selections from this book, write to
Permissions, W. W. Norton & Company, Inc.,
500 Fifth Avenue, New York, NY 10110

Composition by Pine Tree Composition
Manufacturing by R. R. Donnelley-Harrisonburg
Production Manger: Leeann Graham

Library of Congress Cataloging-in-Publication Data

Wehrenberg, Margaret.
   The anxious brain : the neurobiological basis of anxiety disorders and how to effectively treat them / Margaret Wehrenberg, Steven Prinz.
       p.   cm.
         "A Norton professional book."
         ISBN-13: 978-0-393-70512-6
         ISBN-10: 0-393-70512-9
         1. Anxiety—Physiological aspects. 2. Anxiety—Psychotherapy. I. Prinz, Steven. II. Title.

RC 531.A594 2007
616.85'22306—dc22   2006047314

ISBN 13: 978-0-393-70512-6
ISBN 10: 0-393-70512-9

W. W. Norton & Company, Inc., 500 Fifth Avenue, New York, N.Y. 10110
www.wwnorton.com

W. W. Norton & Company Ltd., Castle House, 75/76 Wells St., London W1T 3QT

0 9 8 7 6 5 4 3 2

For Fred and Marge Polzin. Thanks for creating and tending this brain.

—Margaret Wehrenberg

To my wife Deb and my three beautiful boys, Ryan, Scott, and Kyle. They are my continuous inspiration for all that I do. I love you!

—Steven Prinz

CONTENTS

ACKNOWLEDGMENTS

I may sit alone at the typewriter, but there have been many who have graciously and generously helped me to bring this book to publication. First of all, my editors, Michael McGandy and Andrea Costella, have been enormously helpful in shaping the work and getting me through the details. Casey Ruble did an outstanding job in copyediting, always improving what she worked on. Personal encouragement from Lurlene McDaniel and Mary-Lou Carney, fine writers both, gave me courage and practical advice from the beginning to the end. Steve Prinz, who worked together with me, gets a big dollop of appreciation for his contributions in getting these ideas to print. And finally, the incredible support of my (large!) family frees me from anxiety about taking new steps. Throughout my life, they have been my safety net so that failure is no threat and success is shared joy. Thank you each and all for the different and necessary ways you love me, help me, and celebrate with me.

Preface

Jon came into my office with a thick file folder and told me he was sure he had been misdiagnosed by his medical doctor, who had suggested he suffered from attention-deficit disorder and avoidant personality disorder. After researching his symptoms on the Internet, Jon concluded that he had social phobia, and he wanted me to treat him. He handed me his folder of downloads, apparently assuming I needed to be educated about anxiety, as none of the therapists he had seen since he was 12 had ever considered these diagnoses. As Jon began to talk about his symptoms, it became clear that there was a lifelong history of anxiety: panic, social anxiety, generalized anxiety, and a subsequent depression that was situationally induced when his wife left him due to his social anxiety. Jon had indeed discovered a key to his condition that his doctors had not identified. However, it was also clear that he had no idea what the underlying causes of his anxieties were, and he had been unable to apply the treatments he read about in his research.

CLIENT EXPECTATIONS AND THE TREATMENT OF ANXIETY

As the story of Jon illustrates, it is no longer uncommon for clients to enter therapy with ideas about their condition. Between watching late-night drug ads and doing Internet research, many people have a good sense of what disorders they may have before they seek therapy. This is both positive and negative as treatment gets underway. On the positive side, they are more likely to seek treatment because they know it is available. On the negative side, they are often more inclined to believe that drugs alone will cure them.

Self-diagnosis does not help people know why they have a disorder or what successful treatment will entail. They may have read that psychotherapy is a good idea, and they may know terms like *cognitive-behavioral* or *exposure and response,* but they do not fully comprehend these treatment methods or know how to apply them to their own situations. Therapy must expand and personalize the understanding of anxiety for people who, like Jon, are eager to know what their condition is and learn how to treat it.

Client expectations about psychotherapy may differ radically from the treatment clients actually need, because most people are unaware of the various causes of anxiety and do not understand what it will take to recover. Consider how different the course of treatment will be for a man who has a panic disorder caused by post-traumatic stress from childhood abuse versus a panic disorder in a 16-year-old girl that came "out of the blue" as she finished puberty. Some people will benefit from short-term symptom management; others will require longer treatments to heal trauma. Still others, like Jon, whose lives have been altered by anxiety over years, need time to develop more adaptive thoughts and behaviors to better interact with other people. Clients often have misconceptions about how fast they should get better. Educating them about their brain-based symptoms helps them understand why therapy takes time.

In this TV- and Internet-educated society, people still need psychotherapy to eliminate anxiety. Research on the Internet is no substitute for interpersonal feedback and cannot address individuals' questions about their particular situation. It also does nothing to eliminate people's irrational fears, which are a hallmark of anxiety disorders.

For example, Jennifer, a 20-year-old secretary, finally confessed in a session that she was convinced that her drinks could be poisoned if she left them at the bar while she went to the ladies' room. She could not leave a glass unattended on a restaurant table and then drink from it when she returned. Replacing her beverages was sometimes embarrassing and expensive. But worse, Jennifer thought this irrational fear meant she was seriously mentally ill. Her fear of poisoning seemed crazy, but it was still real and powerful.

Internet research would not have helped Jennifer because she had no way of knowing whether her fear was caused by serious mental illness or by more treatable anxiety. She needed feedback from a therapist who could respond specifically to her situation and reassure her that such irrational fears are common and very treatable. She also appreciated knowing they are a result of brain function as well as life experience. That knowledge gave her a start on interrupting the symptom's hold on her. She said, "I'm so glad I know this is my brain going haywire. I thought I was crazy." Just as Jennifer needed to know she was not crazy in order to begin treatment, many people need to know what their symptoms mean and why our treatments might help.

UNDERSTANDING THE BRAIN

New information about the complexity of the brain has proved that mental disorders develop from the complex interaction of neurobiology and life experiences. Advances in understanding brain structure and function have forever changed how we look at behavior. We are learning how neuro transmitter activity shapes experience as well as records it. We know without doubt that nature and nurture are interdependent processes in development of identity, personality, and mental health.

The new brain science can tell us about how our methods will affect an anxious brain and change the symptoms we want to eliminate. It makes our methods more effective. How do we learn the implications of this new research? Most of us do not have the fundamental language of the neuroscience field nor the training to understand the research methodologies being used. For the majority of clinicians who studied the brain in training to do psychotherapy, neurophysiology was more of a sidebar than a focus of learning. A few great integrative thinkers like Daniel Siegel, Allan Schore, and Candace Pert have been seriously looking at how this flood of neuroscience helps us to understand the psyche and mind/body. Their stunning ability to draw together work across the wide field of neuroscience, including their own research and clinical work, has contributed enormously to making psychotherapy interventions more targeted. Reading their work is worth the effort for those who seek a deep understanding of the physical brain and its interaction with psychological development.

But how can we clinicians in the daily practice of psychotherapy find the time to educate ourselves about this sophisticated work and apply it to our practice? In this book, we lay out the practical implications recent research on anxiety disorders has for psychotherapy. We describe brain structure and function in simple, relevant terms so that people can better understand why they are anxious and how psychotherapy can change their brains. This knowledge is an important part of making therapy for anxious people more effective.

AN OVERVIEW OF THIS BOOK

This book begins with a generalized discussion about how the "anxious brain" causes various types of anxiety disorders and how treatment can be used to both manage symptoms and address the underlying problems causing the anxiety. Chapters 1 and 2 describe the physical brain and the role neurotransmitters play in generating anxiety. The book goes on to examine three distinct types of anxiety: panic disorder, generalized anxiety disorder, and social anxiety disorder. Separate chapters are dedicated to the brain-based origins of each disorder, the psychological treatment of the disorders, and the medications for symptoms of the disorders. Differences in symptom expression and treatment methods for different ages are highlighted throughout the book.

The psychotherapeutic treatment methods build on each other throughout the book. For example, certain methods for treating panic disorder can be used for treating other anxiety disorders because they decrease physiological arousal—a condition that affects all people with anxiety. Descriptions of both psychotherapeutic and pharmacological treatment methods are augmented by case examples derived from composites of clients we have treated.

Our decision to separate chapters on medication from those on psychotherapy treatment was motivated by a desire to make the book more readable and easy to reference. We do not want to imply that medication and psychotherapy are independent. Many people in psychotherapy do best when medication is used simultaneously. Therapists and psychiatrists working in close coordination with each other provide the best integrated treatment.

Our goal in writing this book was to integrate research on neurobiology and psychotherapeutic treatment of anxiety disorders and present it in a practical, down-to-earth way for mental health clinicians. Although new research continually adds to the compendium of knowledge about the brain and psychological disorders, we have structured the book in a way that allows you to integrate new information as it becomes available. It is our hope that this book will help readers learn how an anxious brain generates symptoms and how treatment methods can be used to control symptoms and eventually calm the brain.

The Anxious Brain

INTRODUCTION

How necessary is anxiety treatment? Statistics from Kessler, Chiu, Demler, and Walters's (2005) comorbidity study indicate that nearly 26% of adult Americans suffer from anxiety in any given year. Of those, approximately 2.7% have panic disorder (PD), about 3.1% have generalized anxiety disorder (GAD), and about 6.8% have social anxiety disorder (SAD) (National Institute of Mental Health, 2006). Other anxiety disorders include post-traumatic stress disorder (PTSD), obsessive-compulsive disorder (OCD), specific phobia, and agoraphobia.

Anxiety disorders are frequently comorbid with several psychological complaints, including other anxiety disorders. People with GAD have PD in about 25% of cases, and 15–30% of people with PD also have SAD. (The wide range of this percentage may reflect that panic attacks can induce social anxieties.) A whopping 50% of people with panic and generalized anxiety also suffer from depression. Some personality disorders tend to be linked to anxiety. For example, avoidant personalities are susceptible to social anxiety, obsessive-compulsive personalities are prone to generalized anxiety, and borderline personalities are vulnerable to PD (and possibly to all forms of anxiety, considering their likelihood of having post-traumatic stress as well). Because these disorders tend to overlap, it is often necessary to treat multiple kinds of anxiety in the same person.

ANXIETY ACROSS DIFFERENT AGES

Children, adolescents, and elderly adults all suffer from anxiety disorders. Symptoms are quite similar across the various age groups, although clients' descriptions of symptoms vary with age and their ability to express themselves.

Estimates of how many children suffer anxiety vary widely, but most suggest that 8–11% of individuals will develop anxiety during childhood or adolescence. It is thought that if school refusal and childhood sleep problems were reported as anxiety, the overall numbers would be higher (Vasey & Dadds, 2001). At present there are no good criteria for looking at the overlap between anxiety and attention-deficit hyperactivity disorder (ADHD) or externalizing disorders such as oppositional defiant disorder. The overlap between these disorders and mood disorders may be significant.

How many children can be diagnosed at different ages depends on how the criteria are applied, as children naturally experience some anxiety appropriate to their developmental stage. For example, almost all small children have a fear of strangers or other phobias such as fear of the dark, and young adolescents suffer pangs of social embarrassment as they learn social skills. Young people may go through a stage when they technically meet the criteria for an anxiety disorder but grow out of the stage without difficulty and with no adverse affect on psychological development. Thus, when looking at demographics of children, it is important to distinguish between individuals experiencing normal developmental anxiety and those who suffer anxiety that persists across developmental stages or whose anxiety impairs their ability to achieve the goals of their social and academic activities. Whereas in adults and adolescents we look for debilitation, in children anxiety-related impairment may not be a loss of functioning so much as a failure to make expected progress.

Elderly adults also suffer anxiety due to significant life changes that entail loss or uncertainty, and they often adjust well when given sufficient information and support. However, times of crisis—illness, declining physical functioning, loss of spouse and friends—can trigger anxiety disorders even late in life. Elderly clients also may have a first onset of anxiety due to decrements in the levels of neurotransmitters in the aging brain. The slower pace of neurotransmitter production may make their responses to stress less effective or may create anxiety, but medication and psychotherapy can help correct these problems.

The elderly respond very well to the same techniques as adults (Ayers, Wetherell, Lenze, & Stanley, 2006; Blumenthal et al., 1999; Stanley, Hopko, & Diefenbach, 2003). The caveat seems to be the importance of coordinating services. "Too many cooks spoil the broth" is an adage that applies to treatment for the elderly. Having one primary clinician who coordinates psychological interventions and medical interventions and who facilitates information flow between service providers can help eliminate problems with medication interactions and confusion of services for the elderly adult.

TREATING THE ANXIOUS BRAIN

Today's mental health practitioners are in an unusual bind. We can effectively treat anxiety with the methods now available without knowing how those methods actually work. But the last decade of brain research, made possible by advances in brain imaging, has moved the understanding of anxiety disorders into a new dimension. The flood of new information improves our ability to treat people effectively, even if it is difficult to keep up with those advances.

Psychotherapists now know why it is *not* necessary to work on clients' underlying psychodynamic conflicts as a means to eliminate the symptomatology of generalized anxiety. We know why it *is* necessary to eliminate the impact of trauma. We see the power of medication to relieve overwhelming symptoms. Imaging research demonstrates how activity in specific regions of the brain contributes to different kinds of anxiety. Based on our current level of understanding, clinicians can diagnose brain function by behavioral and emotional symptoms. The most exciting direction in research is exploring the interaction between life experience and brain development—the foundation of psychological states (Amen, 2003; Pert, 1997; Schore, 2003; Siegel, 1999; van der Kolk, 1997).

Although we can successfully treat clients without knowing the implications of the research, we can be more effective with more people if we have a better grasp on how and why our treatment methods change brain function. This book provides both a compendium of the best techniques for treating anxiety disorders and an explanation of how they work to change the underlying neurobiology of the anxious brain.

The treatment methods we outline are described in the same order that actual treatment often progresses:

1. Address the aversive and intense physiology (the primary focus of panic treatment).
2. Manage the cognitions that continue to hold symptoms in place (the primary focus of generalized anxiety treatment).
3. Moderate avoidant behavior that has developed to diminish anxious symptoms but which also diminishes the quality of life (the primary focus of social anxiety treatment).

HOW THE BRAIN CAUSES ANXIETY

Underlying all the anxiety disorders is an anxious brain—a physical organ that is generating anxious thoughts and feelings. The anxious brain can lead a person to develop panic, generalized anxiety, or social phobia symptoms in the absence of any immediate or underlying psychological causes. Anxious brains develop due to:

- Heredity and genetics
- Trauma or stress that alters healthy brain function
- Physical conditions such as hormones, drugs, illness, or aging

How does the anxious brain create the state of anxiety? The anxious brain is an interactive brain. Scientists may identify specific functions of the physical organ of the brain, but when we refer to our "mind" or "psyche" we mean something more than just physical brain functioning. We all experience ourselves as a fluid state of mind and body without separation. Anxious people experience their brain as an unpleasant set of *sensations* (queasiness, dizziness, heart pounding) and *emotions* (tenseness, fear, dread, panic, and so on). People don't "feel" their brains, but rather feel an integrated experience of anxiety—a state that is at once physical, emotional, mental, and behavioral. It may be that people who develop anxiety have more sensitivity to that anxious state and feel strongly averse to it (McNally, 2002; Reiss, Silverman & Weems, 2001).

How do people respond to the anxious state? Anxiety states contribute to the development of mood and personality disorders. A person cannot feel such intense feelings and sensations without generating a response to them. No matter at what age the brain starts to produce anxiety, a person changes in relation to it. Life events or physical health may create the anxiety, but once the anxiety is experienced, responses to it are always patterns of avoidance intended to circumvent the anxious feelings. Those avoidance patterns may be solely mental, such as attempts not to think about or deal with topics that are anxiety-producing. They may be behavioral, such as avoiding school, avoiding crowds or restaurants, avoiding conflict, or avoiding the limelight of success at work. Eventually, personality, coping skills, social interactions, self-image, and even mental health or substance use are affected by anxiety in an interactive way. The physical state of anxiety and the emotional, mental, and behavioral states that develop in response to anxiety or that cause the anxiety become the criteria by which anxiety disorders and their comorbid conditions are diagnosed.

Treatment: Immediate Symptom Management, Ongoing Psychotherapy

Early symptom management creates the space to do the deeper work of therapy. The psychotherapy of anxiety uses practical interventions during the beginning stages of recovery (Ninan, Liebowitz, Dunlop, & Feigan, 2005). Treatment immediately targets symptom management and can progress rapidly. But symptom improvement is not a guarantee that anxiety will not recur. Life stressors can prompt a new cascade of symptoms. Preventing recurrence of anxiety means continuing to treat long enough that: (1) the anxious brain can change and heal itself, and (2) any other causes of the anxiety, such as underlying psychological dysfunction, can be addressed.

The management of symptoms is just the first step in the treatment of anxiety. When symptoms subside, people must then address any psychological origins of their anxiety that may exist, as they will continue to create anxiety if left untreated. Psychological origins may include:

- Unresolved effects of trauma
- Psychodynamic conflicts
- Skills deficits
- Personality disorders

Symptom management allows people to focus on psychotherapy for life events, traumas, personality factors, or developmental causes without having to deal with the distressing and distracting symptoms of anxiety. Because anxiety disorders tend to make a comeback under various stressors, effective long-term treatment must include a lifetime management plan to cope with anxiety should it recur.

A CAVEAT ABOUT BRAIN INFORMATION

New studies about the brain become available at an astounding rate, presenting a significant difficulty in writing about neurobiology. Each new piece of research may cause us to review former assumptions about how the brain operates. The potential for new information to invalidate former ideas always exists. For example, a new study may reveal that an often-researched neurotransmitter has a surprising interaction with another neurotransmitter, or demonstrate how a brain system responds differently to a medication than previously thought.

The most rapid shifts in understanding derive from medication research, and the neurobiological conceptualization of anxiety disorders has benefited from this research. A recent example of new information changing ideas about how neurotransmitters work and how medication changes them was a discovery in a study about the selective serotonin reuptake inhibitors (SSRIs), which have been prescribed in the United States since the late 1980s. Although some of the actions of SSRIs were understood, it was only recently discovered that they may stimulate growth of serotonin (SE) neurons (Korn & Pollack, 2002) and that action may be more responsible for their effects than reuptake inhibition. Other medications, such as the tricyclic antidepressants, have been utilized for decades. The use of these medications has not changed much, but research has helped us know when they are most effective and how to use them in augmentation regimens.

With every scientific advance, the understanding of how and why psychotherapy works has also developed. We now know that effective psychotherapy changes the brain (Amen, 2003; Roffman, Marci, Glick, Dougherty, & Rauch, 2005; Rossi, 1993; Schore, 2003; Schwartz, 1998; Siegel, 1999; Siegel & Hartzell, 2003; Stein, Hanna, Koverola, Torchia, & McClarty, 1997; van der Kolk, McFarlane, & Weisaeth, 1996). Like many medications, psychotherapy methods that have been used for many years are still effective. Now we know more about how they work and under what conditions they are most effective. New information about brain structure and function will undoubtedly contribute to the development of better psychotherapeutic treatment. However, current scientific knowledge is sufficient to provide an excellent basis on which to examine the underlying neurobiology of anxiety disorders and how to effectively treat them.

TEN REASONS WHY UNDERSTANDING
THE ANXIOUS BRAIN MAKES THERAPY WORK BETTER

How can knowing about the brain improve psychotherapy practice? Following are ten important outcomes of boosting our brain power about the brain.

Education improves treatment compliance. We have found that when people know *why* they are doing therapy techniques and understand *what can happen* if they follow the homework, they are more likely to comply with whatever regimen we lay out for them. Explaining what symptoms your technique is targeting and how it will accomplish the task of controlling the mind will improve your credibility with people who have experienced therapy failures. They will be more willing to give your ideas a chance if you explain the *why* of the technique.

Education creates a climate for success. Being able to explain how the brain functions in anxiety increases our credibility as experts in using our treatment methods. In the early stages of anxiety treatment, people want to lean on your expertise to solve their problem. They want to believe in your ability to help, and they want to believe in your vision of how they can succeed. Expecting success improves the chance of success. Your confidence in the potential of your methods, conveyed by explaining how symptoms will respond, increases clients' motivation and thus increases the likelihood that they will succeed.

Learning about the biochemistry of anxiety increases clients' ability to apply thought-management methods. This knowledge promotes an objectivity that is crucial to the correct application of thought-stopping and thought-replacement techniques.

It is important to tell people that brain function is not purely physical. Rather, the mind/body is one inseparable entity (Pert, 1997), and the mind is much more than just activity in the brain. The mind is a flow of information and energy, experienced both physically and emotionally (Siegel, 1999).

People tend to forget that the brain is a physical organ and that shifts in this physical organ show up as emotional or mental symptoms. Knowing that the physical brain can create a real feeling that something is "wrong" relieves people of the powerful tendency to go looking for reasons for why they have anxiety. Jeff Schwartz (1998), in his work with obsessive-compulsive disorder (OCD) patients, incorporated this idea in his method for stopping obsessions and compulsions. He taught people to notice an obsession, remember that their brain is producing a signal that is false, and then ignore it without giving it significance.

Many different methods may help people achieve such objectivity about their anxious symptoms. We strongly influence treatment outcome when we help people utilize the higher function of the brain (observing ego) to notice how their anxiety is flaring without reason.

Knowing how lifestyle affects brain function improves motivation for change. Clients are more likely to make lifestyle shifts if they understand how those shifts will change brain activity. You might explain, for example, that exercise causes increased blood flow to the brain, or that eating nutritious food provides fodder to make neurochemicals. When we ask clients to make lifestyle changes, we must back up our suggestions by explaining the brain outcome we anticipate.

Knowing which kind of brain activity might underlie a person's specific anxiety symptoms improves our ability to select methods to change those symptoms. Whether we are recommending medications or applying therapy methods, targeting a specific aspect of brain function will enhance our selection of treatment. This increases the likelihood that treatment will work. When one method helps, people become more likely to try other methods we suggest for homework or lifestyle changes. It's a win-win situation.

Knowing about the brain increases people's patience with their rate of change. Many people have tried what I call "Nike therapy" to push past anxiety symptoms: They want to "Just Do It." When their quick-fix approach fails, they feel discouraged and helpless. We must explain to clients that although it takes very little time to learn how to do a symptom-management method, it takes a long time to eliminate the sensations. I often tell people, "Treatment is simple. It just is not easy." When people know they are working on a process that will *gradually* alter brain function in a natural way, they don't blame themselves for slow change. They learn that they are training their brains, just as they would train muscles for a marathon—a little at a time.

Learning about the brain causes of anxiety lessens self-condemnation. Prior to talking about their symptoms, people develop ideas about why they have the symptoms. These often include pejorative interpretations regarding themselves or others and misunderstandings about why they have symptoms. Attributing anxiety to brain functioning helps clients get past the self-blame that stunts therapeutic improvement.

Understanding brain functioning helps psychotherapists make better referrals for medication and improves their communication with the doctors who prescribe medication. Psychotherapists will be more clear about what benefits people can get from the medication and why it is helpful to psychotherapy.

Knowing how anxiety affects psychological development and interferes with learning allows therapists to assess for missing skills and identify experiences that affect overall psychological function. This allows us to make better referrals to outside sources for training in areas such as social skills, job or interviewing skills, conflict management, assertiveness skills, parenting skills, and public speaking.

Education improves our overall effectiveness. Our highest aspiration is to improve our clients' welfare. Working to the best standards of professional care enhances not only the well-being of our clients, but our own well-being as individual clinicians and as a profession.

This last reason—promoting the well-being of those who suffer with anxiety—is at the heart of this book. Knowledge is power. Enhancing knowledge of what causes people to be anxious and why treatment methods work will give people more power to conquer their anxiety.

CHAPTER ONE

THE PHYSICAL BRAIN
AND THE MIND OF ANXIETY

There is no longer any doubt that symptoms of anxiety originate in neurobi-ological functions. There is also no doubt that we can intentionally *use* our brains to *change* our brains. You may wonder, "How hard is it to deliberately change your brain?" Take a deep breath. (Really—take a nice, deep breath and release it slowly.) In that simple act, you just demonstrated why psy-chotherapy works for anxiety symptoms. In deciding to take a deep breath, you thought about breathing and used that thought to control the otherwise unconscious function of breathing. Put another way, by utilizing one of the executive functions (decision-making) of your prefrontal cortex (PFC), you allowed your PFC to override your medulla to change your respiration.

There are many techniques that allow us to use our brains to change our brains. Effective anxiety treatment includes learning not only *how* to do these techniques but also *why* to do them. This maximizes their efficacy and fosters compliance with trying the techniques. This chapter on brain structure and function and the next on neurotransmitters are intended to provide enough brain basics to make your explanations about how therapy works to change the brain clear and helpful.

THE PHYSICAL BRAIN: TWO HEMISPHERES

As seen in Figure 1.1, the brain is divided into two hemispheres. Although the structures of the brain are symmetrical between the left and right sides, the functions they serve are lateralized (performed more on one side than

9

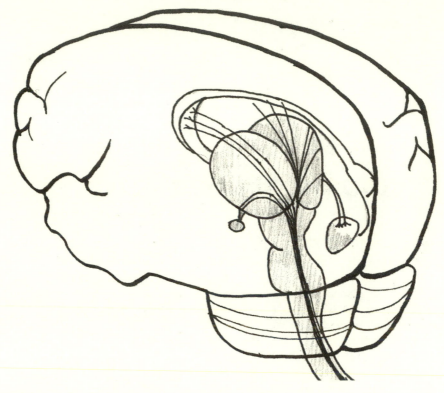

FIGURE 1.1.   A transparent view of the two hemispheres of the brain, and their relationship to the limbic system.

the other) to efficiently process information and create physical, mental, and emotional responses.

Left Hemisphere

This side of the brain is where verbal work and making meaning of experience occur: categorizing, problem-solving, and analysis. The left brain organizes information, makes sequences, and comprehends time in conjunction with activities or events, putting events in sequential order and placing them in time. Thus, people know that an event is over and done, they can recall when in the course of their lives an event occurred, and they remember that certain tasks must be performed in specific sequences. In the left hemisphere the brain forms symbols (language and math) for experience, and it creates explanations and meanings for experience. It plays a role in inhibiting the activity of the right hemisphere, which deals with emotion, by moderating the emotional information coming from that part of the brain. In this way the left brain can mediate memory and the non-verbal, emotional responsiveness of the right-sided structures.

Right Hemisphere

This side of the brain is specialized for nonverbal recognition and emotional memory, both of which are vital for quick and accurate responses to the world around us. The right hemisphere is responsible for recognizing faces, reading emotion, and assessing the emotional significance of an event in conjunction with data from the senses, which it interprets. The right hemisphere has a strong role in creativity and nonverbal problem-solving, creating novel responses to both practical and emotional situations. The right hemisphere sees spatial relationships and listens for and creates cadence and rhythm in speech, movement, music, and so on. It also regulates the nervous system and hormonal responses coming in from the senses.

REGIONS OF THE BRAIN FROM A "TOP-DOWN" PERSPECTIVE

Although the brain functions as a whole, we can examine the primary work of each region. Starting with the outer (top) layers of the brain and moving to the inner structures, we will describe the activities that affect psychological functioning. In Figure 1.2, these regions are shown in a side view of the brain, seen as if the right half is removed so the inner regions are visible.

The Cerebral Cortex

The cortex is the outer layer of the brain that contains the capacities for analysis and abstract thought. The cortex receives messages from all the parts of the brain and maintains executive control of other parts of the brain. The front of the cortex, on both left and right hemispheres, has three primary divisions:

- The *motor cortex,* which mediates motor activity
- The *premotor cortex,* which plans complex motor activity
- The *prefrontal cortex* (PFC), which conducts executive reasoning

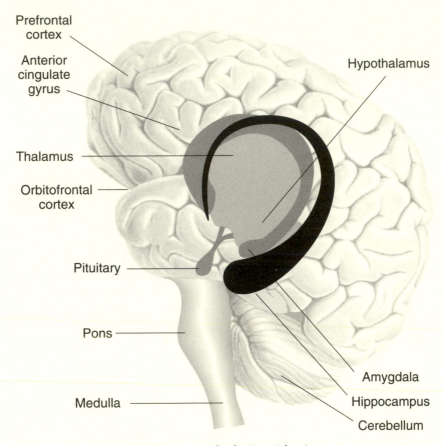

Prefrontal cortex

Anterior cingulate gyrus

Hypothalamus

Thalamus

Orbitofrontal cortex

Pituitary

Pons

Amygdala

Medulla

Hippocampus

Cerebellum

FIGURE 1.2.   The brain, side view.

The Prefrontal Cortex

The PFC is critical for sequencing behavior. With the motor and sensory cortex, it integrates motor activity and speech with recent sensory information, and it communicates in all the pathways that both plan motor activity and carry it out. It handles working memory, which is the temporary holding and manipulating of information necessary to do daily tasks such as dial a phone number or remember how much salt to add to a recipe. The PFC does not finish its development until mid-adolescence, and it is not until the mid-twenties that full, efficient operation of this part of the brain is achieved (Walsh, 2004). The PFC has two subdivisions of major interest in discussing anxiety, due to their impact on assessing and controlling anxiety symptoms.

- The *orbitofrontal cortex* (OFC), which controls working memory
- The *anterior cingulate gyrus* (ACG), which filters and amplifies information from lower regions to and from the prefrontal cortex

These two regions will be discussed more fully later in this chapter.

The Corpus Callosum

The corpus callosum is the nerve bundle that connects the two hemispheres. It is vital for integrated thought, feeling, and action. The corpus callosum thus has an impact on temperamental reactions. It functions directionally in communication between hemispheres, with information funneling toward and from the left PFC.

The Subcortical Brain

The parts of the region surrounded by the cortex, the subcortical brain, that are especially relevant to anxiety include the basal ganglia (BG). Ganglia are concentrated groupings of neurons forming nuclei. The BG are comprised of several nuclei: the ventral striatum (caudate, putamen, nucleus accumbens, pallidum, and olfactory tubercle), the dorsal striatum (caudate and putamen), and the globus pallidus. The BG are part of the subcortical systems that integrate behavior with drive and motivation, regulate emotion expression and impulse control, and mediate executive cognition. They strongly affect arousal and energy. They connect between the thalamus and the cortex for regulation of cognition and mood, attention or vigilance, and motivation.

The Limbic System

The term *limbic system* comes from the Latin word for "ring" and refers to the structures that ring the upper part of the brainstem. The parts of this system play separate and important roles, but they function together to regulate emotion and memory. These structures integrate incoming stimuli and initiate rapid, autonomic (involuntary) responses to stimuli without the intervention of cognition. They create context for sensory information.

The concept of these connected structures in the brain was developed over many years. The limbic system was initially considered to be the deep, central brain structures of the amygdala, hippocampus, thalamus, and hypothalamus. Now many expand this system to include the anterior cingulate gyrus (ACG) and the orbitofrontal cortex (OFC), both of which are technically part of the prefrontal cortex (PFC). The limbic system may also include the subcortical structures of the ventral striatum (including the nucleus accumbens) and the connecting structures between them, including the fornix and the stria terminalis.

For the purpose of differentiating aspects of function as we discuss how the brain generates anxiety, we will consider the anterior cingulate gyrus (ACG) and the orbitofrontal cortex (OFC) to be connecting regions between the limbic system and the prefrontal cortex (PFC). As we discuss the etiology of anxiety disorders, the parts of the limbic system that are of greatest interest are:

- The *amygdala,* which is responsible for recognizing changes in the environment and assigning positive or negative emotional valence to the stimuli. It communicates with the other structures of the limbic system to alert the brain to danger and communicate the immediate need for response to external changes or events. The amygdala could be called the brain's "early warning system."
- The *hippocampus,* which has a critical role in memory storage and retrieval. It is part of the behavioral inhibitory system, a system postulated by Gray (1995) to facilitate withdrawal in the face of anxiety-provoking stimuli. The hippocampus stores short-term details of events without interpretation or emotional tone. It is memory's "Joe Friday" ("just the facts, ma'am").
- The *thalamus,* which is the main relay station for the brain. It relays sensory information from the outside world directly to the amygdala to identify importance. It relays information from and to the cortex and between most parts of the brain. The thalamus also is involved in the regulation of brain waves.
- The *hypothalamus,* which is the relay station for the *internal* regulatory system. It monitors information about the functioning of the organs, including reading the blood for oxygen and glucose levels, monitoring all information from the autonomic nervous system, and commanding the body through those nerves and the pituitary gland.

The Pituitary Gland

The pituitary is often called "the master gland." It directs activity in the endocrinological system, which produces secretions in the body. The pituitary is important to the function of the stress response system because it alerts the adrenal cortex to release the glucocorticoids (especially adrenalin and cortisol) in response to a stress signal.

The Pons

The pons (bridge) is the connection between the lower brain and the mid-brain. One part of the pons, the locus coeruleus, has a dense concentration of norepinephrine (NE) and thereby affects physical arousal, including blood pressure, and is responsible for the heightened physical arousal in anxiety. Nuclei within the pons are important in rapid eye movement (REM) sleep.

The Medulla

The medulla is the primitive brain, the "Energizer bunny" that keeps everything ticking even when the rest of the brain is not conscious to the outside world. It controls respiration and heart rate.

The Cerebellum

The cerebellum is responsible for body and limb position, relating to balance, posture, walking, and so on. It plays a significant role in integrating information. The functions of the cerebellum are not yet completely understood. It contains as many neurons as the cortex and connects to so many other parts of the brain that the importance of its functions are probably greater than currently known. It is assumed that the cerebellum plays important roles in dreaming, memory, and other functions.

THE NERVOUS SYSTEM

The nervous system is responsible for sensing and reacting to the environment and for coordinating the functions of body organs. The central nervous system (CNS) includes the brain and the spinal cord as well as the peripheral nervous system (PNS) and the autonomic nervous system (ANS).

The Peripheral Nervous System

The peripheral nervous system (PNS) affects the heart and the muscles and directs communication between the organ of the skin and the brain. The skin is vital for receiving data about the external environment and the safety of the body. Changes in pressure, temperature, and so on immediately cause both conscious and automatic adjustments to the environment. People with anxiety are often too aware of minor changes, which they interpret as symptom onset (for example, they might interpret the feel of a draft of air as a "chill of anxiety"). Also, norepinephrine (NE) activates the PNS, in turn activating heart, muscles, and extremities. As NE rises, so does heart rate and blood pressure, and anxious symptoms such as sweating, flushing, and tremor occur.

The Autonomic Nervous System

The autonomic nervous system (ANS) enervates and controls the action of all internal organs. It has three parts:

- The *sympathetic nervous system* (SNS), which is responsible for the arousal of the brain and body. It is particularly important in creating the physical responses of anxiety, including initiating arousal under stress and trauma.
- The *parasympathetic nervous system* (PSNS), which inhibits arousal. It restores balance to internal organs and stress response systems. Many therapy methods for anxiety aim at triggering or enhancing parasympathetic activity.
- The *diffuse enteric nervous system,* which controls digestion and peristaltic action (the "rippling" movement of the digestive track).

THE ANXIOUS BRAIN AND THE CORTEX

The prefrontal cortex (PFC) in both hemispheres has significance in the development and treatment of anxiety disorders. Tasks of the PFC include processing information, maintaining conscious attention, and forming behavioral responses. The work of the PFC also includes making meaning of sensory information. A lower part of the PFC, the orbitofrontal cortex (OFC), is, as noted earlier, involved in working memory and the consolidation of long term memory. Working memory holds pieces of information just long enough to use them to complete tasks of everyday mental functioning. The OFC also compares information with other data, such as anxious emotions generated by the limbic system with other signs of potential risk. The anterior cingulate gyrus (ACG) is the lowest part of the PFC and connects directly to the structures of the limbic system. In the ACG information is filtered and amplified. When the ACG is too rigid or "stuck" on a piece of incoming data from the limbic system, flexible thought and problem-solving is compromised and anxiety rises. Then the overall control that might be exerted by the PFC over anxious states is diminished.

The Left Prefrontal Cortex

The left PFC is the verbal side of the brain where analysis and synthesis of information occur. Language and mathematic functions are performed dominantly on the left side of the brain in the temporal lobe. It is the left PFC that does the work of putting words to emotional experience. The OFC in this hemisphere is integral to encoding memory. After a person is about 4 years old, the left PFC, with its executive decision-making and interpretive functions, predominates over other brain areas, including the right PFC (Figure 1.3).

The left PFC is the target of cognitive-behavioral therapy in treating anxiety disorders. It can be used to consciously, intentionally control emotional states—to "talk down" a heightened emotional state, think about emotions, and decide how to handle them. Thus, it is significant to the quieting of anxiety states. The left PFC is also the site for planning for how to handle problems, which is the antithesis of worry, so it can circumvent worried states. Table 1.1 outlines the many functions of the left PFC that affect anxiety.

With consistent, persistent, consciously intended activity, the left PFC exerts control on lower cortical and other brain structures, and it can slow neural activity. It can even decide how to increase blood flow to itself and carry out the plan. That is essentially what happens when a person makes a decision to get some exercise and then goes outside to do so.

Good PFC function requires sufficient energy. When energy is insufficient, medications may help, as will physical interventions through nutrition, sleep, and other means.

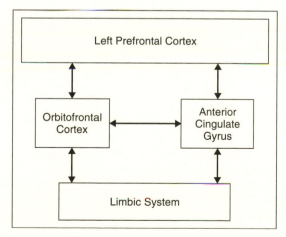

FIGURE 1.3.   The left prefrontal cortex interacts with the limbic system.

TABLE 1.1 The Activities of the Left Prefrontal Cortex and Anxiety

Function of the Left Prefrontal Cortex	Relevance to Anxiety Disorders
Analyze information	Incorrect assessment of situations leads to anxiety. Improving this function helps clients gain new perspectives.
Synthesize experience and information	Cognitive-behavioral therapy targets this ability to change perceptions of anxiety-producing events.
Plan and prepare to execute plans, including motoric plans	Allows the brain to recognize the necessity of therapy homework and carry it out.
Understand time and place events into sequence	The effects of trauma disturb this function. Therapy can correct for it.
Create procedures from information	This ability allows therapy to break anxious experiences into segments so small steps for progress can be planned. This is important in creating anxiety symptom hierarchies for desensitization and for planning in vivo exposure.
Interpret experience and modulate emotional states	This ability has a direct influence in stopping anxious reactions caused by lower brain regions.
Concentrate and purposefully attend to the environment	This allows for objective observation, important in recognizing triggers for anxiety and in desensitizing.
Purposefully direct inner experience, including physical functions like respiration	This makes it possible to trigger parasympathetic calming.
Controlling impulses and deciding how best to meet needs	People can draw on this function to stay in an anxiety-provoking circumstance, perform calming functions, and relearn how to decrease fear.
Make goals and plans to attain goals	The decision to act in counterintuitive ways to the feeling of anxiety is vital to initiating therapy and following recommendations.

TABLE 1.1 (continued)	
Function of the Left Prefrontal Cortex	**Relevance to Anxiety Disorders**
Analyze obstacles and assess failures. Improvise revised solutions to attain goals	This function is vital in therapy to assess what stops people from releasing anxious reactions to events.
Create structure for use of time and activity without external control	This function is most important in motivation and creating structure. Without a sense of internal organization people tend to feel more anxious.

The Right Prefrontal Cortex

The right PFC is specialized for nonverbal functions. The "language" of the right temporal lobe is a language of melody, physical gesture, and facial expressions. The right PFC, and especially the OFC, are vital to the retrieval of memory. The right PFC handles spatial recognition, which is crucial in all nonverbal problem-solving. Problems that might stem from poor functioning of the right PFC include:

- Nonverbal learning disabilities
- Poor rhythm and coordination of body moving through space
- Social fear
- Social ineptness
- Impaired ability to modulate or interpret social cues or plan nonverbal responses

Table 1.2 on the following page highlights how functions of the right PFC affect anxiety.

What Cortical Blood Flow Shows About Brain Activity in Anxiety

Cortical blood flow is a measure of activity in the brain. When people are in an anxious state, blood flow to the left PFC is diminished. In cases of extremely heightened anxiety, as in post-traumatic stress disorder (PTSD), right PFC blood flow may be increased (Bergman, 1998; Siegel, 1999; Stein et al., 1997). This implies that the left PFC has a role in modulating negative emotional arousal. When the left PFC is active (has good blood flow) it can calm the anxiety generated from excess activity in the limbic system. When blood flow in the left PFC is diminished, it has less control over the limbic

TABLE 1.2 The Activities of the Right Prefrontal Cortex and Anxiety

Function of the Right Prefrontal Cortex	Relevance to Anxiety Disorders
Recognize people by their faces and recognize meaning of facial expression	Overreaction to negative faces causes social anxiety and may trigger panic.
Recognize and interpret others' emotions via tone (melody) of voice, posture, and gesture	Overreaction to negative implications of tone or gesture or previous sensitization to risk associated with specific looks or tone may cause anxiety.
Coordinate emotional relevance with information about previous life experience (i.e., recognize, interpret, and modulate information with the right-sided limbic structures)	The lower-right hemisphere structures specialize in appraisal of risk and warning of risk. The right prefrontal cortex assists in interpreting stimuli and coordinating the feeling of risk (i.e., creating anxiety states).

system, allowing anxiety to build and cognitions to become more negative. Heightened blood flow in the right PFC occurs when emotions are intense and nonverbal information is being registered. The left PFC can modulate that heightened arousal, but only when it has enough energy or blood flow to do so.

The Orbitofrontal Cortex

The orbitofrontal cortex (OFC) is an area of the PFC that is sometimes called *paralimbic* and is closely connected to the limbic system. It is highly involved in regulation of mood and behavior, especially in regulating impulses. Thus it plays a major role in personality (personality being defined as the typical patterns of behavior, cognition, and emotion seen in one's personal expression and interpersonal interactions). The ways in which a person may control mood, express emotion, or show self-control are activities of the OFC and are what psychotherapists evaluate to diagnose psychopathology.

This part of the cortex has connections from and to the amygdala and the thalamus and sends those signals forward to other areas of the PFC via the temporal lobes. It encodes information from the environment and can link it with bodily representations of experience. It is also involved in retrieval of information (Siegel, 1999). It shifts signals between the PFC and the limbic system to regulate emotional tone and physical responses to the environmental information. This means that the OFC is central to connecting motivation and cognition. Figure 1.4 illustrates how the OFC compares emotional context with information and memory and connects the PFC to limbic structures.

When this part of the brain is damaged or is over- or underfunctioning, behavior and personality problems appear, such as difficulty suppressing urges or impulses, controlling obsessive thoughts, and diminishing negative moods. Hypoactivity in the OFC has been linked to secondary depression, but the types of mood problems that typically are related to damage in the OFC more often include mood lability, poor impulse control, and inappropriate behavior or social judgment.

The Anterior Cingulate Gyrus

The ACG is a bridge between the limbic structures and prefrontal cortex (PFC). It makes connections for processing emotional, sensory, cognitive, and motor information. It has close neuronal connections to the

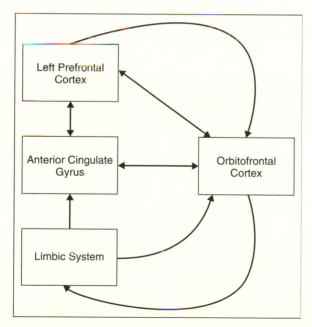

FIGURE 1.4.   Activity of the orbitofrontal cortex.

reward/pleasure center of the brain, the nucleus accumbens (NAc), which is part of the basal ganglia (BG). From the NAc, activities and relationships are imbued with desirable emotional tone, and motivation to participate in the activity or be in relationship to a person depends on that positive emotion tone (reward).

Through that connection to the NAc, the ACG is a vital link to the PFC. It helps the PFC to recognize and feel motivation and to direct activity toward goals. Motivation is a primary factor in new learning—we learn what is useful, important, or desirable to remember. By connecting reward and emotion with the hippocampus (the brain part key to short-term memory), the ACG connects details with emotional tone (Figure 1.5). It also connects to the orbitofrontal cortex (OFC) to transfer data from the limbic structures to assist in the comparative and working memory functions of that region. Then it transfers that information to the PFC, where executive functions of analysis, synthesis, and long-term memory occur. It connects PFC conscious attention and limbic motivation (Figure 1.6). Lack of activity in the ACG would result in apathy.

An essential function of the ACG is shifting between cognition and emotion. The ease and flexibility with which the ACG transfers its integrated information affects the ease with which humans develop new solutions to problems of both verbal and nonverbal natures. It is thus linked to creative process and to cognitive flexibility. In other words, when one way of thinking or behaving is not working well, the ACG plays a role in finding a new direction to pursue. When there is healthy ACG function, one sees behavioral qualities of cooperation and adaptability, both of which are important aspects of negotiation and conflict resolution. When there is the right amount of neuronal activity in the ACG, a person can see options and move from one idea to another with ease.

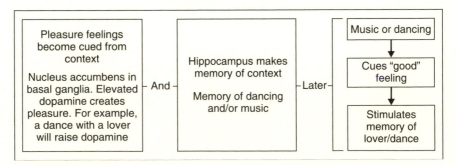

FIGURE 1.5.   Pleasure feelings become cued from context.

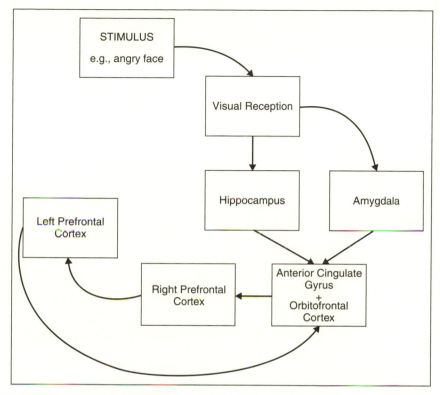

FIGURE 1.6. Pathway between emotional stimulus and left prefrontal cortex.

The Overactive Anterior Cingulate Gyrus

When the ACG is overactive, the anxious brain emerges. Instead of shifting smoothly from one idea to another or viewing problems as having many possible solutions, the ACG ruminatively holds onto hurts or mistakes. It creates worrying by looping negative thoughts instead of shifting them. When the ACG is highly overactive behavior may become oppositional, because the first connection it makes between emotion and cognition gets stuck and does not shift smoothly to another, preferable option. Argumentative behavior may result. Consider what may happen when a child with an overactive ACG interacts with a parent making a request. When the parent says it is time to get ready to go to Grandma's, the child's first emotion is "no!" because it means stopping the current fun activity. When the overactive ACG gets stuck on the "no", the prefrontal cortex (PFC) will have a harder time communicating back to the limbic system information about why "yes" might have a better result. The following case example illustrates this problem.

Thirteen-year-old Abby was highly anxious and also oppositional. Her parents offered her a later bedtime on the weekend if she agreed to complete her chores by noon on Saturday. Abby's first response was "No! I don't want to clean my room!" because her initial thought was that she did not want to have to do the work. She couldn't get to the second thought, "If I get it over with by noon, I'll get a reward," which would have correctly connected positive motivation with clear cognition for good problem-solving. The ACG was not smoothly making the connection between the second motivation, desire for a reward, because the first motivation of not working was more powerful, got stuck, and wouldn't give way due to excessive activity in the ACG. It took time, patience, and careful distraction to allow Abby to come around to a more positive solution. If her parents had dug in and pushed on her first response, she would only have become more oppositional or argumentative. This is because the hyperactivity in the ACG needs to cool a little to the first "no!" in order to get to the second motivation, desire for reward.

THE ANXIOUS BRAIN AND THE SUBCORTICAL STRUCTURES

Several structures of the subcortical brain play separate but interrelated roles in generating anxious symptoms. Each contributes specific qualities of anxiety, but dysfunction in one structure may trigger dysfunction in other structures of the subcortical and cortical regions.

The Basal Ganglia

The basal ganglia (BG) are dense with dopamine receptors. Dopamine (DA) is the neurotransmitter associated with feeling reward, interest, and motivation. For this reason, the BG have a significant impact on overall energy for work, interest in social experience, desire to achieve personal goals, and energetic tone in general. Dan Amen (1998, 2003) called the BG "the idle" of the brain, setting the general level of energy for all mental and physical tasks. The BG are highly implicated in the anxiety disorders for different reasons, depending on which part of the BG is considered. Spontaneous, kindling activity can trigger panic, and constant overarousal sets the tone of generalized anxiety.

The BG are connected to the cortex and to the lower regions of the brain (Figure 1.7). They receive information directly from the cortex and communicate to the thalamus, which in turn is connected directly back to the cor-

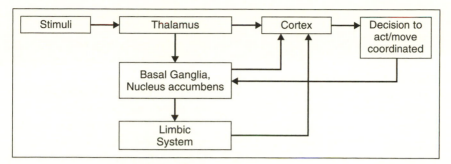

FIGURE 1.7.   Basal ganlia connections.

tex. The nucleus accumbens (NAc) in the BG receives and sends information to the cortex and directly communicates with the various parts of the
limbic system. It plays an especially significant role in the experience of
pleasure (a profound motivator!) and also in PTSD, as is discussed later.
The NAc is the site that receives dopamine (DA) signals of reward, but it is
also an area rich in opiate receptors, a factor that plays a role in feeling that
movements and thoughts are complete. Figure 1.8 illustrates how the BG
reacts to DA to stimulate motivation.

High levels of neuronal activity in the BG are related to general tension
and high drive. There are many gamma aminobutyric acid (GABA) neurons
in this region. GABA is a neurotransmitter that tones down activity in the
brain. When GABA fails to properly diminish neuron firing in the BG, several consequences occur:

- *Emotional and cognitive negativity.* Excess arousal of limbic and basal
  ganglia areas cause emotional and cognitive negativity, as seen in the
  anxious tendency to predict the worst possible outcome of a situation.
- *Irritability and aggression.* People with anger-management problems
  usually have a high tension level (a result of overactivity in the BG),
  which translates into irritability and a quick temper. Anxiety thus may
  underlie aggression.

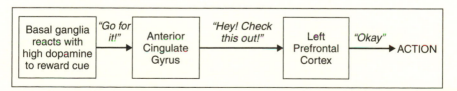

FIGURE 1.8.   Dopamine stimulations motivation.

- *High reactivity.* When people are tense, they may constantly feel a high degree of overall arousal. They may startle more easily or react strongly to small changes or stressors. People with high baseline tension levels are often described as "up tight" or "wired." It does not take much to trip their wire and send them into states of anxiety, aggression, or negativity.
- *Shakiness and panic attacks.* The BG are very important in motor control and thus may be involved in the motoric shaking accompanying social anxiety, as the body prepares to respond physically to threat. Erratic firing of neurons in the BG, a mild seizurelike activity resulting from problems with GABA function, triggers panic attacks.

THE ANXIOUS BRAIN AND THE LIMBIC SYSTEM

As noted earlier, the limbic system is comprised of the thalamus and hypothalamus, the hippocampus and amygdala, and the connecting structures. It may also be considered to extend to the anterior cingulate gyrus (ACG) and the orbitofrontal cortex (OFC), because the direct connections to and from the cortex through those structures are the sites of emotion recognition and modulation. This is the emotional brain, and it supplies necessary information about the importance of whatever happens so the prefrontal cortex (PFC) has a context for understanding the significance of new sensory data.

How the Limbic System Generates Fear, Worry, and Negativity

When the limbic system is overactive, emotional things seem too important—too frightening, threatening, negative, difficult, or unattainable. The limbic system may be severely deficient in serotonin (SE) or may have enlarged structures causing an overemphasis on whatever is negative. It essentially filters experience for what is negative, alerting the rest of the brain to threat even when the actual threat level is low. Each part of the limbic system plays a role in generating anxiety. Table 1.3 summarizes the various activities of the limbic structures that pertain to anxiety.

The Thalamus

The thalamus is the relay station for incoming information from the external world. It is connected by only one synapse to the amygdala, where instantaneous evaluation is made of the sensory information. The thalamus also relays the information to the prefrontal cortex (PFC), but the connecting pathway is literally longer, so the amygdala gets thalamic input first. The PFC gets both direct data about the nature of the stimuli and its con-

TABLE 1.3   The Activities of the Limbic System and Anxiety

Function of the Limbic System	Relevance to Anxiety Disorders
Thalamus: Processes external stimuli and relays it to cortex, hypothalamus, and amygdala	The instantaneous connection of incoming stimuli to other parts of the system may trigger panic or anxiety. Brainwave activity may lead to sleep and appetite problems typical of anxiety.
Hypothalamus: Processes internal stimuli and initiates stress response	Oversensitivity or overproduction of corticotrophin release factor (CRF) neurons causes overactive stress response; thus, physical anxiety symptoms are heightened.
Amygdala: Sets the emotional tone	Moodiness, negativity, and recognition of threat may be excessive, triggering alarm even in neutral situations. Overreaction to facial expressions creates anxious expectations of rejection or humiliation.
Hippocampus: Stores details of experiences for short-term memory	Creates context for emotional reactions, providing information for the cortex (PFC, OFC, ACG) to respond to the anxious emotion.
The combined limbic data is transferred to the PFC via the OFC and ACG.	This data is processed through the OFC and ACG to diminish or enhance appraisal of threat. Intense sensations of anxiety influence thought to see threat and danger even in otherwise neutral contexts.

text—emotion and memory from the limbic system. The thalamus serves a variety of complicated functions; it is involved in the regulation of brainwave activity and the coordination of information about motor activity, so it may be relevant to sleep problems in anxiety. Because the thalamus relays sensory information so rapidly to the amygdala, as well as to the rest of the limbic system, it is the starting paint for all anxiety triggered by an external stimulus.

The Hypothalamus

The hypothalamus consists of several nuclei. It monitors and controls internal systems, making it a vital link in sleep, circadian rhythm, and appetite and thirst. It is the hypothalamus that initiates the stress response to prepare the body to handle stressful events. When it is overactive, it generates too much stress response, causing people to overreact physically and be anxious disproportionately to the event.

The Amygdala

The amygdala gets special attention for its role in generating anxiety because of its function as the brain's early warning system. It is constantly alert to changes in external environment because novelty may contain a threat. The olfactory sense is the only one processed directly by the amygdala. Other sensory cortices send input via the thalamus to the amygdala. The amygdala assigns an emotional significance to incoming stimuli, like "Danger!" "Unpleasant!" "Threat!" It directly stimulates the stress response and the sympathetic nervous system before the PFC can exert modulating influence onto the amygdala. The amygdala directly connects to:

- The *parabrachial nucleus* for panting respiration
- The *hypothalamus* to initiate stress response, which, if intense enough, will trigger fight or flight sympathetic nervous system activation
- The *locus coeruleus* (pons) to step up norepinepherine (NE) and thus raise blood pressure, alertness, and behavioral fear response
- The *periacquaductal gray,* which may initiate freezing and modulate pain responses

The amygdala thus plays a direct role in creating the symptoms of anxiety connected to acute anxiety, stress, panic, and social anxiety. Figure 1.9 shows the complex pathway of a stimulus to the limbic system structures and to the cortical structures.

Learning Negative Experiences

The amygdala learns what is dangerous. It learns from experience if sensory inputs are threatening or not threatening. It very quickly forms associations between specific situations and pain, danger, or negative outcome. Therefore, after a frightening experience, and especially after a trauma, the amygdala maintains alertness to all future signals that a similar experience is about to occur. For example, if a person is in a car accident that is significantly frightening or painful, all of the aspects of that experience are learned by the amygdala as signals of danger: tires squealing, smells of fuel

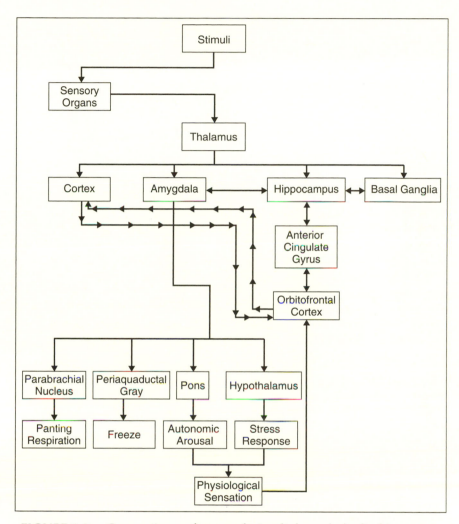

FIGURE 1.9. Connecting pathways of stimuli through the limbic system to the cortex.

or smoke, sirens, and even the specific place on the road, the weather conditions, or other features of the accident. Any aspect of a genuinely frightening experience could be learned by the amygdala as a signal to watch for in the future. Whenever one of those signals is perceived by the amygdala, the person will feel frightened. Even when the sound, smell, or place is not presently dangerous, the amygdala may react as if it is, because the association formed in the amygdala between danger and the stimulus will cause the amygdala to start the fear or panic response.

This learning or associative process also works in reverse when a person has a panic episode. The situation in which the person has a panic attack—a state of terror—may not be dangerous in any way. However, the situation *feels* dangerous because of the panicky sensations. In that way, a neutral stimulus may become a signal of danger. This kind of fear learning can occur when a panic attack strikes while people are driving. Whatever road condition is present at the time of the panic is learned by the amygdala as dangerous. If they feel panicked when on a highway with limited access, the amygdala may associate the inability to get off the road with danger. On a subsequent trip down a limited access highway, they will experience feelings of fear that could even lead into panic. Or if the person experiences a panic attack while driving in the rain at night, the next time he or she is in that weather condition, the amygdala, having associated dark and rain with fear, may trigger a panic reaction. In that way, neutral situations can be learned as dangerous by the amygdala, and until unlearning occurs, the amygdala will signal fear in that situation.

Consistent but less intense overreactivity is a feature in generalized anxiety in which the amygdala, sensitive to nonverbal signals from people, may overinterpret those signals as negative. The amygdala may be enlarged in those with social anxiety compared to controls in research studies, causing overreactivity to changes in facial expressions. Such overreactivity is seen in the expectation of rejection or pending humiliation that typifies social anxiety.

Unlearning Negative Experiences

The amygdala can also unlearn the association between a sensory input and a state of danger. If a person is in a situation that previously caused panic but does not panic this time, the amygdala learns not to panic in the future (Bouton, 2002). Although unlearning can occur naturally, it can also be accomplished with therapy methods intended to desensitize the response to a cue. There are several different methods that can be used, but all essentially pair the cue with a relaxed, safe state of being and with calming cognitions. The same process applies to unlearning cues to feel socially anxious or to worry, as in generalized anxiety.

The Hippocampus

While the thalamus is relaying sensory input and the amygdala is evaluating its importance, the hypothalamus is initiating a stress response and the hippocampus is registering the details of the events that are happening. The hippocampus plays a vital role in mapping events across space and time (Siegel, 1999). It is vital to the development of memory, and it creates context by holding the details of a situation next to the emotion generated by the amygdala. Consequently, fear generated by the amygdala becomes associated with environmental stimuli. Later similar environmental cues may elicit the fear/stress responses again, even when no threat is present (Bergman, 1998; Labar & Cabeza, 2006; Rothschild, 2000; Yehuda, 1997).

The hippocampus plays a role in anxiety and the development of PTSD as well. It relays information about the events of the day to the left prefrontal cortex (PFC) for memory storage and processing during REM dreaming (Stickgold, 2005). Long-term storage of significant information occurs as a result of processing during REM. The insignificant details of life are discarded during sleep, and the hippocampus is freed to take up a new day of details (Bergman, 1997; Mellman, 1997).

When people suffer anxiety and do not sleep well, this stress-relieving, healing process is shortchanged, and sleep is not as emotionally restorative as it could be. It is possible that people with anxiety and sleep problems may remain in the sleep stage of hippocampal relay without getting to the REM dreaming. This can cause fretful dreaming that is not really nightmarish but is definitely unpleasant. The dream process for the hippocampus can also be disrupted when neuronal activity from a trauma blocks REM from occurring; the hippocampus holds onto the detail memories of the traumatic event but without the benefit of interpretation or placing the event in time. Thus, when memory of the trauma is triggered by an environmental cue, the memory is without the context of when in time it occurred. It does not feel like it is in the past; it feels like it is happening now. This is the basic concept of a flashback (Bergman, 1998; Nemeroff, 1998; Stein et al., 1997).

THE ANXIOUS BRAIN AND THE SYMPATHETIC NERVOUS SYSTEM

The stress response of the brain is very important to understanding anxiety, and it starts in the amygdala and the hypothalamus. As illustrated in Figure 1.10, the hypothalamus-pituitary-adrenal (HPA) axis is the brain system that initiates the stress response, which is the preparation of the body to respond to the stressor. The hypothalamus initiates the response by releasing a peptide called corticotropin release factor (CRF) to the pituitary gland. The pituitary releases adrenocorticotropin hormone (ACTH) to the glands. The ACTH goes to the adrenal gland, and the adrenal gland releases adrenalin and a series of corticosteroids, among them cortisol. Adrenalin helps stimulate the organs of the body to handle the demand for action to fight stress. Cortisol stimulates the release of fat and glucose to fuel the stress response, and it is part of the feedback loop that helps turn off the stress re-

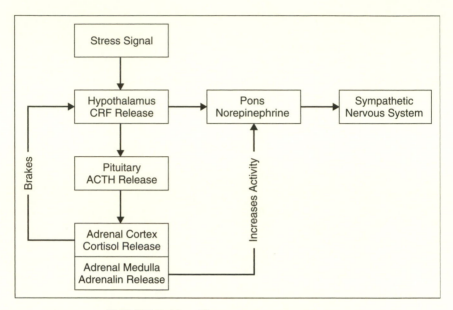

FIGURE 1.10. The stress response system.

sponse by alerting the hypothalamus that the stress signal has been received (Davidson et al., 2004; Rothschild, 2003). When stress continues at a high rate, a state of hypercortisolemia can occur. High levels of cortisol can cause the death of neurons, and under conditions of chronic stress or traumatic stress it is responsible for damage to brain structures, such as the hippocampus (Bremner, 2005).

How Does Stress Affect the Body?

The physical sensation of "being stressed" is unpleasant. When people have the opportunity to physically react to a stressor, their bodies use the chemicals of the stress response. The muscles burn the glucose and fat and use the adrenalin. When no physical activity occurs under stress, adrenalin causes sensations of shakiness and muscle weakness. The HPA axis starts the sympathetic nervous system (SNS) arousal that results in increased heart rate and respiration and in redirection of blood flow (Figure 1.11). The SNS arousal has far-reaching effects. It may cause a brief surge of immune function, protecting against illness, and it uses up neurochemicals like serotonin

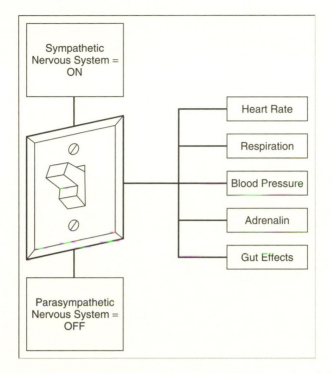

FIGURE 1.11. The sympathetic nervous system for arousal and the parasympathetic nervous system for calming.

(SE), dopamine (DA), and norepinephrine (NE). These responses are intended to be short-lived.

When stressors are constant, the stress response functions continuously and anxiety results (Shekhar, 2005). Stress responses burn out the immune system, making one subject to illness, and can deplete the supply of neurotransmitters that keep brain functioning in balance (Talbott, 2002). Anxiety and even depression can be an outcome of diminished stores of neurotransmitters that have not enough time to replenish themselves. Stress can also lead to the death of neurons from the impact of chronic elevations of cortisol (Bremner, 2005).

How the Stress Response Causes Anxiety Disorders

Even when the actual situation does not warrant it, some people may still have a strong stress response. This is typical with anxiety disorders. One possibility is that they were born with hyperresponsivity in the HPA axis. They may have an overabundance of CRF-producing neurons or they may be very receptive to CRF at the receptor site. Trauma research suggests that this is also a likely outcome of childhood traumatic stress; the HPA circuitry gets reset at a more sensitive level when a child has been abused or traumatized by a life event (Bremner, 1995; Felitti et al., 1998; Yehuda, 1997). Whatever the cause, the result is that small life events are experienced physiologically as if they are major events (Heim, Owens, Plotsky, & Nemeroff, 1997). They are literally felt in the body as important because the sensations are so strong (Rapee, 2002; Rothschild, 2000).

When a particular stress is serious, the sympathetic nervous system (SNS) may trigger the body into fight or flight through strong activation of norepinephrine (NE). The strong surge of HPA activity stimulates adrenalin to be released. That is necessary to get the physical energy and mental concentration for extraordinary response. If the fight or flight response is warranted, the arousal of the body is appropriate and the surge of adrenalin is utilized by the physical actions. However, fight or flight responses can be triggered unnecessarily by erratic firing of neurons in the brain, very much akin to a short circuit in the SNS. That can start fight or flight without a stress. This is the experience of people whose panic comes "out of the blue." It is like a small, short-lived seizure activity, sometimes called a "kindling of neurons," and it happens for no good reason. It is under this condition that people with panic deliberately look for reasons for the panic and often make incorrect and unhelpful interpretations of why they panicked.

Other Aspects of Heightened Arousal Under Stress

The hypothalamus initiates the stress response for adrenalin to activate the body and sets off sympathetic nervous system (SNS) arousal for fight or flight. While that is happening, the amygdala may already have connected to the parabrachial nucleus to initiate the panting respiration typical of panic attacks. It may have connected to the locus coeruleus to raise norepinephrine (NE) levels to increase blood pressure and generate high levels of alertness. And if the stress is traumatic, the amygdala will start activity in the periacqueductal gray to cause the "freeze" that is associated with dissociation from the psychic and physical stress of trauma (van der Kolk, McFarlane, & Weisaeth, 1996; Murburg, 1997). Traumatic stress disrupts brain activity and may even change brain function or structures (Cortes, 2005; DeBellis et al., 2002). For example, extremely heightened NE intensifies right-brain activity while diminishing left-brain activity (Siegel, 1999; Southwick et al., 1997) and later blocks consolidation of memory of the trauma, including REM dreaming (Mellman, 1997). After exposure to serious or chronic stress, the brain may be structurally different (Stein et al., 1997; Teicher et al., 1997; van der Kolk, Burbridge, & Suzuki, 1997) and the stress response may be permanently sensitized (McEwen & Magarinos, 1997; Yehuda, 1997).

Calming the Stress Response

A goal of symptom management for anxiety is to find methods that will trigger parasympathetic nervous system (PSNS) activity to slow the physical arousal. Once symptoms are underway, they can be reliably stopped if a person can master the techniques. Preventing panic and anxiety attacks is another therapy goal that focuses on intervening at the level of the preanxiety attack with stress reduction, cognitive control, and physical self-management such as nutritional changes, exercise, and meditation.

HORMONAL SYSTEMS

Although not a focus of the psychological treatment of anxiety, hormone levels and anxiety are intimately linked in varied ways, both causal and consequential (Leibenluft, 1999; Pert, 1997). Whenever physiological causes are part of the etiology of anxiety, they must be corrected before anxiety management can be effective.

Thyroid Function

When thyroid function is low, depressive symptoms result and medications are inefficiently metabolized. This means that levels of medication in the bloodstream may be lower than they need to be to work. When thyroid is too high, even within normal range, the sensations experienced are those of anxiety, and it is harder to calm the body (Bunevicius, Vilickiene, & Prange, 2005). Thus, the interpretation of the experience is that something is wrong (anxiety-producing) and the brain goes on a search to locate the source of the anxiety. Worry is the result.

Female Hormonal Fluctuations

Hormones that fluctuate with the female monthly cycle and over the life cycle affect the receptor sites for serotonin (SE), an important neurotransmitter for regulating emotion. When estrogen is lower, the receptor site is less receptive to SE. Women who have lower levels of SE may suffer more anxiety when their estrogen levels are low. Additionally, estrogen and progesterone function in balance with each other, and at times of the month or at times of life, such as perimenopause, when progesterone is too low in comparison with estrogen, feelings of anxiety can result (Leibenluft, 1999; Northrup, 2001).

Hypoglycemia

Blood sugar is another major contributor to feelings of anxiety, especially when it falls precipitously, as it might in sugar-sensitive people after a breakfast of doughnuts and coffee. Persons with hypoglycemia may experience these sensations frequently and develop anxiety disorders because they have the perception that the anxiety is caused by events or stress in their lives.

CONCLUSION

Brain regions and systems are involved in both creating and eliminating anxiety. The task of psychotherapy is to identify the possible brain triggers for anxiety and utilize methods that will eliminate them. Medications for anxiety target activity in the neurotransmitters that affect the way the regions and systems of the brain work. The combination of these treatments is highly effective to eliminate anxiety symptoms and prevent their return.

The descriptions of brain function in this chapter and the next chapter are simplified to make the connections between the cause of anxiety and the correction for it accessible to those of us who are not specialists in neuroanatomy. As we go on to examine neurotransmitters and their impact on brain function, keep in mind that the brain is highly complex, integrated in structure, and functions in vastly complicated ways.

CHAPTER TWO

NEUROTRANSMITTERS: MESSENGERS OF THE BRAIN

The organ of our brain is physical, and it does a lot of physical work. But to speak of it as a *part* of the body is wildly misleading. The brain directs internal organ and hormonal systems and keeps the whole of the body in homeostatic balance to both internal and external stimuli. It monitors internal processes and external messages and responds without our conscious attention to those signals. For example, our heart rate changes several times within the space of only a second to adjust to internal changes like temperature and oxygen levels (Childre & Martin, 2000). Interacting continuously with the other body organs, the brain also creates our mental state. In short, the brain and body are one. Hence, it would be accurate to use the phrase "mind-body" to imply the continuously interactive state of body and brain in sensing anxiety (Pert, 1997).

Not only is the brain highly complex, but it is also fluent, meaning that neurons can grow and change. The brain is a unique organ that can compensate for other parts of the brain when functions are interrupted, such as after a stroke. This means that new growth appears to be possible in all parts of the brain. Barring cell disease and damage, the brain can continue to grow new neurons until we die (Rossi, 1993).

In psychology we differentiate the 3-pound organ of the brain from the mind. "Mind" implies something we might call "self," an entity that is not static but rather continuously integrates new information, changing itself as it does. Each of our minds involves a unique process of the physical, emotional, spiritual, developmental, and experiential aspects of the self, and it integrates all those aspects into a self that can have coherent communication with other selves. The development of anxiety is the result of the activity of the mind, and the treatment of anxiety disorders takes all of the aspects of the mind and the self into account. But we first need to understand the functions of the organ of the brain to understand how it can create anxiety in the absence of a good psychological explanation.

Discussing *parts* of the brain may create an impression that they work in isolation. Nothing could be further from the truth. Ten billion neurons can each communicate with about 10,000 other neurons. The way in which those neurons communicate is with the exchange of chemicals called neurotransmitters. Neurotransmitters are chemical messengers in the brain, and their communication processes constitute the thoughts and physical reactions relevant to anxiety disorders.

Neurotransmitters are released at the end of a neuron's axon, which can extend at length across the brain or body. Many neurons have dendrites receiving neurotransmitters in the same synaptic space, so these chemical messengers can send their signals to many parts of the brain at one time.

NEURONS

Again, the human brain is comprised of billions of cells (neurons) that communicate with each other via neurotransmitters. Figure 2.1 shows the parts of a neuron. The neuron parts important to this discussion include:

- *Dendrites,* which have receptor sites to receive the neurotransmitters from other neurons
- *Axons,* which carry the signal initiated from the neurotransmitter received at the dendritic site
- *Synaptic spaces,* which are located between the end of the axon of one neuron and the beginning of another neuron. Neurotransmitters travel in this space, from which they are taken up by a receptor site, destroyed in the synapse, or taken up by the neuron that released them ("reuptake").

Other parts of the neuron include the body of the neuron (soma), which contains vesicles that hold neurochemicals (neurotransmitters). These neurotransmitters are released from vesicles located at the end of the axon (the axon terminal) into the synaptic space. Surrounding the neuron are glial cells, which serve many purposes, including helping transmit the neuronal message down the axon. Glial cells assist in nutrition and waste removal for the neurons, and some of the latest research indicates that glial cells play an important role in memory as well.

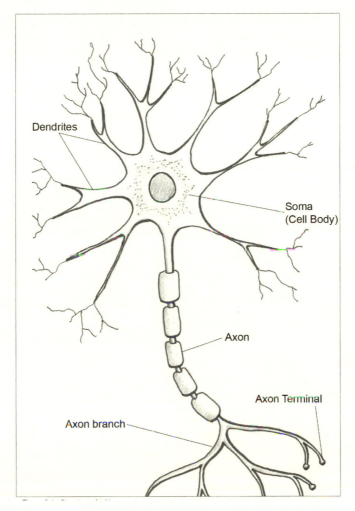

FIGURE 2.1. Structure of a neuron.

Neurons produce and store the neurotransmitters and release them when stimulated to do so. The presynaptic neuron releases its neurochemicals into the synaptic space. (The signal to release neurons is the result of excitatory exchange of chemicals from the synapse to the receiving neuron.) When the neurotransmitters are released from the vesicle into the synapse, there are up to 10,000 other neurons whose dendrites are waiting to receive the signal, meaning the possible connections form a complex network astonishing in its possibilities.

Figure 2.2 shows the cells connecting to each other. All of the dendrites shown can receive signals from many different surrounding neurons, so that the cell body can be directed to fire by many different neurochemicals. The phenomenal, densely packed brain is thus highly networked.

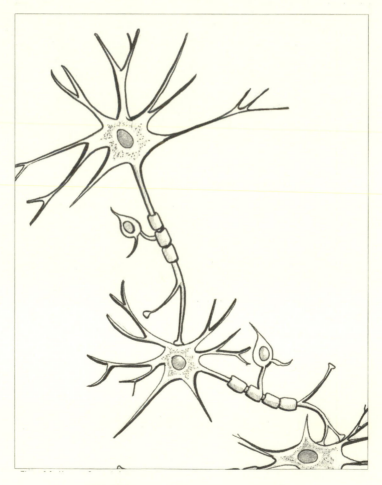

FIGURE 2.2.   Neurons connected.

Neurotransmitters are produced in the neurons. It was thought until recently that each neuron made only one kind of neurotransmitter, but it now appears that more than one kind of neurotransmitter may be made in the cell (Pliszka, 2003). Neurons release neurotransmitters when excited, thereby sending a message to other neurons, which are excited by the reception of the neurotransmitter and may go on to release their own neurotransmitters.

Each neuron can receive signals (neurotransmitters) from many other neurons. The postsynaptic neuron receives a neurotransmitter at a receptor site, which is prepared to receive only certain types of neurotransmitters. It was once thought the receptor site was like a lock and specific neurotransmitters were like keys that fit only one lock, but it is now known that this is not a rigid process. How well a receptor site accepts a neurotransmitter is affected by how the site is primed to be receptive. It is made more or less receptive by the influence of other neurotransmitters, hormones, peptides, and other neurochemical messengers. There are many different types of receptor sites for neurotransmitters, which affect how that neurotransmitter will be received and how sensitive the receiving site will be. The basic interaction between the neurotransmitters and the receptor sites is diagrammed in Figure 2.3.

Action Potential: The Opening of the Receptor Site and Stimulation of the Neuron

The movement of neurotransmitters occurs when they are released from the presynaptic neuron and activate a receptor site on a postsynaptic dendrite. When the receptor site is activated by the reception of a neurochemical, it opens (chemically changes) to allow for an exchange of chemicals in the postsynaptic neuron that may be strong enough to send a signal down its axon (Figure 2.4).

When a transmitter is received, the receptor site opens the neuron to a flow of ions (sodium, potassium, chloride, or calcium), thus changing the polarization of the neuron and creating an electrical charge that causes it to fire. (This is called the *action potential.*) The reception of the neurotransmitter starts a chain of other activities in the neuron, including the further release of neurotransmitters.

SPECIFIC NEUROTRANSMITTERS AND THEIR ACTIVITY

The neurotransmitters all function in relation to other neurotransmitters in complicated feedback loops. The neurotransmitters that are of most interest in understanding anxiety are:

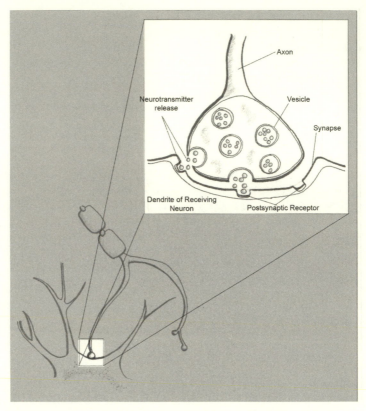

FIGURE 2.3.   Neurotransmitter release.

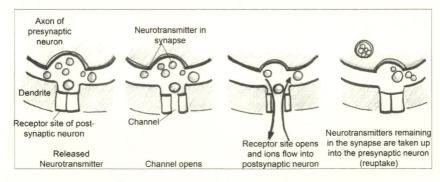

FIGURE 2.4.   Neurotransmitter activates postsynaptic cell.

- *Glutamate.* Glutamate is excitatory and is responsible for activating neuronal firing. It is distributed throughout the brain and functions in balance with GABA.
- *Gamma aminobutyric acid (GABA).* GABA is inhibitory and is necessary to stop the path of neuronal firing. It is found all over the brain and is very significant to anxiety because of its role in slowing or relaxing neuron activity.
- *Serotonin (SE).* Serotonin is found in many areas of the brain and body, but SE neurons are dense in the raphe and connect to the limbic system, where they are vital in the regulation of mood, appetite, sleep, libido, and impulse control and are involved in sensory reception, stress response, pain response, and perception and memory. Serotonin is also involved in recognizing reward.
- *Adrenalin.* Adrenalin, also called *epinephrine,* is involved in heart rate and respiration. It is a major player in activating the stress response system.
- *Norepinephrine (NE).* Norepinephrine is also called *noradrenalin,* and is key to arousal in the brain, as adrenalin is to arousal in body systems. It is localized in the pons, part of the mid-brain, where it is part of the sympathetic nervous system (SNS). It is also involved in autonomic arousal, including peripheral nervous system arousal, and it modulates blood pressure and other aspects of physiological arousal. It has a profound impact on memory and attention.
- *Beta-endorphins (BEs).* Beta-endorphins are peptides, named for their role as endogenous morphine and responsible for diminishing the sensation of pain and triggering dopamine release. They are natural opioids and are vital to the sensations of satiety and completion.
- *Dopamine (DA).* Dopamine is highly localized in the nucleus accumbens (NAc), where it is responsible for the sensation of pleasure or reward, and its function in the cerebral cortex is for alertness and attention. In addition to influencing many important physical functions, including motor activity (as in Parkinson's disease), it plays a significant role in many aspects of mental health, such as addiction, ADD, psychosis, and PTSD.

The Importance of Balance in Neurotransmitter Levels

The brain likes balance (Figure 2.5). It achieves balance via feedback loops. Every function of the brain and the body is initiated, monitored, and controlled by the brain in feedback loops of great complexity. It functions

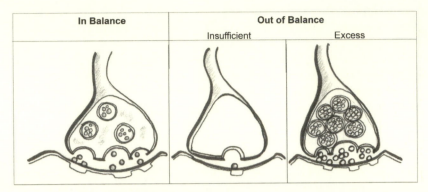

FIGURE 2.5. The brain likes balance.

best when there are only minor imbalances between levels of neurotransmitters.

Neurotransmitters affect each other differently under different conditions of balance. For example, when serotonin (SE) is low, norepinephrine (NE) functions to boost production of SE. When SE is too high, NE puts the brake on it. That alternate function of both stimulating and braking is an excellent example of the complexity of the interactions between neurotransmitters as well as of the need for balance. When balance cannot be achieved due to interference of disease, insufficient nutrition, genetic flaws, and so on, symptoms will appear. With regard to mental health, these symptoms may show up as problems with attention, cognition, depression, anxiety, and the like.

The varied types of anxiety symptoms can be explained through examining the impact of neurotransmitters on physical, emotional, and cognitive functions. When you know the basics of neurotransmitter effects, you can readily see why medications are selected for different symptoms of anxiety and when medication is necessary in the treatment for anxiety disorders.

Glutamate and GABA

Glutamate and gamma aminobutyric acid (GABA) are ubiquitous neurotransmitters that affect all chains of neuronal firing. Glutamate is responsible for activation of cell firing. It is not only found in the brain, but also functions in stimulating smooth muscle activity. In the brain it is necessary for starting activity.

GABA is the brain's braking system. It functions to slow and stop chains of firing. Networks of firing neurons set off other networks of firing neurons, and there must be a point at which the chain reaction ceases or every cell would fire constantly. There would be no time for the cells to recharge (literally) or to restore and replenish themselves. Different kinds of problems may occur in GABA functioning. There may be insufficient quantities of the GABA neurotransmitter. There may be neuron problems with receiving GABA on a receptor site. There may be problems with transmitting GABA across the synaptic space. Depending on where the GABA problems occur and how severely GABA function is impaired, anxiety problems related to excessive activity in the brain occur, such as rumination, unremitting acute anxiety states, and erratic panic.

Serotonin

Serotonin (SE) neurons are most dense in the raphe, and they connect to most parts of the brain, strongly influencing activity in the limbic system. Serotonin neurons are few in comparison to GABA or glutamate, yet their impact on the balance of other neurotransmitters, and thus on systems throughout the brain, is pervasive. When you think "serotonin," think "regulation." Serotonin modulates internal body temperature, appetite, libido, cognition, perception, mood, impulse control, pain, and sleep patterns. Serotonin in different parts of the brain relates to different types of anxious symptoms.

Serotonin is involved in the ability to recognize reward or positive experience. Different from feeling pleasure, this is an appreciation that it was *good* to do an activity, that the activity has been satisfying or useful. People who have difficulty recognizing positives are more prone to anxiety, depression, and addiction. The activity of the left prefrontal cortex (PFC) creates positive cognitive interpretations. This part of the brain is called the "optimistic brain"; it sees options to handle negative situations and resolve problems satisfactorily. Without SE, the left PFC cannot do its optimistic work.

Serotonin affects functioning in the anterior cingulate gyrus (ACG) and is necessary to promote smooth shifting between emotion and cognition. We cannot make good decisions without emotional information. We cannot solve a problem without knowing the significance of the different aspects of it. For example, making a decision about which apartment to rent means being able to weigh how important available parking is against the size of the bedrooms and the cost of the rent. Shifting between those concepts without getting stuck on one, and then being able to decide and take action, requires activity in the ACG, which filters and amplifies the various emotions and thoughts that are going back and forth. Without sufficient SE, anxiety-ridden people may not be able to do efficient problem-solving, and they may become ruminative. They may be unable to interrupt ruminative thoughts about a negative emotional state or they may have unreasonable cognitions.

Serotonin plays a significant, if indirect, role in creating the mentally stuck symptoms of OCD, one of the disorders in the spectrum of anxiety, by its influence in a circuit of activity between the cortex and the thalamus related to planning movement (Pliszka, 2003; Schwartz, 1998). Low SE or poor transmission in the cerebral cortex leads to a different kind of thought problem: distorted cognitions, as those seen in social phobia (Figure 2.6). The tendency to exaggerate the likelihood of rejection or to catastrophize (such as about a minor conflict with another person) is much greater when SE levels are low.

There are other cognitive aspects of SE function in the cerebral cortex. Serotonin is quite important in impulse control. When it is deficient in amount or transmission in the cerebral cortex, cognition is affected. The ability to restrain an impulse and think through a correct course of action is modulated by SE levels. When SE is sufficient, a person can make plans and fully utilize the higher-level executive functions of decision-making and deferring gratification instead of acting first and thinking later. This plays directly into anxiety, as the impulse with feelings of anxiety is to protect oneself. Poor SE transmission may result in an irritably anxious person's striking out verbally or physically when high levels of tension need to be dissipated. Serotonin contributes to clear cognition about what a person

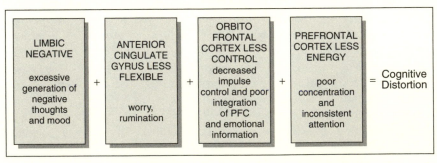

FIGURE 2.6.   Cognitive distortion.

needs and how to get it. Without clear thinking and good self-control, tension may be released in aggression or a bout of drinking.

Many of the medications used for anxiety are SSRIs, and they are currently indicated for all of the anxiety disorders. Even though the parts of the brain in which the anxiety is generated may differ among different disorders, serotonin plays such a significant role in so many brain systems that it has a profound effect on mental health.

Norepinephrine

Norepinephrine (NE) is important to the generation of anxiety symptoms in several ways. It is dense in the pons, a primitive part of the brain in which blood pressure is controlled. When people are panicky, NE triggers blood pressure to rise as part of the fight or flight response to fear. Norepinephrine is stimulated during the stress response by adrenalin. When it is stimulated intensely or for long durations, it can contribute to PTSD. This is discussed in more detail later.

Levels of NE that are too high create sensations of hyperarousal. Levels that are constantly too high lead to hypervigilance, a hallmark of generalized anxiety disorder and trauma. Relatively high levels of NE are highly correlated with generalized anxiety. People with overall heightened arousal have trouble relaxing both physically and emotionally, and they may suffer from too much tension. Figure 2.7 shows the impact of excessive NE on anxiety states.

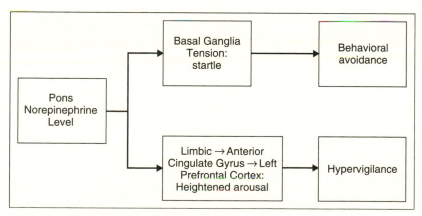

FIGURE 2.7.   High overall level of norepinephrine.

High levels of NE can cause too much responsiveness to stimulation in the environment and make it difficult for people to relax into sleep. They may startle easily or become exhausted from their constant alertness to the world around them. People who are already tight and tense can be easily irritated by small things; when they also have poor impulse control (as seen with those who have low SE levels or other neurotransmitter problems), they can be easily catapulted to rage, as are some children with rage-control problems or adults who explode with little provocation.

Norepinephrine can be too high for several reasons. When a child is traumatized by abuse of any kind, the levels of NE can remain constantly too high. In the case of single-incident trauma or adult traumatization, NE can also be dysregulated. (See the discussion on stress response in Chapter 1, p. 33, for more on this.)

Additionally, NE may be insufficient from too few NE-producing neurons or from too few receptor sites. Norepinephrine is modulated by other neurochemicals such as hormones, so how well it is sent and received is affected by other conditions. Norepinephrine is responsible for overall arousal, which is a necessary state. The brain needs to be aroused to pay attention to important or unusual stimuli. When the brain is insufficiently aroused and has insufficient energy for general alertness, attention deficit may result. Low NE can also cause lethargy and lack of arousal as may be seen in depression.

Beta-endorphins

Beta-endorphins (BE) are neurotransmitters called peptides, which are larger molecules than SE, DA, and NE (the monoamine neurotransmitters). They play several important roles in brain health. Among the roles important to anxiety is that of modulating pain. Beta-endorphins are the body's natural morphine—an opioid in the brain. When pain occurs (you stub your toe or your heart is broken by a romantic breakup), BE is released in large amounts, dulling the perception of pain. This allows you to take action by responding to the problem the pain is making you aware of.

Beta-endorphins also serve other important roles, depending on where they are received in the brain. (Remember that there are many receptor sites for the same neurochemical.) Beta-endorphins are intricately related to a sense of satiety or of being finished with an activity. When a person has enough to eat or is finished with a sexual experience, the sense of "enough" is the result of opioid activity in the brain. Without it, the sense of completion is missing. It is thought the opioid receptors in the brain are somehow not working correctly in OCD, so that people do not register an action's being completed, such as turning a lock in a door or hand-washing. Thus they repeat the action until they feel finished. Many OCD clients describe this state quite exactly, saying they just do not "feel done."

How is BE related otherwise to anxiety? Beta-endorphins are connected to dopamine (DA) and are highly involved in serious stress and trauma. When a person is in pain and BE is strongly active, it triggers the release of DA. In this case DA is complementary for the needs of a person in pain. The interrelationship of BE and DA in the context of stress and trauma is discussed after the following section on the functions of DA.

Dopamine

Dopamine (DA) has different functions in different parts of the brain. Among its most important roles is motor control. Sufficient DA in the basal ganglia (BG) is needed for efficient fine motor control, and losing DA results in tremors, as in Parkinson's disease.

Dopamine in the BG is also related to motivation. It is necessary to have enough DA to feel drive to meet goals and pleasure in accomplishment. When the BG is set a little too high, people may be highly motivated but also be subject to tenseness. When high levels of NE are accompanied by high DA in the BG, the kind of tension we call "wired" occurs. These people are tight, tense, and nervous but also motivated and energetic and have trouble sitting still (Amen, 2003). They get a lot done, but they pay a price in mood and tightness of muscles.

When prompted by an emotional "heads-up" from the limbic system about a situation, people need flexible, rapid, clear thinking to decide what course of action to take, and they need to be able to rapidly coordinate movement in conjunction with their decision. Dopamine activity in the BG helps us form rapid responses to emotional situations, as in seeing a car roll over on the highway in front of you. The BG coordinates with the rest of the brain to respond to the sense of emergency by making a quick decision to call 911 or run to the aid of the person in the car. High DA may cause too much tension for a smooth response, and NE and SE levels in other parts of the brain affect the coordination as well. When the neurotransmitter levels do not permit that smooth, flexible, rapid coordination, a person may feel frozen with anxiety or fear and respond slowly or inappropriately, with poor coordination of emotion and cognition.

Every person needs DA to feel pleasure. In the nucleus accumbens (NAc) of the BG, DA flows when an experience is good. The amount of DA triggered sends the message of how good it was. A chocolate sundae can be registered in the NAc as pretty darn tasty and a euphoric sexual experience can be registered as fantastic. In fact, both chocolate and sex are stimulators of DA.

Many drugs of abuse are strong triggers or mimickers of DA. They cause the transmission of the neurotransmitter in amounts far above what would be produced under normal experience. Thus, the user feels intense euphoria. Likewise, the ordinary "drugs" of caffeine and tobacco also raise DA, but at far lower levels and within more ordinary boundaries.

Logically, the less DA that gets transmitted, the less pleasure is felt. People with depression may have problems with low levels or poor transmission of DA. People with anxiety, especially generalized anxiety, also have trouble feeling pleasure. This may be caused by low DA (as in comorbid depression and anxiety), but it is also possible that pleasure is being overwhelmed by fear. For example, a person with anxiety might experience great pleasure in having met and chatted with an interesting person whom they would like to ask on a date but then be overwhelmed with fear of rejection. The pleasure in the meeting is not enough to compensate for the fear about the outcome.

Dopamine and Pain

The pleasure-producing aspect of DA is related to pain reduction. A person suffering pain needs to be able to ignore the pain long enough to get help or find relief. Beta-endorphins, the natural pain killers that help diminish the awareness of the pain receptor, trigger release of DA in direct proportion to how much BE was needed. The greater the pain, the greater the BE release and the greater the DA release. In this case, the euphoria produced by high levels of DA is not euphoria per se, but rather a state that allows a person enough ability to ignore the pain and take action to repair the injury.

Another major function of DA is also relevant in this scenario of pain. Dopamine in the cerebral cortex is responsible for attention and concentration. It plays a very important role in cognition. Sufficient DA is necessary to concentrate awareness on important stimuli and to block attention to insignificant stimuli. This means that we need not pay attention to the waxing and waning sounds of traffic outside the window as we read, but rather hold attention to the information on the page. When people have ADHD, they may have low levels of DA in the cerebral cortex.

When people are hyperaware of the stimulation around them, they are in a state of anxious alertness. When it is not concentrated on a specific activity that compels interest, a brain with high levels of DA is scanning incoming signals from the environment in a conscious attentive and overly anxious manner. People with social phobia are often in this state, scanning signals from the faces of others for signs of rejection or humiliation.

Dopamine, Beta-endorphins, and the Memory of Trauma

Dopamine helps people learn, and the more significant an event is, the more we remember it. When a person is in pain, DA, triggered by BE, is transmitted in large amounts in the cortex. This allows the person to concentrate on the cause of the pain in order to learn what is dangerous (painful) and to avoid the problem in the future. Thus, DA focuses attention on aspects of the stimuli in order to memorize them as important. This important learning process keeps us safe from exposure to future similar situations. People with ADHD often have trouble learning from their mistakes, and their low DA level may be a big factor in that problem.

Conversely, in situations of trauma or serious pain, a person may concentrate on irrelevant aspects of the painful situation. For example, in a car accident or medical crisis, the smells, sounds, and color of the light may all be registered as warning signs of danger when in fact they have nothing to do with the cause of the pain. This means that subsequent experiences of a smell like the burning car or the hospital E.R. may trigger fear, even though no actual danger is present. A person being mugged may focus on the color of the attacker's jacket but not notice the attacker's face, and PTSD flashbacks may be triggered by such irrelevant cues. After the event the jacket color seems trivial, but it is locked in the brain as interrelated with fear and pain, even if the victim is not consciously aware of it. This can lead the person to have flashbacks that seem to occur "out of the blue."

CONCLUSION

Neurotransmitters, the messengers of the brain, are the focus of attention for treatment with medication. Their activity, when in balance, underlies healthy cognition, emotion, and physical function. When neurotransmitter activity is excessive, insufficient, or out of balance, mental health dysfunction occurs. In the case of anxiety disorders, we look for those symptoms in physiological arousal or lethargy, in cognitive errors, and in behavioral avoidance.

Many researchers have demonstrated that psychological treatment methods change the activity of the brain. (Amen, 1998, 2003; Bergman, 1998; Roffman et al., 2005; Schore, 2003; Siegel, 1999; Siegel & Hartzell, 2003; Schwartz, 1998; Shapiro, 2001; Winston, Strange, O'Doherty & Dolan,

2002). Gaining access to the brain through engaging the executive pre-frontal cortex is what we do in psychotherapy. The methods we employ have the effect of connecting the various parts of the brain for the purpose of modulating emotion, behavior, and cognition. When the methods are employed consistently and with persistence, brain activity eventually changes. Thus, in psychotherapeutic treatment of anxiety, we help people use their brains to change their brains.

CHAPTER THREE

PANIC DISORDER: MINDLESS FEAR

Panic disorder (PD) is the disorder no one can miss and no one wants to live with. The symptoms are profoundly disruptive of normal functioning. However, many people with PD are not diagnosed quickly or properly because the symptoms suggest a physical rather than psychological cause.

In any year, nearly 2% of the adult population in the United States will experience panic disorder (National Institute of Mental Health, 2006). The majority are female, although men certainly suffer from it as well (American Psychiatric Association, 2000). Panic disorder is not typical in children but begins to strike more frequently at puberty. In women, PD may appear at any time when rapid or dramatic changes in hormone functioning occur, such as during postpartum or perimenopause changes (Leibenluft, 1999).

When diagnosing and treating the elderly for PD, it is very important to rule out any condition involving dementia. Early stages of dementia can include panic symptoms. That said, PD can have its first onset late in life and confuse the diagnostic picture regarding competence. The elderly brain does continue to produce neurochemicals, but at a lower rate, so depletion of brain chemicals, especially serotonin (SE), may cause PD when a person did not previously have it. People who develop PD in later years may have shown signs of anxiety or depression earlier in life, even if it was untreated, and a good diagnostic interview will look for those premorbid symptoms. Current situations that involve loss—death of friends or family, loss of health or abilities (like driving), or loss of independence—can trigger panic. Research about treating elderly patients without cognitive impairments indicates that the elderly respond to the same treatments as the younger adult population (Ayers, Wetherell, Lenze, & Stanley, 2006; Blumenthal et al., 1999; Stanley et al., 2003).

DIAGNOSTIC CRITERIA

According to the *Diagnostic and Statistical Manual IV-TR* (*DSM-IV-TR*), a diagnosis of PD requires that a person:

- Have panic attacks (physical symptoms)
- Have psychological distress (fear of having more attacks) that is severe enough to:
  - Impair mood
  - Interfere with behavior

Three Clusters of Symptoms

Panic disorder is characterized by identifiable aspects of physiology, behavior, and cognition, all of which are typified by high levels of arousal and activity. There are three clusters of symptoms that are evaluated:
- The *physiological symptoms* of a panic attack
- The *cognitive symptoms* of fear of future panic attacks
- The *behavioral symptoms* developed to avoid future panic attacks

Physiological Symptoms
The physical symptoms that may appear in a panic attack include sudden and intense sensations that are often interpreted as medical crises. These include:

- Palpitations (accelerated pounding sensation of the heart)
- Sensation of choking
- Shortness of breath
- Chest pains
- Nausea or diarrhea
- Light-headedness or dizziness
- Psychological sensations of derealization (feelings of unreality)
- Depersonalization (feelings of being detached from oneself)

Whether they feel one or many of these symptoms, people experience the heightened arousal as extremely aversive—frightening, physically unpleasant, and confusing. The symptoms may be medically confusing as well, because they are undeniably present when a person is highly anxious or panicky. Furthermore, because these symptoms are similar to those indicating serious physiological problems, such as a heart attack, they cannot be ignored without risking missing a medical problem. Medical personnel must perform extensive tests to ascertain whether the pounding heart, dizziness, elevated blood pressure and other feelings are attributable to a medical event.

Although frequency of panic is not necessarily a consideration in the diagnosis, people often have attacks with increasing frequency because their fear causes them to worry themselves into a panic. Once people suffer a panic attack, they begin to worry about whether they will have another attack, and they will do just about anything not to experience it again. Part of the diagnostic criteria for PD involves worrying so much about future attacks that daily life is interrupted. Daily life may also be disrupted by the measures people take to avoid having the potential attack.

Cognitive Symptoms

The cognitive symptoms of PD develop *in response* to the physical symptoms. The panic attack itself comprises highly aroused sensations that develop, crest, and diminish within 10–15 minutes. That is a short period of time, but it is long enough to develop the belief that you might be dying, and it is plenty of time to think you never want to go through the experience again. The cognitions come from the most startling aspect of a panic attack—the intense, sudden, and shocking realization that this might be what it feels like to die. Driven to the emergency room with a terrorizing, "What if I am dying?" fear, people develop the *cognitive error* that their symptoms are evidence of a serious problem, which expands their panic attacks into PD. In PD, people make incorrect assumptions (thoughts) that lead to cognitive errors:

- "I am going to die."
- "I am going crazy."
- "I am losing control."

But these thoughts rarely are examined or thought through logically. They are an important treatment target because they freeze people in this frightened state. The erroneous thoughts that the person is dying, losing control, or going crazy maintain the mindless fear of another panic attack. In other words, people react to the sensations without using logical thought to examine their frightened, reactive cognitions.

The more often the brain goes into a panic attack, the more easily a panic attack can be set off the next time, regardless of why the panic started. This process is called *kindling*. The faulty cognitions that develop during a panic attack do not disappear when the rapid heart rate goes down. Fear causes hypervigilant attention to physiological arousal and

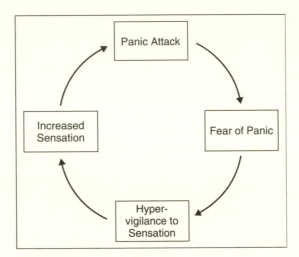

FIGURE 3.1. Circular nature of panic.

magnifies every small tingle or twitch. The fear that those sensations will develop into panic will actually create panic (Casey, Newcombe, & Oei, 2005). This vicious circle is illustrated in Figure 3.1.

The inner dialogue may go something like this:

"I have felt panic before. I have a physical sensation. I wonder if it is panic. I'd better pay attention.

I will hypervigilantly monitor my physical sensations. Uh, oh! I feel every sensation getting faster—heart rate, breathing.

Yes, I am sure this is panic! Oh, *no!* I hate this. Now my heart is really fast and my breathing is shallow."

Sure enough, the panic attack comes on full swing, as self-talk made all the sensations worse. This circular interaction between physiology and thinking is easily begun.

People usually think that whatever they were doing at the time of panic caused the onset of the attack when in fact the attack occurred "out of the blue" due to erratic brain activity. They may develop the idea that certain locations or situations are triggering panic attacks. From those ideas linking panic and situations, the behavioral symptoms of panic disorder are born.

Behavioral Symptoms

The behavioral symptoms of PD begin as a result of the combination of the intensity of the physiology and the fearfulness of the cognitive errors, which spur panicky people to take action to avoid the panic and fear. People quickly establish behavior patterns to stay out of the circumstances they believe caused the panic—*believe* being the operative word. There may be no evidence that a specific situation causes the panic, but they will do whatever it takes not to feel the panic again. Clear patterns of avoidance—mental, physical, and emotional—develop. This is the third cluster of symptoms that is part of the criteria for PD:

- *Mental avoidance* (trying not to think about anything that might cause panic). People with panic mentally plan complicated and circuitous ways to negotiate their world without getting into situations that are distressing.
- *Avoiding activities.* This may may include avoiding any activity they may formerly have done with ease–driving on highways, returning phone calls, eating in restaurants, and so on. The more people avoid activities, the less able they are to ward off panic.
- *Avoiding the feeling of fear.* As people with panic become increasingly vigilant about preventing another attack, their whole emotional goal soon becomes avoiding fear. They may sacrifice opportunities to feel joy or competence, even when such things previously marked their personality. Now they just focus mental and physical activity on avoiding feeling fear. Fear of fear becomes the dominant emotional state.

Whatever the pattern of avoidance, it must be identified and eliminated, because avoiding fear keeps panic in place.

THE ORIGINS OF PANIC DISORDER

Panic disorder may begin in different ways, but it always ends with an overreactive brain that sends the body into a state of fight or flight—often for no good reason. The neurobiological explanations of the panic attack are important to grasping basic treatment for the disorder, but effective, lasting treatment also requires an understanding of how the attacks first began. Panic disorder may begin in several ways:

- *From a state of trauma,* leaving a person hypersensitive to cues and reminders of the initial event
- *From early disturbances in the attachments to parents or caregivers,* which leave a person with a sense of insecurity
- *From psychological conflicts* born of irresolvable tension between needs

- *From neurobiological causes,* such as neurotransmitter imbalances, which may be genetic or which may develop over the lifetime from different physical causes

The correct treatment entails symptom management at the outset and usually requires therapeutic attention to identify and resolve the underlying causes of the panic. This was the case with Mary, as the following vignette illustrates.

Mary came to treatment in her thirties, when, out of nowhere, she began to experience panic attacks. Her doctor had given her every medical test in the book—with no positive result. Finally, he prescribed antidepressants and antianxiety medications because, as he told her, the medications could control the symptoms and there was nothing else medical to do. Not in favor of taking medication, Mary finally took a friend's advice to talk to a "shrink."

Mary described herself as "high-strung," with a tendency to feel her stress physically, but said she had no history of abuse or neglect and no accident, injury, or trauma that could explain the onset. As a therapist I was, of course, very interested in knowing why the panic attacks had begun when they did, but the answer to that question was not immediately clear. So, rather than trying to uncover that mystery, we began our course of treatment with learning to stop the panic.

Mary did learn to stop panic once it started by using breathing, relaxation, and other physiological methods (described in Chapter 4). But the panic attacks kept getting triggered, and Mary wanted to stop them from ever starting. Therapy helped her track the onset of panic. It became clear that she regularly had panic attacks after phone conversations with her sister, Sally Ann, who had recently moved to town and was calling much more than she used to.

Mary felt that her sister was leaning on her for advice about money problems but that she really just wanted to complain instead of taking action. Mary, the pragmatic sister, had clear ideas about how Sally Ann could eliminate her constant money woes. But she was in no position to control Sally Ann's budget or spending. She also felt responsible for helping her sister, because their parents were no longer alive.

The combination of being relied upon and responsible for her sister but having no control over the situation was a bad match for Mary's personality. She was intelligent, perfectionistic, and exceedingly disciplined. As Sally Ann's phone calls increased, Mary felt intensified inner conflict that tipped her into panic. Once Mary could see what was triggering the onset of the panic, she was able to examine her sense of responsibility, develop new ways of relating to her adult sister, and work out a better approach to her sister's calls. This stopped the panic from being triggered.

MINDLESS FEAR: THE INTERACTION BETWEEN THE PHYSIOLOGY
AND PSYCHOLOGY OF PANIC DISORDER

The intense arousal of a panic attack is the physical state of terror, without a reason for the terror. As humans who think about our condition, we want reasons for what our bodies feel. It feels psychologically disorganizing not to have an explanation for what we feel physically (Gazzaniga, 2005).

Terror without explanation—or mindless fear—is an unwelcome state, so how does the brain handle it? It *makes up reasons* for the physical arousal. But the human brain, observing and experiencing panic for the first time, does not reason in a cool, objective manner, "Would ya look at that? I am experiencing a state of high arousal generated by my basal ganglia!" Instead, the brain draws connections between the panic and what you were doing, thinking, or feeling at the time the attack began. If you were driving on the highway, you might decide that the panic was caused by the highway driving rather than assume you were having a biological event, and you would be inclined to avoid highway driving in the future. Thus, thought and behavior follow the brain's explanation of a panic attack, even though the explanation is not rational.

Panic is a condition of experiencing the stress response without a stressor. How does the stress response play a role in the development of PD?

The Stress Response Is a Necessary Reaction to Events

Stress is triggered from both internal conditions (such as hunger, thirst, illness, or distressing thoughts) and external stimuli (such as a loud noise, an angry voice, or the smell of smoke). The sensations of stress are the physical changes needed to fight or flee from danger.

The beauty of the stress response system is that it works continuously without intentional monitoring to provide the kind of energy we need to meet the ordinary ups and downs of everyday living. It kicks up when we are given a pop quiz in chemistry. It works immediately when we hear an angry voice. It starts when the front door slams. Without the need to think it over, the body responds to the need for action. The stress response turns itself off when it becomes clear that the stress is manageable—when you know the answers on the quiz, or the angry voice has nothing to do with you, or your child yells, "Sorry about slamming the door—the wind caught it."

When a stress is perceived, the hypothalamus kicks off a whole cascade of hormones and neurotransmitters (Bremner, 2005; Rothschild, 2000) that light up all the internal organs to prepare the body to fight off or flee from the cause of the stress:

1. The hypothalamus releases corticotrophin release factor (CRF), often called the *stress response hormone.*
2. CRF causes the pituitary to release adrenocorticotropin hormone (ACTH), which instructs the adrenal gland to release adrenalin (from the medulla) and cortisol (from the adrenal cortex). The release of cortisol and adrenalin energizes the body.
3. The hypothalamus signals for the release of norepinephrine (NE) in the pons, which sets off "fight or flight" activity.
4. "Fight or flight" sympathetic arousal stimulates the whole body for a strong and effective response to the danger.

The stress response system turns itself off with cortisol. As the end point in a feedback loop, cortisol signals to the hypothalamus that the CRF has done its work and does not need to be released any longer. The CRF has produced the necessary heightened arousal, and the cortisol is received in the hypothalamus as a "turn off" so the body and brain can go back to normal after the brief arousal caused by the adrenalin-norepinephrine spike.

Cortisol in long duration is damaging to the brain. There is evidence that cortisol causes atrophy in the hippocampus of people who have been under stress for long periods of time, such as a child living in conditions of abuse (Bergman, 1998; Bremner et al., 1999; Stein et al., 1997). People with depression show levels of cortisol that are too high; currently it is not known whether the high cortisol level is the result of or the trigger for depression. Learning to control and diminish the stress response lowers cortisol levels and helps prevent the excessive duration of cortisol that can damage the brain.

Panic and the Stress Response

Panic is the outcome of the stress response when there is no real danger and the response is triggered for some other reason. Without a stressor to trigger the stress response, the body and mind are confused. You are feeling danger and physically preparing to fight or flee from it, but instead you are sitting in a traffic jam, or talking on the phone, or standing in the grocery store checkout line. Thus, instead of using the physical arousal to move, your body may:

- Increase your respiration
- Increase your heart rate
- Increase adrenalin flow, making you feel shaky and weak
- Divert blood flow from the stomach, making you feel nauseated
- Make you feel an urgent need for urination

This is a truly aversive state. The only way people can begin to ward off PD is to understand that although this state of terror is real, it is not necessary.

The Stress Response and Child Development

Evidence from research for the Child Anxiety State Index (CASI) identifies that overresponsiveness to states of anxiety in children is a good predictor of developing PD in adulthood (Reiss, Silverman, & Weems, 2001). Children who find feelings of anxiety very aversive are more likely to develop PD. The "chicken or the egg" phenomenon applies here. Were they born with sensitivity, making early experiences harder? Or was sensitivity developed as a result of early life experience, shaping subsequent experience as more anxiety-provoking? Knowing how the stress system develops sheds some light on this problem. Good diagnostic interviewing can clarify how it applies to individual clients.

Although the stress response system is automatic, unconscious, and immediately responsive to internal and external stimuli, the system is not efficient from birth. Exploring early life experience provides clues as to whether a person has a genetic predisposition to anxiety or had early life experiences that created the sensitivity. When working with children, having this information can lead to planning better corrective experiences. When working with adults, the information will clarify what kind of treatment, including the use of medication, will be best for putting anxiety into remission (Grover, Ginsburg, & Ialongo, 2005). Let's start by exploring how the stress response system is trained in infancy.

The profound and intense relationship of an infant and an emotionally healthy caregiver trains the infant's body-brain stress response to function smoothly and efficiently. Continuing interactions between caregiver and child teach the infant's stress response system how much arousal is necessary in what kind of situations and how quickly to calm down (Schore, 2003). A newborn baby is a little like a furnace whose thermostat has not yet been programmed. The furnace can kick in and heat up, but it does not know how hot to get or how long to run. The caregiver's responses to the infant program the thermostat.

Stress arousal continues until it learns to shut off. The infant stress system must be trained for how excited to get over each stress—cold, hunger, pain, fear, and so on—and how quickly to calm down. The infant brain, born with the capacity for stress management, can release the stress hormone that causes the stress response system to kick in. However, that stress arousal gets too high and continues for too long because the infant has not yet learned how stressful various conditions actually are. The child needs repeated experiences to learn how quickly his or her needs will be met, how accurate the caregiver will be in anticipating the child's needs, and how effective the child's cries are at gaining a response. Repeated experience trains the brain.

How does the interaction with the caregiver train the brain of the infant? Under stresses like cold or hunger, the infant's brain releases CRF and initiates the stress response, demonstrated in physical agitation and crying. Training the stress response system occurs in the most basic, intuitive way. When an infant is screaming with hunger, the caregiver's voice soothes the infant long before the food is provided. She will usually croon some version of "It's okay, food is on its way" while she warms a bottle or gets ready to nurse. Much of this soothing behavior—rocking, patting, crooning, humming, and the like—emerges intuitively from an empathic caregiver. It is part of the symbiotic relationship between the two. When the caregiver soothes, the child registers that it will get what it needs, and the stress system is programmed to recognize that it has produced and expressed enough arousal and now can turn off the stress response. The demand for relief (feeding) is underway. The response turns all the way off and pleasure/satiety is experienced when the food is provided.

The system is programmed by repeated experience. Reasonably consistent caretaking is all that is necessary for the stress response system to become trained. Perfection is not required or even desirable. Anticipating a child's needs so perfectly that it never has a moment of cold, hunger, pain, or fear would not train the stress response system for arousal, meaning that it would be at risk for overarousal when it eventually encountered a stress. Without frustrations, an infant would become a sensitive or bratty child, overreactive to little bumps or frustrations in life. Over time the experiences of getting hungry and then fed, wet and then dry, cold and then warm, program the infant's stress response system to produce a reasonable degree of arousal under similar conditions. Literally, the brain circuitry for the CRF-ACTH-adrenal activity and sympathetic arousal becomes trained and the parasympathetic calming is easily initiated.

Inborn Overactive Stress Response Systems

Even with good-enough parenting, however, there can be problems with an infant's stress response system. Children may be born with a stress response system that reacts too quickly or too intensely. They may have too many CRF-producing neurons that generate too much stress response in relation to the intensity of the trigger. People with too many CRF neurons make mountains out of every molehill. They can be identified from diagnostic interview information that reveals lifelong problems with being "temperamental" and from reports of strong childhood emotional responses and behaviors. Such dramatic, intense children may well have been shaped developmentally by the stress response system (Lobaugh, Gibson, & Taylor, 2006; Winston, Strange, O'Doherty, & Dolan, 2002).

The stress response affects personality. The intensity of the child's stress response has an impact on the development of future responses to stress and on personality as well. It is easy to imagine how a child with an intense response can appear to be dramatic. The dramatic style then becomes a personality style—a habitual reaction to stress that intensifies the stress response rather than soothing it (Millon, 2000; Schore, 2003).

Caregivers shape the impact of the stress response. The impact of parenting is quite important to shaping stress responses in these conditions. If a highly reactive child has caregivers who are calm and who talk the child down, thereby modeling and teaching self-soothing skills, the child will absorb self-quieting skills that will modulate the impact of his or her stress response. Caregivers can model fear reactions (Dadds & Roth, 2001) or model soothing. The child may continue to have strong reactions (high CRF output), but caregivers will be able to calm the child down rather than exacerbate the stress. The stress response will be modulated and the feeling of stress lessened. Thus the child learns to control stress response output, having learned self-soothing from the parental calmness in the face of a stress. For example, if the mother of a child screaming loudly over a little bump on the knee remains calm and croons that it will be fine while she gets a Band-Aid, the child will internalize the mother's calm response to a bump. The child may respond equally intensely to subsequent bumps, but parasympathetic calming will be activated when he or she remembers the maternal calmness.

Imagine now instead that the high-CRF-output child has anxious or angry parents who screech or get agitated when the child responds intensely to a stimulus. Suppose this child scrapes her knee and instead of receiving soothing, hears fear and upset in her mother's voice as the mother yells, "What have you done now?" or "Why can't I ever have a minute without you ruining it?" The child will certainly be even more upset than she might have otherwise been. The mother's negative response causes the child's level of stress to increase, and her hypothalamus will output even more CRF, exaggerating such normal life stressors. That particular molehill doesn't just become a mountain, it becomes Mount Everest, and the child does not learn how to calm herself. Rather, she feels intolerable degrees of upset over what might otherwise be normal degrees of stress (Yehuda, 1997).

Such a child's personality style is likely to become more dramatic and less effective over time. Future stressors that are handled with the same high CRF output will be made worse, because instead of curbing her CRF output through soothing, she intensifies it via the internal model of parental overreactivity (Schore, 2003; Siegel, 1999).

People with high CRF output and few self-soothing skills are at high risk for both anxiety and depression later in life. Their stress response systems continue to produce damaging levels of stress at a biological level. At the psychological (personal or interactive) level, the inability to effectively manage stress is detrimental to stability of mood and interpersonal relationships.

THE PANICKY BRAIN AND TRAUMA

A history of abuse or other negative life experiences can also create a stress response that is triggered unnecessarily or disproportionately to the stressor. Negative life experiences set up cues that danger is on the horizon, and these become psychological triggers for panicky states. A person may start to panic even though he or she is not consciously aware of the cues.

How Are Triggers Created?

Signs of danger are created in the limbic system of the brain and remembered unconsciously. They are marked by the amygdala working in concert with the hippocampus and the stress system. The actions of these parts of the brain are inseparable. From birth the amygdala, the brain's early warning system, is memorizing the emotional tone of life experiences, noticing and remembering anything that could be a warning that trouble is on its way. When an infant's gaze is fixed on its caregiver's face, the feeling of the interaction is memorized by the amygdala. When the caregiver's face is warm and loving and the infant feels good and safe, that expression is memorized with a bodily state of well-being.

When the infant's body (its *self*) is feeling uncomfortable, the look on the caregiver's face is memorized as well. A negative outcome could result if the infant, in a state of hunger or pain, cries without stopping and the caregiver becomes increasingly agitated. If the caregiver's face begins to reflect frustration, anger, or rage at the infant's tears, rather than calming the infant, she increases her child's agitation. The child's stress response keeps on working and creates that very aversive state of high arousal. The child's state of discomfort is matched with caregiver's expression. The stronger the caregiver's state of anger, the more likely she will show it on her face, and the more likely the infant will be to mark the expression as related to the state of negative arousal it is feeling.

It is the amygdala, highly specialized to notice and memorize negative facial expressions, that will record the emotional tone of the exchange and associate the facial expression with the negative arousal (Phan, Fitzgerald, Nathan, & Tancer, 2006). Repetition makes for stronger memories. The more often the facial expression is connected to negative stress arousal, the more the amygdala will remember to watch out for that facial expression as a sign of trouble ahead. After enough experiences of the caregiver's becoming angry and rough when the child cries, the child's amygdala will learn that an angry look presages aggressive action (a danger). Even though the child may eventually be fed (or changed or covered with a blanket), the next time he or she experiences hunger or cold, the stress response will start intensely.

If the child sees an angry face, the face itself becomes a stress. A CRF stress response in reaction to that angry face will start without thought about what the face means. In fact, the stress response starts so quickly that conscious thought about a facial expression either does not occur or occurs long after the physical stress response has been triggered. Thus, the child might learn to cower or run from an angry face on any person. More importantly, his or her stress response will surge without conscious thought, causing distressed feelings in response to even slight expressions of anger on a person's face. When caregivers' reactions are abusive, the child's stress response is going to become proportionally more intense.

From birth, children busily notice faces and develop an internal code book of what is dangerous and what is not. In addition noticing to faces, a child's amygdala is recording information from all the five senses. Cues to feel fear may therefore be associated with smell, touch, taste, or sound, and with visual cues other than facial expression. This is illustrated by the case of Suzanne, whose trigger involved the sense of smell.

Suzanne had been in treatment for anxiety in the past and had done very well, but she came back to see me when she faced a problem she could neither understand nor solve. "I just cannot stand the way he smells," she said, and with a stricken look, she talked about her fear that she would not be able to accept her newly adopted toddler. Suzanne could understand it might take time to get used to having a new child in her home, but she could not understand the absolute revulsion she felt when she held him and smelled the natural scent of his body. It made her want to escape when they were physically close.

Her young son had been adopted from Russia. She was stunned at how smelly he was when she picked him up, and the first thing she did was throw away the clothing he wore from the orphanage. On the 3-day trip home, she spent long hours in the hotels helping him soak and splash in the tub, trying to eliminate the actual dirt and the body odor. Despite cleaning him, she feared the smell would never go away, and she felt disgusted both by his scent and her reaction to it.

This emotional response was out of proportion to the reality of the child's scent. Although Suzanne knew he was clean on the outside and that changing his diet to healthful and familiar foods was already changing his natural scent, her revulsion remained. She feared that having formed this reaction to her son, she would not be able to love him as she wanted to. She had no idea why she felt this way, but she knew that the feeling of wanting to escape was so strong that she did not want to hold him, touch him, or cuddle him. She did these things, but she feared her reluctance would show and affect him.

I suspected her response was an emotional reaction based on a memory of this type of smell that her amygdala was holding. We used the EMDR method (discussed in Chapter 4) to identify, reprocess, and desensitize her reaction, and she found a surprising connection. In childhood she had experienced significant abuse and neglect, much of it at the hand of a stepfather and his family. When she targeted the feeling of disgust and the memory of the smell, she became immediately aware of the similarity of her feeling toward her son and her childhood reaction to visiting relatives—something she was required to do no matter how she argued against it. She felt sick when they visited and she hated being there without any way to get away. She recalled them as living in disgusting conditions: intense smoke from cigarettes, stale food and garbage in the house, and poor personal hygiene. The sensation of being "stuck" with her new son was exactly like this emotional memory of having no option to leave the relatives when she was a child. Once she had identified the source of the feeling and worked it out in therapy, she was able to let go of the first memory of her boy and the smells of the orphanage. She was able to see—and smell—her son as he was at this moment: a clean, sweet boy for whom she felt great love and affection. Until she could connect the emotional memory of the amygdala to an actual recollection and learn that the old experience was over and done, she could not shake the feeling she had in reaction to the smell.

Suzanne's experience is a classic and singular example of a flashback memory, stored without a sense of time or other factors. It illustrates the way the amygdala recalls cues and serves as the early warning system for safety. Such a cue could be associated with any sensory stimuli, such as the smell of smoke or a clanging siren, as when people have been endangered in a fire or a storm.

Of course, not all cues have the clarity and simplicity of Suzanne's example, but everyone has an entire repertoire of experiences associating sensory stimuli with emotional states. These form the basis of intricate, sensitive social responses. But these responses are based in *preverbal* social experience, which is why many people with panic responses do not know why they are anxious.

Therapists must remember that life-threatening events may be one-of-a-kind and not the result of abuse. A traumatic experience may be caused by a necessary medical intervention or a single event involving a natural disaster, accident, or crime. People may also be traumatized by ongoing life experiences in adulthood, such as combat or working for police or emergency-response teams.

Regardless of the type of trauma experienced, survivors' brains are changed in several ways. One aspect of trauma is that the prolonged and intense release of norepinephrine (NE) alters the processing of the event, which is shown in Figure 3.2. Right-brain activity is heightened by the neurochemical impact of trauma and activity in the left prefrontal cortex (PFC) is shut down during the event (van der Kolk, Burbridge, & Suzuki, 1997). Subsequent memory of the trauma thus involves fewer of the explanatory and modulating effects of the left PFC and more overreactivity in the right brain to cues of the trauma, which can trigger panic (Kent et al., 2005; Kent, Mathew, & Gorman, 2002). Traumatic experience thus results in both overall heightened NE function and also specific overreactions to stimuli that trigger the stress response.

Trauma Changes the Brain to Increase Panicky Reactions

Brain imaging shows that the brains of traumatized people have been altered in size, with the hippocampus shrinking by 8–12% (McEwen & Olie, 2005; Stein et al., 1997). Traumatized brains also show altered blood flow in the left prefrontal cortex (PFC) and the amygdala, with the amygdala

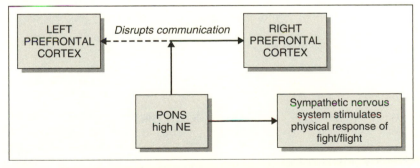

FIGURE 3.2.   Effects of high, prolonged norephinephrine from trauma.

becoming preferentially stimulated by certain triggers associated with the trauma (Bremner et al., 1999; Lobaugh, Gibson & Taylor, 2006; Phan, Fitzgerald, Nathan, & Tancer, 2006). Scans also show less metabolism of energy in the prefrontal cortices and the right limbic structures under conditions of stress. In other words, trauma physically changes the brain and becomes a predictor of later anxiety (Grover, Ginsburg, & Ialongo, 2005; Libby, Orton, Novins, Beals, & Manson, 2005).

Additionally, the stress response system becomes overreactive to new stressors, resulting in excessive output of CRF, ACTH, and adrenalin, all of which affect physiological systems. Although there is some debate about cause and effect (it is possible that people who are more negatively affected by trauma have preexisting differences in brain structure that make them more vulnerable to such negative effects), it is evident that the brains of people who have been traumatized at young ages are more significantly changed than those of traumatized adults. There also appears to be a causal relationship between intensity and duration of abusive situations, so that the younger the age, the longer the abuse went on, and more severe it was, the worse the outcome for brain health (Anda et al., 1999; Chaffin, Silovsky, & Vaughn, 2005). What is clear is that trauma-related brain changes make people more susceptible to feeling stress and anxiety in subsequent circumstances.

When the body feels the impact of the overreaction to a stressor, the stressor not only *seems* but *is* more intense, and new experiences are changed by the heightened intensity of that reaction. Many adults who were neglected as children have powerful stress responses when they feel alone. So being alone, by itself a minor stress for most people, becomes painful and a person could begin to feel highly anxious whenever she or he faced "alone" time. A stressor that may have been mild or unimportant is subsequently perceived as a big deal and causes a serious stress response. The implications are serious for the development of personality disorder as well as for Axis I anxiety disorders. The goal of psychotherapy for anxiety is to assist the client in bringing the sensitized brain back under some control. How much healing can occur depends on many factors, including seriousness of the damage, physical health, lifestyle factors such as nutrition and exercise, and the consistency of applying symptom-management techniques.

"Out of the Blue" Panic Versus Cues of Trauma

The impact of living with aversive stress can have several outcomes. It may function as trauma, creating unconscious cues to panic; it may shape reactions that affect the development of personality; or it may sensitize the stress response. Sensitizing the stress response will result in higher degrees of generalized anxiety rather than unconscious cues to panic.

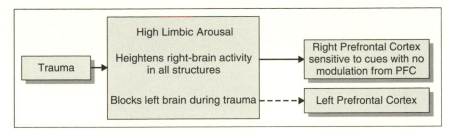

FIGURE 3.3. Trauma changes the brain.

Ongoing traumatic experience changes the way the amygdala identifies cues and alters the stress response, a change that is diagrammed in Figure 3.3. The cues generalize more widely to different kinds of situations, prompting more frequent panic attacks. Additionally, when people are conditioned by these increasing panic attacks to learn that panic is a likely response, the fear of another panic attack becomes more intense. Thus learning, which is itself a brain activity, affects the likelihood of panic.

Alternatively, "out of the blue" panic experiences may be the result of activity in the basal ganglia and be unrelated to life events. Sporadic firing of neurons in this region of the brain may trigger panic in the way a short in an electrical circuit may sporadically cause an electrical connection to be made. Panic attacks may result from this kind of electrical activity in the brain system, similar to seizure activity. This misfiring in the basal ganglia can start at any age, but as in all panic states, once it starts it quickly develops into the psychological state of PD. It can be a great relief to people who have this history of panic development to know it is just a neurochemical "glitch" and not evidence that they are crazy or losing control.

Another theory is based on the finding that people with panic disorder have about a third fewer serotonin (SE) neurons in the raphe and the limbic areas, which affects basal ganglia neuronal activity. It is possible that there is not enough serotonin to allow the anterior cingulate gyrus (ACG) to dampen limbic signals of distress (Maron et al., 2004).

PANIC AND HORMONES

People may be born with brains that have or will develop biological triggers to panic. They may experience panic from an early age or develop panic at times of biological adjustments in hormone levels. Genetic makeup determines some of this developmental potential of panic, and this is probably why women have a greater likelihood of developing panic. When women hit puberty, their estrogen/progesterone levels begin a rapid monthly change, which affects neurobiology. The 20% of women who are genuinely sensitive to hormonal changes during their monthly cycles, pregnancy, postpartum, perimenopause, or menopause experience the estrogen-progesterone balance differentially affecting transmission or reception of SE neurotransmitters (Leibenluft, 1999). Because the gonadal hormones sensitize receptor sites for neurotransmitters, changes in their levels can affect the transmitter functions that modulate anxiety states. When the receptor sites are less sensitive to neurotransmission, they do not function as efficiently, and SE levels that are minimal or insufficient have less chance of maintaining their necessary levels of functioning. Without sufficient SE, the norepinephrine (NE) levels may increase and the resulting arousal may make the brain more easily triggered into panic states.

Additionally, the thyroid hormone is intensely connected to states of panic and anxiety. High thyroid function alone can cause the sensations of anxiety and panic (Bunevicius, Velickiene, & Prange, 2005). When there is too much thyroid, physiological arousal may include rapid heart rate, fatigue, difficulty sleeping, and feelings of agitation. It would be difficult to tell the difference between feeling exceptionally anxious and have high thyroid levels. When certain thyroid diseases such as Hashimoto's disease cause erratic levels of thyroid hormone, the symptoms may come and go, and panic may appear to come "out of the blue." This was the case with Karen, who began to have panic attacks during her first year of graduate school.

Karen was a hard worker and accustomed to school success. Although it was tempting to ascribe her panic to the stress of harder coursework than she had previously faced, her panicky state was unpredictable and intense, and she was not conscious of feeling the stress any more acutely than she previously had. When a careful diagnostic interview was conducted, the pattern of symptoms, coupled with a family history of both Hashimoto's thyroid disease and hypoglycemia, suggested that an endocrinological exam was necessary before diagnosing PD. While she waited to get a medical evaluation, Karen made good use of calming techniques (described in Chapter 4) for the high arousal. Eventually the medical testing revealed that her panic was indeed caused by biological factors.

As this case illustrates it is important for therapists to consider the possibility of hormonal sensitivity or malfunction when diagnosing PD.

CONCLUSION

Panic disorder can be triggered by many things. Therapists must be watchful for the impact of negative life experiences, noting the age or developmental stage of a person at the time of the experience. Therapists must also be willing to consider that brain activity alone might be triggering the panic—and evidence of the contribution of an anxious brain should be considered with each factor. In reviewing clients' history and planning treatment, various factors should be weighed:

- Psychological history
- Family history (genetic contribution, life events)
- Medical crises
- Evidence of hormonal dysfunction
- Developmental indicators (age of onset and life events)
- Patterns of onset of the symptoms

When people know why the panic has come on, they are better prepared to use every therapy tool provided in each stage of treatment.

Panic disorder is among the easiest of all psychological disorders to treat. People experience rapid, dramatic improvement when they are able to follow the treatment recommendations specific to their situation. The most difficult aspect of treatment is gaining compliance, so teaching the reason for the techniques must be part of the program. In the next chapter we review the major techniques for eliminating panic attacks, changing false beliefs about the cause (or outcome or meaning) of panic attacks, and eliminating the avoidant patterns that typically accompany PD.

CHAPTER FOUR

TREATING PANIC DISORDER

Sara entered therapy after a full year of medical tests—a situation commonly seen in psychotherapy. Her intense onset of panic included all of the physical symptoms. These symptoms had been brought on a couple of years ago, after she had experienced a severe allergic reaction during a routine medical treatment. She had been treated with high doses of steroid medications. Sara assumed that the symptoms would disappear after the medical situation was resolved, but she continued to suffer tachycardia, surges of high blood pressure, and a sensation of dying—classic panic symptoms.

Sarah was baffled about these symptoms. She doubted that they reflected a sudden change in her cardiac health, because she had always been athletic and in good shape, but she couldn't come up with any other explanation. Too exhausted to maintain her normal workout schedule and worried about her physical health, Sara sought medical help. Her primary physician sent to her to three specialists—a cardiologist, an ear-nose-throat specialist, and an endocrinologist. None of them produced positive test results.

Meanwhile, the frequent panic attacks were reducing Sara to a shadow of her former self. Her level of physical activity and energy continued to drop precipitously, and she began to feel out of control and confused. Her cognitions became distorted. Her first thought had been "I feel like I am dying," and this had taken her down the medical pathway. After a year's worth of failed treatments and inconclusive tests for possible medical conditions, Sara had to acknowledge that she was not dying. So she shifted her cognition to "I am losing control."

In trying to get her attacks under control, Sara changed her normal behavior dramatically. She began avoiding all things that might cause her to panic. She stopped driving on highways and tried to stay on local routes. She reduced her work hours. She kept social commitments to a bare minimum. No longer highly energetic and sociable, she was staying inside, napping often, and otherwise withdrawing from the active life she had led. Her marriage was also beginning to suffer.

Sara was mentally on her way to "I must be going crazy" when she switched her primary care physician. Her new doctor listened to the symptom picture and insisted she see a psychiatrist and a psychologist to treat the panic. Sara had gone through MRIs, blood work, heart monitors, and every test recommended. She had drawn the line at taking high blood pressure medication "just to see if they help." Yet, she could not believe her problem was psychological—she was not a panicky person. However, lacking any better idea, Sara went along with the doctor's recommendation. She sought therapy and started on medication for PD. After learning some breathing and thought-changing techniques, Sara found her panic beginning to subside.

Sara's case illustrates how panic brought on by any type of cause can lead to a cascade of change in thought and behavior. Once people *believe* they will panic and *believe* that avoiding places or situations will circumvent panic, PD is in place and treatment must be psychological. The treatment targets for Sara were typical of those used for PD. Therapy consisted of a series of methods that allowed her to change her brain to control symptoms, to slow down the frequency of the onset of panic, and to change thought and behavior patterns by using cognitive-behavioral techniques (CBT) for the short term and insight-oriented work for the longer term.

The first step of treatment is to address the physiology. Once this has been done, the second and third steps (addressing cognitions and addressing behaviors) can be conducted simultaneously in an interwoven process.

Step 1. Address Physiology. Stopping the attack is the first part of the therapy process. This involves:

- Psychoeducation about how panic is generated and why the physical methods will work to stop panic attacks.
- Learning calming techniques such as breathing and relaxation.
- Decreasing the frequency of onset of panic. This is a byproduct of stopping the attack and of desensitizing triggers.

Step 2. Address Cognitions. This step, done in conjunction with the next step, involves:

- Identifying unrecognized triggers.
- Minimizing known cues and triggers through CBT and other methods.
- Challenging distorted cognitions.

Step 3. Address Behavior. The goal of this step is to stop avoidance behaviors and face the fears. This involves:

- Learning to tolerate or ignore physical sensations.
- Confronting previously avoided situations.
- Identifying and desensitizing unrecognized triggers through Eye Movement Desensitization and Reprocessing (EMDR), insight-oriented therapy, and CBT methods.

STEP 1. ADDRESS PHYSIOLOGY

Panic disorder is the easiest of all anxiety disorders to treat. There is no brain-based function that prevents people with PD from stopping panic attacks—*if* they do what they learn in good psychotherapy. That may sound like a bold claim, but controlling the worst of the panic symptoms is simply an issue of learning to turn off the sympathetic arousal causing them. This can be learned very quickly.

Identifying Triggers

The journey down the path to recovery from PD ends when the brain itself is changed by therapy that alters thought and action. Stopping an attack is the first step on the path for everyone. This step is easy for many, particularly those for whom panic comes out of the blue. For others, it may not be as easy, due to a host of psychological reasons that depend on the origination of the panic and the life circumstances of the client. Recall that:

- Panic attacks are triggered when the basal ganglia (BG) generate a signal (for no good reason) that the person is in imminent danger. The BG are likely to generate panic attacks over a lifetime, but frequency of onset can be decreased and the attacks can be warded off so that the person need no longer have panic *disorder*.
- Panic attacks may also be triggered by a cue that the person does not even recognize. These cues may be internal sensations or psychological triggers from some earlier experience or even from prior panic attacks.
- Panic attacks may be triggered by physical conditions that must be treated before the panic can abate.

Ruling Out Physical Causes

Several physical symptoms of panic attacks are characteristic of medical disorders. Thus, as in all psychological treatment, it is imperative to rule out medical conditions that may underlie the psychological state. Some of the similarities between anxiety and medical conditions are outlined in Table 4.1.

Assessment should include questions about known medical conditions and about the date of the person's most recent physical exam or medical visit. Regarding medication, ask whether:

- Prescribed medications are being used.
- Medications are being used *as prescribed.*
- Medications are being prescribed by more than one physician.
- All physicians are aware of the other physicians' prescriptions.

TABLE 4.1 Similarities Between Anxiety Symptoms and Medical Conditions

Anxiety Symptom	Possible Medical Condition
Shortness of breath	Heart problems
	Respiratory problems (e.g., pneumonia)
	Asthma, pulmonary obstruction
Dizziness, faintness	Anemia
	Benign positional vertigo
	Blood pressure
Palpitations	Tachycardia
	Mitral valve prolapse
	Thyroid problems
	Hypoglycemia
	Perimenopause
Sweating, flushing	Hormonal imbalances (e.g., menopause, thyroid)
Depersonalization	Temporal lobe epilepsy
Numbness or tingling	Hyperventilation
	Circulatory/respiratory problems
Chest pain	Heart conditions
Nausea	Many possibilities

Therapists treating PD must work with a psychiatrist or have contact with their clients' medical doctors to review the medical symptoms and history and to advise on the necessity of medical examination. Many clients come to treatment already using medication, and contact with the prescribing physician is quite useful to discuss treatment. Therapy can begin while a person is obtaining necessary medical evaluations because initial therapeutic treatment does not vary.

Psychoeducation: Convince the Brain That It Can Change Itself

Psychotherapy works because it helps clients utilize the function of the executive brain to control, shape, and change other brain functions. Offering a complete course on brain physiology is not necessary, but giving clients a general sense of brain function helps them understand how therapy techniques work. We teach clients that panic is a biopsychosocial problem. We also discuss:

- Causes of the disorder
- Potential for recovery
- Required preliminary psychological and medical testing
- Methods of treatment

Knowing how panic attacks start is absolutely necessary for success with physical panic-stopping methods. By helping clients understand the physical nature of panic we:

- Help them understand why the treatment methods work
- Help them come to *believe* that treatment will work
- Engage the learning and decision-making functions of their brains to increase compliance
- Improve confidence that has been undermined by panic

Psychoeducation is best done in small groups. Being in a group implicitly suggests that clients are neither unique nor alone, which is marvelously reassuring for people who believe themselves to be crazy or wrong. Small groups are better than larger groups because these clients typically become anxious when there are too many people to relate to at one time. In fact, many people with panic also have agoraphobic symptoms.

The Panic Record

Individualized assessment and information-gathering helps the thinking brain to fully engage. Assessment always requires an accurate picture of the symptoms and their severity. In addition, objective measures of frequency and severity become a reality check device later in therapy.

The panic record is very simple. For a few days or even a week at the very beginning of treatment, clients keep track of the time of day the attack occurred, how severe it was, how long it lasted, where they were when it occurred, and what situation or thoughts preceded the attack (even if there is no obvious relationship between what they were doing and feeling panicky). This can be done on an index card or a page in a notebook. A sample version of this chart is shown in Table 4.2.

If clients do this for even a few days, they will document an important standard against which to measure progress. Additionally, and even more importantly, they will have practiced the art of observing their panic from an objective standpoint. This becomes an important tool in the cognitive therapy of panic.

TABLE 4.2 Sample Panic Record Chart

When	Severity (1–10)	Duration	Where	Situation or Thoughts That Preceded It
Tues., 10 A.M.	8	12 minutes	classroom	test announced

Changing the Brain by Changing the Body

As noted earlier, the brain is a physical organ that is constantly interacting with the body in highly complex, intertwined ways. Thus, addressing physiology to treat panic involves changing lifestyle habits that affect the body. These include:

- Nutrition
- Exercise
- Sleep

Nutrition

Addressing nutrition includes eliminating the CATS—caffeine, alcohol, tobacco, and sweeteners (sugar and aspartame)—in our clients' lives. Caffeine is a stimulant, and brains that are already overactive do not need added agitation. However, there are surprising genetic reasons why some people's panic is triggered by caffeine. Adenosine is an inhibitory neurotransmitter connected to creating sleepiness. Caffeine interferes with adenosine receptors in the basal ganglia—it stimulates the brain in that area. People with a specific genetic variation of this receptor have stronger reactions to caffeine ingestion. Those with PD are likely to have this genetic variation, and when they ingest caffeine, it brings on a panic attack.

Alcohol also has a connection to panic. When it is first ingested, it calms the brain down through its impact on GABA reception, but after the sedating effect wears off and before it is completely eliminated from the body, it leaves cells in the brain irritated, creating agitation. Many anxious people induce drowsiness or relaxation with a couple of drinks. Even that amount of alcohol can cause brain cell irritation and may wake people a few hours after they go to sleep. The more a person drinks and the more frequently, the greater the likelihood of anxiety stemming from alcohol use. Some people have an imbalance in the GABA glutamate system, which may create sensations of agitation that are diminished with alcohol use, leading to a vicious circle of agitation/sedation/increased agitation.

There is some disagreement regarding tobacco's impact on anxiety. The act of smoking is a relaxing activity, and nicotine is known to increase focus, but smoking is linked to increased sensations of panic (Goodwin, Lewinsohn, & Seeley, 2005; Zvolensky et al., 2005a; Zvolensky et al., 2005b). A big "but" here is that the thought of eliminating tobacco can also make people highly anxious. Thus, eliminating smoking should only be considered as a long-term anxiety management goal. An interesting sidebar to the problem of smoking is that it appears to intensify trauma and increase the risk of PTSD (Beckham et al, 2005; McClernon et al., 2005).

Sugar is an issue for people with hypoglycemia. People vulnerable to hypoglycemia may experience panic attacks triggered by low blood sugar levels. When people ingest sugar the blood sugar level rises rapidly. Then the sugar level falls rapidly, causing the body to feel shaky, nauseous, and sweaty—very much like when a panic attack comes on. The sweetener aspartame has been linked to increased anxiety among many other problems, so clients should curtail drinking beverages and eating sweets that contain this sweetener.

Eliminating CATS from clients' diets is an important first step in curbing anxiety. The results of such nutritional changes can be immediate and profound, as was the case with Ellie.

Ellie could not figure out why her panic attacks returned with a vengeance two months after she returned to college from summer break. She had done so well over the summer, even discontinuing the medication she had taken for years prior to consulting me for panic that would not stop despite medication. In therapy, Ellie had practiced breathing and worked on eliminating catastrophic thinking, but now the panic was suddenly back. I considered the possibility that Ellie's discontinuation of medication was the culprit, but before I suggested that she see her psychiatrist, I asked her to keep a panic record.

Flashing her big, beautiful smile when she came in for her next session, Ellie showed me her panic profile: "Look!" she grinned. "I figured it out!" She could directly trace attacks to days after she drank heavily and to times when she smoked a cigarette—neither of which she did while living at her parent's house over the summer. Her caffeine use had risen dramatically to help her wake up for classes after partying at night, and her diet had devolved to pizza and doughnuts. Ellie did not relish the idea of giving up these habits, but her panic record had made it clear: Her anxiety symptoms were physical, and calming her body had eliminated her panic triggers. Taking care to eliminate the CATS from her body, Ellie got back on track without returning to medication.

Exercise

Exercise has been proven to decrease the impact of stress on anxious people, but it has other significant effects as well (Babyak & Blumenthal, 2000; Blumenthal et al., 1999; DeAngelis, 2002; Lancer, 2005; Manger, 2005). People with PD have high degrees and often long duration of stress response. When they engage in regular, vigorous exercise, they diminish the impact of stress on the physical body:

- Physical activity dissipates the adrenalin released in the stress response.
- Exercise helps the body rid itself of toxins more quickly; the stress response releases cortisol, which is toxic to brain cells.
- Exercise uses up the fat and glucose released by the stress response.
- Exercise raises levels of neurochemicals that promote positive mood and energy.

The prescription is simple: Exercise 5–7 days a week, for 25–45 minutes, at 70% of your maximum heart rate. (That can be measured by the talk test. You know you are exercising vigorously enough when, while continuing to move, you have difficulty catching your breath and talking at the same time.) The exercise can be walking, running, or any form of activity that keeps the body moving. For maximum stimulation of neurochemicals, repetitive and noncompetitive activities are best.

Sleep

Shakespeare wrote in *Macbeth* a wonderful line, "Sleep that knits up the ravell'd sleeve of care." Getting enough sleep does important things for the body-brain. During the cycles of a night's sleep, the brain is busy accomplishing important tasks of learning, eliminating unnecessary information, and restoring itself physically (Stickgold, 2005). A normal night of a sound

8-hour rest includes four cycles of deepening brainwave patterns, each of which is followed by a period of REM sleep. The first of the four REM dream cycles lasts about 10 minutes, and they gradually increase in length. The fourth cycle lasts 50–60 minutes, just before we awaken, and is the dream cycle we are most likely to remember.

The brainwave cycles allow the hippocampus to send information learned during the day (short-term memory) to the left prefrontal cortex (PFC). The PFC examines the stimuli presented and establishes a long-term memory if the information is important. The process consolidates knowledge. If we have had a stressful day, the hippocampus and the amygdala send neurochemical signals to the PFC that the PFC can release—not unlike sending computer data to the recycle bin. The kind of dreaming that occurs while the hippocampus is sending information to the PFC includes lots of detail.

Rapid eye movement (REM) sleep is necessary for calming and relieving stress. During REM, the PFC discharges unnecessary stressful input. When people fail to get enough sleep, they cheat themselves of REM and its important functions related to stress relief. It is during REM that the neurons produce more neurotransmitters and regenerate themselves. If the REM cycles are disturbed, the brain cannot fully restore balance in the neurotransmitter systems. Additionally, during REM the PFC modulates the emotional reactivity of the amygdala.

The importance of sleep is relevant to all anxiety disorders, and establishing a healthy sleep pattern is a goal of treatment. Ways of improving sleep are discussed in Chapter 7.

Calming Techniques: Diaphragmatic Breathing

Diaphragmatic breathing diminishes panic attacks in two ways. The decision to breathe is made in the prefrontal cortex (PFC); it is an executive decision that overrides the primitive brain (the medulla), where respiration and heart rate are controlled without conscious intention. Thus a panicking person can, by making a decision, change the rate of respiration. That stimulates activity of the parasympathetic nervous system (PSNS) to reduce physiological arousal (Figure 4.1). Further, when breathing reduces panicky arousal, it also stops the firing in the basal ganglia (BG) that triggered the panic. Stopping firing in the BG over time reduces overactivity in the BG, thus reducing the likelihood of a panic attack.

Diaphragmatic breathing is the first thing to teach people, as it is the most reliable means of stopping a panic attack once it has begun. It is the only thing that a person can do as an act of will, even without believing it will work. It is guaranteed to change physiology immediately. If clients are

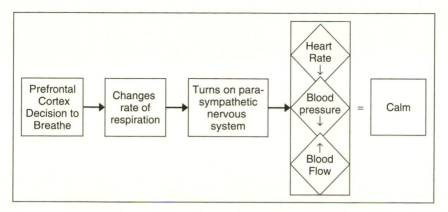

FIGURE 4.1.   The effect of diaphragmatic breathing.

tense, their breathing is probably affected even before they start to panic. In panic, breathing gets shallow and rapid, and people feel as if their breath is coming in gulps or gasps. They hyperventilate, eventually becoming dizzy. Diaphragmatic breathing counters that kind of breathing. Although used differently, this method is also important with generalized anxiety, so it should be learned by all clients with anxiety disorders. The following instructions for diaphragmatic breathing can be given to clients as a printed worksheet or simply conveyed verbally.

THE DIAPHRAGMATIC BREATHING TECHNIQUE

Before you start, carefully observe how you breathe. Take a moment to write down what you observe about your breathing right now. Is your breathing regular in its pace on inhaling and exhaling? Do you pause in your breathing? When? Do you feel short of breath or rushed? Can you tell if you are filling your lungs or breathing into your chest only? What can you notice? Fill out the chart (Table 4.3) by putting a checkmark next to the descriptions that apply and add notes describing any other observations you may have about your breathing.

 The next time you are under pressure, set aside a part of your attention to observe how your breathing changes when you are tense. If you have to speak at a meeting and that makes you nervous, notice your breathing. If you are having a disagreement, note how you breathe. If you are feeling pressure from time, take a moment to feel your breath-

TABLE 4.3 Breathing Checklist

Short or impeded intake		Even, but fast		
Gasping		Relaxed		
Long in, short out		Holding breath		
Shallow		Panting		
Gulping		Hyperventilating		
Additional Observations:				

ing. It may surprise you to find that you have not been filling your lungs or that you have been holding your breath after you inhale.

Instructions

This technique can be done anywhere, anytime. Whether you are tense at work or home, in public or alone, you can breathe without being obvious. When you are at home practicing this technique, you may be more comfortable lying down as you do it.

1. Lie down flat on your back or stand in a relaxed manner with your feet slightly apart and your knees loose. You must have a straight passage for air to flow. If you are seated, make sure you are sitting straight and that your head is upright, not hanging forward or tilted back against a couch cushion.
2. Rest your hand on your abdomen. This will help you to notice if you are breathing deeply enough and whether your chest is tight. One way to imagine this is to think about how a balloon fills with water when you attach it to a faucet. The bottom fills and widens first and then the water expands the upper portion. This image of heaviness as you fill is something to hold in mind as you imagine your breath. Form an image of your breath filling your abdomen, feeling heavy and warm. This will help your body to relax and fill your lungs completely. If you have trouble feeling this, raise your arms and clasp your hands behind your neck. It will help you breathe more fully.
3. Next, blow out all the air in your lungs until you feel empty.
4. Then begin to breathe in. Inhaling must be done evenly, as if you can fill your lungs from bottom to top in equal, even amounts.

Breathing evenly is easier when you find a pace that works to measure your breathing in and out. Count your breathing until you feel exactly full (e.g., a slow 1, 2, 3, 4) to help you get a measured, even breath. It will probably take 3–6 counts to fill your lungs. If you do not like the idea of counting, breathe while thinking a sentence with an even rhythm, such as "I notice I am breathing in. I notice I am breathing out."

5. Fill up evenly, with no gulps or gasps, so the top is reached physically (as in the image of the balloon) just in time to release the breath at the same even, measured pace.

6. Exhale evenly. Count the breath out of your body, with no sudden release. Never take less time to exhale than you took to inhale. Your body needs time to exchange the oxygen and carbon dioxide, and inhaling too rapidly can make you dizzy.

7. Exhale longer than you inhale. If you get dizzy breathing in and out at the same pace, exhale for 2 counts longer than it took you to inhale or pause for 2 counts at the end of the breath.

8. Practice! This kind of breathing will calm you down during a panic attack. Most people who panic immediately forget their panic control measures unless they have practiced them. It is essential to use diaphragmatic breathing the moment you sense a panic attack beginning, so you must practice frequently, whether or not you are sensing panic at the moment.

How to Practice Breathing

Most breathing and relaxation books suggest 10 minutes of breathing per day, but that might seem like a monumental task. It is better to start with a manageable goal and build up to the longer period of breathing, which will set the stage for deep relaxation.

For 7 days, practice this breathing for 1–2 minutes at a time, up to 10 times a day. Decide to practice whenever you are:

- Stopped at a stoplight
- On hold on the phone
- Brushing your teeth
- Watching the commercial breaks during a television show
- In line at a store
- Waiting for a friend at work or school
- In the car to pick up someone
- Waiting for the computer to boot

- Waiting for the teacher to hand out the test papers
- Waiting for the phone to ring
- Waiting for a meeting to start

On the eighth day, pick one time of day when you can predict that you will be uninterrupted for a few minutes. Early morning, late evening, or lunchtime work best for most people. During this one uninterrupted period per day you are going to *add one minute of breathing per day.* You can have music on during this time—preferably classical or new age music, which is specifically composed to enhance brainwaves for relaxation. For the second 7 days, you will continue the 1–2 minute practices seven to nine times a day but you will add one minute each day to the time you picked when you can be uninterrupted. By the end of the week, you may be breathing during this time for 7–8 minutes. This period of time is the foundation for profound tension release, meditation, and cueing of the relaxation that helps the stress response turn off.

The more you practice the diaphragmatic breathing technique, the more you will notice about your breathing. This technique is simple to do, but not easy to master. For breathing to effectively reduce tension, you first have to remember to use it! Until it becomes a habit, you may forget to breathe under anxiety or tension. It takes time, practice, and attention for this process to feel smooth, easy, and natural. As they used to say about driving a stick-shift Volkswagon Beetle, "After a while, it's automatic!"

You can use diaphragmatic breathing for panic attacks right away. You will immediately notice a reduction in the length of the panic attack. Over a period of a few weeks, if you successfully diminish the impact of your panic attacks, you will see a decrease in frequency of the panic. Stopping panic in its tracks calms the basal ganglia and causes it to trigger panic less often.

Obstacles to Diaphragmatic Breathing

Most people encounter obstacles before they make breathing work. Following are some of the common obstacles.

Clients may forget to practice or forget to breathe when anxiety strikes. This is why we link breathing to *many* times, places, and activities throughout the day. If clients find themselves forgetting to practice, suggest the following:

- Visualize yourself practicing, for example, breathing at the sink, in the car, in front of the computer while it boots up, on the phone, or in front of the television. This will help remind you to practice in those places.
- Keep track of when you practice. Some people remember better if they do this. You can keep an index card handy and make a tally mark whenever you practice. The reinforcement of noticing when you practice sets it more clearly in your mind and helps you remember the next practice more readily.
- Post a reminder note in a prominent spot. You can also write the word *breathe* on a notecard and pull it out of your pocket or purse whenever you start to feel anxious.

Breathing may create anxiety. Some people become anxious when they start to breathe deeply. Some fear they will panic while doing something new or something that reminds them of their symptoms. Discuss these fears openly. There are many reasons why a person may resist, so exploring fear of the technique is necessary.

Breathing may not seem to help. It is very rare for diaphragmatic breathing to have no positive impact on panic reduction. Ask clients to observe how they are practicing. It is likely that they are either filling their chests while keeping the abdomen tight or that they are holding their breath during part of the breathing. It can be hard for clients to recognize what they are doing wrong without having someone observe them. I once debated two graduate students in my class who insisted they must suck in their stomachs while breathing in. (They were a great example of how women are socialized to look feminine—they did not want to let their abdomen move out when anyone was looking.) They were doing the exact opposite of what their bodies would have done naturally, but they had breathed in this wrong way for so long that it felt natural. They were amazed at how different it felt when they finally let their abdomen expand while inhaling.

Clients may have difficulty concentrating when they practice breathing. Thoughts flit through all our minds, distracting us and making us forget what we were doing. This is especially likely to happen when clients are adding a minute a day to their uninterrupted breathing sessions. The best way to handle this is to say:

- Notice that you have been distracted.
- Mentally say to yourself, "Oh. A thought." Just notice, without judging yourself negatively, getting upset, or becoming impatient. Consider thoughts as clouds in the sky, just drifting by. There is no need to stop them, examine them, or be irritated that they are there.
- Redirect your attention to your breath.

- Focus on the physical sensation of breathing: the feeling of the lungs expanding, the increasing and decreasing pressure on the waistband, the shifting of the back against a chair, and so on. Feel the breath move through your nostrils or out of your mouth.
- Count to measure the pace of the breathing to help maintain your focus.

There may be restrictions to inhaling. These can include feeling tight or feeling obstructions, as if there is a block in the airflow, or feeling unable to fill the lungs completely. This is not uncommon when people are very anxious. Clients must first make sure they are upright and loosen any restrictive clothing, such as tight jeans or neckties. If this doesn't work, the source of the problem may be emotional. In that case, discuss in therapy:

- Where is the restriction or obstruction located?
- How does it feel? Is there a word or phrase that describes it?
- What does it look like? What is its shape, color, or size?

Then clients should:

- Visualize it clearly.
- Send their breath to the center of that block.
- Notice what happens as they breathe. (Obstructions or restrictions that have an emotional basis will often disappear when clients become aware of them, as long as they do not fight to push them away.)
- Ask themselves what it would take to make the block get smaller or disappear and then imagine doing it.

A final note on diaphragmatic breathing: Often as clients get better and experience fewer panic attacks or none at all, they discontinue their breathing rituals. This was the case with Ellie, the client introduced earlier in this chapter. When Ellie suddenly began experiencing panic attacks again after her return to college, she feared, like many clients, that her new surge of panic might be too powerful for the old methods to work, and she panicked about feeling panic again. We spent a session reviewing diaphragmatic breathing, and she was able to use it effectively again.

Some people, however, simply refuse to believe this technique will work. They get stuck on the idea that the technique is too simple or they believe their panic is so much worse than everyone else's that they will not benefit from what works for others. This is often a result of interference from personality disorder characteristics. As such it becomes grist for the psychotherapy process. Practicing breathing during therapy sessions can help in identifying what the block is, but these clients may make slower progress than most people do with this method.

STEPS 2 AND 3. ADDRESS COGNITIONS, ADDRESS BEHAVIOR

These two steps are nearly simultaneous. Cognitions of dying or losing control cause people to immediately avoid whatever they are doing when the sensation occurs. Therefore, when trying to change the cognitions, we encourage staying in the situation that may trigger a panic attack. (Staying is the antidote to avoiding.) The goal is to undo any superstitious thoughts about what causes panic. After triggers to panic are identified (a cognitive technique), they can be desensitized, which changes behavior almost automatically. In other words, changing cognition immediately changes behavior, and there are not many behavioral tools independent of cognitive tools with panic that is not coupled with agoraphobia.

Three Common Fears

People with PD have three typical cognitions about the panic attack: "I'm dying"; "I'm losing control"; and "I'm going crazy." Given the physiological symptoms of autonomic arousal (Figure 4.2), these self-statements are understandable, but they make the panic worse.

If you have never experienced a panic attack, just believe this: It is among the worst feelings you can have. People having a panic attack are experiencing sheer terror. They literally feel as if they are dying right at that moment. It is all the more frightening because there is no reason for the terror. That is why people start to think that they are going crazy or losing control. Consider this for a moment: If a man in a ski mask pointing a gun broke into your room right now, you would feel terror. You would be seized by sensations of intense fear and your body would have all of the symptoms of a panic attack. *But you would know why you felt that way.* Your feelings would be reasonable and you would not fear feeling that way again because you would know those feelings were an appropriate response to the danger. People with PD, on the other hand, go into that state of terror when they are not doing anything that would explain it. Three types of fear result:

- Fear about the meaning of the symptoms—usually that the person is dying, going crazy, or losing control. Each person has his or her own individual twist on these fears.
- Superstitious fear. People come to believe that whatever they were doing at the moment of panic is what caused the attack. This triggers future avoidance. If they believe that they can stop panic by avoiding a situation (like driving on the highway or being in a crowd), they will avoid those situations despite the inconvenience.

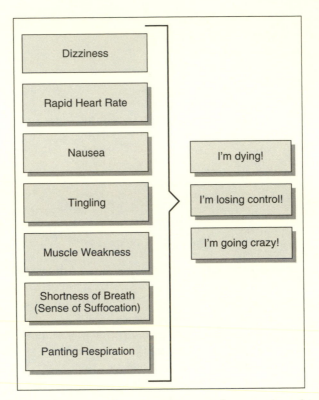

FIGURE 4.2. Symptoms of autonomic arousal create thoughts of panic.

- Fear that this could happen again. People begin to be afraid of their fear's returning.

Changing Fearful Thoughts

Changing the thought pattern, especially altering the fear of being afraid, is a major treatment goal. The fear of fear becomes a self-fulfilling prophecy (see Figure 3.1). When people are afraid of panicking they begin to watch their own physiology very carefully for signs of panic coming on. Consequently, they notice small sensations and start to fear that the sensation is an indicator of fear's getting started. Very quickly, cognitive processes— thinking about being afraid and how to avoid the fear—control the thoughts and actions of the person with PD. In therapy, people can learn to change the impact of the thoughts or the thoughts themselves. There are several ways to change cognition (the activity of the prefrontal cortex) so that the PFC will control or modulate the limbic system arousal:

- Cognitive-behavioral therapy (CBT)
- The Mindful Awareness technique
- Energy therapies
- Eye movement desensitization and reprocessing (EMDR)

Cognitive-Behavioral Therapy for Panic Disorder

Cognitive-behavioral therapy (CBT) is an important component of lasting recovery for anxiety (Craske et al., 2005). CBT techniques for PD include:

- Providing psychoeducation about what is going on during the attack. The explanation of panic dispels the fearful cognitions of dying, going crazy, and losing control.
- Stopping catastrophization that each little sensation is going to become a panic attack and that each panic attack is unbearable.
- Finding panic triggers by observation and record-keeping (as in the case of Mary and her sister's phone calls).
- Finding a counter-cognition that fits each specific fear and identifying and correcting the way a person has individualized the common panic fears of dying, going crazy, or losing control. For example, when the heart rate increases, a person may use a counter-cognition such as "There's the panic again—it's time to breathe," as opposed to "I'm dying of a heart attack!"
- Teaching that fear is unpleasant but not lethal. This is an important part of helping people face situations that they fear might trigger a new attack.

Cognitive-behavioral therapy engages the prefrontal cortex (PFC) executive functions. These executive functions include decision-making, good judgment, inhibition of behavior, and making meaning of experience. Talking through the situations in which a person panics engages the PFC to believe that the panic is unnecessary. Then the decision-making function allows a person with PD to use calming techniques (like breathing) purposefully. In discussion, we change the meaning of the symptoms, undoing superstitions about what they imply. This desensitizes the emotional limbic system and helps decrease the frequency of the attacks.

Finding the disturbing cognitions and changing them is often quite simple, and the changes work well, as the following case study illustrates. Occasionally, however, clients do not respond well to CBT. In these cases, other methods, such as insight-oriented or focusing therapy, may produce better results.

Jeanette had avoided being in crowded public places for years. When she began to avoid restaurants and movie theaters as well, her husband urged her to get help. Jeanette's worst fear was losing control, and she believed that her panic symptoms were signs that she was about to lose control. She refused to risk having those symptoms in public, but she was very vague about what "losing control" behavior would be. When I asked Jeanette, "What would I see if I were watching you lose control?" she stated, "Why, I would look like my mother!" Avoiding a Freudian interpretation at that point, I instead pushed for clarification: "Yes, but what would I see?" Jeanette then described that she would shake, fall on the ground, and be completely incapable of controlling her muscles. Further questioning revealed that Jeanette's mother had poorly controlled epilepsy and had frequently experienced seizures in crowded public places. These events had both terrified and embarrassed her young daughter. Jeanette's fear made sense.

When Jeanette felt her body beginning to shake during her panic attacks, she feared the worst. Cognitive-behavioral therapy involved educating her on how her panicky shaking was a result of adrenalin and did not mean she was having a seizure (establishing a counter-cognition). We then used CBT to formulate thoughts she could use to interrupt her irrational fears about panicking, such as "I have never had a seizure, and I am not having one now" and "I may not like crowds, but I need not panic just because I do not like them." At the onset of an attack she was to remind herself that panic attacks come out of the blue and for no good reason, and then use these thoughts to diminish her fear about those sensations. These reminders helped keep Jeanette's panic from escalating, and eventually she found herself believing her new cognitions fully.

Fear of fear. We can also decrease the likelihood of panic by introducing the cognition that a sensation is just a sensation. Because our clients are afraid of their fear, we teach them that "fear is nothing to be afraid of." It is surprising how often this thought has never occurred to people with PD. They benefit enormously if they come to accept the very real sensations of panic as not lethal but rather merely unpleasant. Therapy introduces the concept: "A feeling is just a feeling. It does not kill me, make me incompetent, or cause me to lose control." The next step for the event is to learn in which situations to apply this.

Mindfulness with Awareness

The wonderfully simple technique of mindfulness with awareness can help clients apply the cognition that "a feeling is just a feeling." Used when a panic feeling is first perceived, this technique helps people divert their attention rather than vigilantly monitoring whether the sensation is turning into panic. The exercise has two simple steps that are repeated several times. (For a lengthier description see Chapter 10.)

MINDFULNESS WITH AWARENESS

1. Close your eyes and breathe, noticing your body—how the intake of air feels, how the heart beats, and so on.
2. Remain with your eyes closed, and purposefully shift your awareness to what you hear or smell, noticing the external world and all of what you can perceive in it.

By shifting awareness back and forth several times, people with PD learn in a physical way that they can control what they notice about their world, whether internal or external. This is a metaphor for the internal locus of control. When people with PD can ignore physical sensations, they can stop making the catastrophic interpretations that actually bring on panic or worry. This helps them feel more in control as they stay mindful of *now* rather than the future.

The mindfulness with awareness technique worked very well with Sara, the client introduced at the beginning of this chapter, who had endured years of medical testing before she sought therapy. As Sara began to master the techniques of breathing and controlling her fear of dying and losing control, she developed another problem: she began to fear that she would always be afraid. "After all," she said, "this took total control over me, and I was always so strong." Sara had started make catastrophic interpretations of small physical sensations, essentially creating panic out of minor changes in her physical state. A slight chill or a momentary flutter in her stomach were enough to make her hyperventilate in fear that panic was on its way. And sure enough, it was—now that she was so focused on it.

Sara needed to stop catastrophizing and divert her attention away from her body. Like most anxious people do when they worry, Sara was thinking about the future and not just *being* in the present moment. Constantly on the lookout for signs of panic, she felt controlled by her body; she had never considered that *she* could manage her body by controlling what she did or did not pay attention to. She did not have to focus on her sensations, and by changing her focus, she could diminish the likelihood of another panic attack. The mindfulness with awareness technique helped Sara do this.

Diverting her attention to the external world was particularly helpful when Sara started to drive again. When she began feeling sensations that seemed like the harbinger of panic, she told herself, "A feeling is just a feeling," and then, breathing, she refocused her attention back on the road. It only took a couple of panic-free trips on the road for Sara to regain confidence that she could resume her driving without fear.

Energy Therapies

There are several versions of energy therapy techniques but all involve tapping with the fingers on acupressure points to decrease arousal of the body when thinking disturbing thoughts. (See Chapter 10 for a full description of this technique.) Energy therapies do not focus on changing cognitions but rather on changing the negative sensations associated with a specific thought. The goal of all versions of the technique is to eliminate fearful feelings associated with specific thoughts that trigger panic attacks, such as "I must drive on the highway."

When this technique works, there is a rapid change in the stirring of panic sensations. It can be a powerful tool to eliminate avoidant behaviors. For example, some people with PD are dreadfully afraid of taking in the middle seat in a theater because they would be trapped when a panic attack might start. This technique could be used to eliminate negative arousal while thinking about being in the theater, ultimately allowing the person to feel free to take the risk of going to a movie.

Eye Movement Desensitization and Reprocessing

Often people have some specific image or trigger that they keep reacting to, even though they know it does not indicate current danger. Car accidents are common on the list of panic-inducing life events, and people who, for example, were hit by a pickup truck may find that pickup trucks continue to serve as triggers for panic long after the original accident is over. Eye Movement Desensitization and Reprocessing (EMDR) is at the top of the list of methods most likely to desensitize traumatic images.

This method, developed by Francine Shapiro (2001), has the person form an image of a distressing scene (a "target" for fear reduction). The therapist then starts rhythmic, bilateral stimulation of the brain by moving a light or his or her fingers back and forth for the client's eyes to follow, by using headphones for sound in alternating ears, or by tapping alternately on the client's knees or hands. This process changes the brain by connecting the left prefrontal cortex (PFC) with the unmodulated emotional memory of a traumatic event, consequently desensitizing the emotional response to memory cues of the event. It allows the client to resolve the event in a therapeutic setting. (See Chapter 10 for a full description of this method.)

Originally developed as a trauma treatment technique, EMDR has evolved into a versatile and effective treatment method for all kinds of anxiety. Its ability to help clients identify and desensitize triggers for panic attacks makes it an irreplaceable tool for therapists treating clients with anxiety disorders, as the case of Jeanette, introduced earlier, illustrates.

As described earlier, Jeanette feared that her panic would cause her to look like her mother, who suffered epileptic seizures. One of the treatment goals with Jeanette was to desensitize her to images of her mother's seizures. In an EMDR session Jeanette revisited a scene of her mother having a seizure. She realized that when she panicked her body was not doing anything similar to what her mother's had done. This helped Jeanette stop fearing that she would look like her mother. Instead, she recognized the sense of helplessness she felt as a child when she could not control her mother's seizures. She subsequently recognized that she did not have to be helpless about her own fear. Jeanette relaxed her fear that her panicky feelings were the beginning of a seizure and she was then more able to use all the self-control measures she was learning in therapy.

MEDICATION OF PANIC DISORDER

There are many times when people with PD have been treated first by medical doctors. They come to therapy because they don't want to be on medication forever or because medication is not fully doing the job. Occasionally, medical doctors require that patients receiving medication also seek therapy.

In some cases, therapists may find that certain clients are just too overwhelmed by their symptoms of PD to get a grip on doing therapy. When the symptoms of panic are severe or intractable, it is wise to refer clients to a psychiatrist so they can use medication while getting started in therapy. The goal is to stop the medication after they are doing better. The following chapter discusses the psychopharmacology of PD.

CONCLUSION

Panic disorder is the easiest of all Axis I disorders and specifically all anxiety disorders to treat. It is often generated by neurobiological causes, although life experiences may complicate it. Even when it is generated by psychological trauma, the correction for the physical symptoms is straightforward. Compliance with treatment is often the most difficult part of the treatment.

We find that treating clients with panic requires us to put on our "expert" hat. Regardless of the strength of their personalities, people with PD tend to believe that panic is stronger than they are, and they feel helpless in the face of their symptoms. They need to believe that we as therapists know what we are doing and that our techniques will give them relief. The good news is that the techniques work and we can be confident in taking on the "expert" role in presenting them. Even more encouraging is the fact that the techniques usually work within several weeks of initiating therapy. However, PD is not often pure and unadulterated by life experiences that require longer-term therapy techniques.

People who are panicking want to know how long it will take before they feel better. Of course, it is impossible to predict how long it will take to prevent attacks completely, but we can reassure our clients that stopping attacks once they have started is something that can be learned relatively quickly. It is possible to say with confidence that if they are able to do the techniques they will feel better very soon.

Treating clients with PD is the closest a therapist can get to immediate gratification in therapy. No other disorder responds as swiftly to the methods we have available. Mastering the techniques of treating PD will reward the therapist again and again with the joy of seeing people feel better fast and feel ready to do the rest of the therapy work from a position of confidence.

CHAPTER FIVE

MEDICATING FOR PANIC DISORDER

Panic affects 2.7% of the adult population in the United States (National Institute of Mental Health, 2006). As noted in Chapter 3, PD consists of (1) symptoms of terror, called a *panic attack,* and (2) anticipatory anxiety regarding having further attacks. Medications target the physical and cognitive symptoms of panic by: diminishing the symptoms, decreasing the likelihood of experiencing panic, and modulating the mood of the PD patient. Medications directly affect neurobiology and are most effective when used in conjunction with psychotherapy for PD.

DO PANIC ATTACKS OCCUR ONLY IN PANIC DISORDER?

Panic attacks can also be associated with other anxiety conditions, including generalized anxiety disorder (GAD), post-traumatic stress disorder (PTSD), and phobic disorders including agoraphobia. Typically, PD strikes more females than males and usually begins in mid-adolescence or early adulthood, unless it is prompted by trauma. There is a definite genetic link with PD.

RISKS ASSOCIATED WITH PANIC DISORDER

Panic disorder has a tremendous, disabling impact on human lives, both for the person manifesting the disorder and also for family members. Among the most disabling risks are:

95

- Inability to achieve potential, especially in career or education, due to fear of having panic attacks in stressful situations.
- Social impairments, especially avoiding social situations due to fear of panic. This tendency may result in higher risk for PD with agoraphobia and may be a factor in comorbidity with social anxiety.
- Heightened suicide risk. There is debate about this risk, but some studies show a risk that is as high as the rates of suicide for depression. Therefore, especially when PD is comorbid with depression or addiction, careful attention to impulsivity and suicidality is required.
- Panic disorder patients have a risk of higher medical costs and of spending time and worry over extensive medical testing. Panic disorder is often referred to as a medical impostor, as patients' physical symptoms mimic emergencies such as heart attack and other medical conditions. That often leads to extensive tests for endocrine, neurological, and cardiovascular conditions, which are expensive and time-consuming.

THE ETIOLOGY OF PANIC DISORDER

Panic symptoms represent dysfunction in any of several possible neurobiological systems, and the symptom constellation reflects the specific abnormal function. Panic can be generated by neurotransmitter dysfunction or by neuroanatomical abnormalities. Therefore, physicians must target different symptoms with different types of medications.

Neurotransmitter Dysfunctions That Can Generate Panic Symptoms

There are several possible ways neurotransmitter activity may be disregulated and cause panic. Three neurotransmitters discussed in Chapter 2, norepinephrine (NE), serotonin (SE), and gamma aminobutyric acid (GABA), are of particular significance.

Norepinephrine

Norepinphrine is also called *noradrenalin,* and therefore one may refer either to the "noradrenergic" or the "norepinephrine" system. For clarity, we will use the term *norepinephrine,* knowing that readers will understand other reference materials may refer to this neurotransmitter with either name.

Some PD patients have an excess release of NE from the NE neurons in the locus coeruleus (the brain center that houses most of the NE nerve cells). Excess NE causes a cascade of symptoms that are anxiety-producing and can lead to panic states. NE may be excessively released in stressful situations, or chronic excess release of NE may sensitize the brain to easily trigger panic.

One way that NE neurons release too much NE is related to a hypersensitivity to an alpha-2 auto-receptor antagonist. When a neurotransmitter is released into a synapse, it can be received at any site—postsynaptic or presynaptic—that is prepared to receive it. An auto-receptor is on the presynaptic neuron and receives the neurotransmitter it releases. An alpha-2 auto-receptor is a presynaptic NE receptor located on the NE neuron that is releasing the NE. If activated (i.e., if it receives an NE molecule), the alpha-2 auto-receptor will *slow down* the release of NE. It has a braking effect on NE release. When the braking action stops, more NE is released. This is how a healthy brain functions to regulate the release of NE (Figure 5.1).

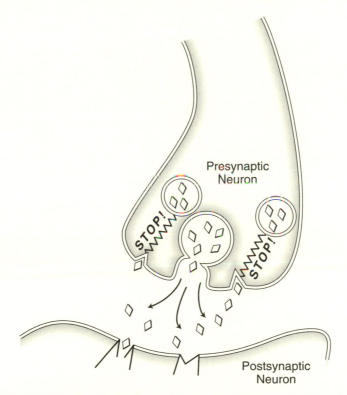

FIGURE 5.1. The braking effect of norepinephrine received at the auto-receptor. Norepinephrine transmitters (represented by the diamond-shaped objects) are released into the synapse. When the auto-receptor is stimulated by a norepinephrine neurotransmitter, the presynaptic neuron brakes the firing of transmitters.

In some cases, however, the alpha-2 presynaptic NE auto-receptor is antagonized (blocked). Therefore, the NE is not braked as it should be. This
results in an *increased release* of NE neurotransmitters, because the braking
action of the alpha-2 auto-receptor is inhibited. So, one cause of PD may be
hypersensitivity to any chemical that blocks the alpha-2 auto-receptor. This
hypersensitivity results in too much release of NE, which causes the heightened physical sensations of panic. This explanation for panic is supported
by the reaction to certain medications that exacerbate panic symptoms in
people with PD. For example, the medication yohimbine is an alpha-2 antagonist. When administered to PD patients, it triggers an exaggerated anxiety response. Caffeine, also an alpha-2 auto-receptor antagonist, similarly
causes heightened anxiety and panic in PD patients. In Figure 5.2, the

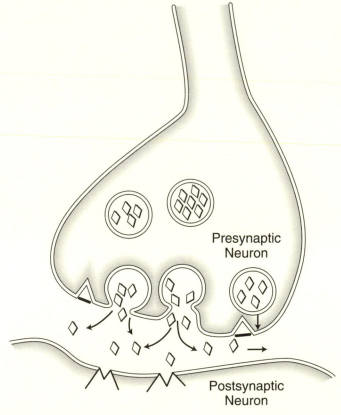

FIGURE 5.2.   The neurotransmitter is antagonized (blocked) at the auto-
receptor, allowing it to continue firing.

neurotransmitter cannot stimulate the presynaptic neuron to brake the firing of the neuron. Thus, excess NE is released.

Another possibility related to NE is that the patient has a *hyposensitive* alpha-2 NE auto-receptor. If a PD patient is not sufficiently sensitive at the alpha-2 auto-receptor site, the receptor will not shut down release of NE. The normal braking action does not occur. The end result is an increased release of the NE neurotransmitter. Some medications function as alpha-2 agonists. Agonists are chemical substances that *stimulate* release of a neurochemical. Extra NE in the synapse allows more stimulation of hyposensitive auto-receptors. Thus, the neuron gets the chemical message to stop releasing NE, and panic symptoms subside. Figure 5.3 demonstrates the neuron being agonized to allow more neurotransmitters to hit the auto-receptors.

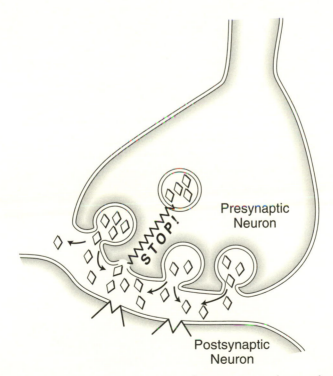

FIGURE 5.3. Receptor being agonized to increase release of norepinephrine.

Serotonin

The serotonin (SE) neurotransmitter is significant to the function of many brain structures and systems beyond panic symptoms, but its role in panic is most clear in its function to help maintain balance in the neurochemical feedback between the neurotransmitters that affect mood, anxiety, attention, and reward. Thus, SE is a neurochemical that has significant impact on brain structures that affect anxiety, and it affects norepinephrine (NE) levels, which are postulated as a cause of panic. SE and NE function in a feedback loop with each other. In a healthy brain, when SE is sufficiently available, NE levels remain balanced.

When SE is insufficient in the nervous system it can contribute to the sensation of panic. Because of the feedback mechanism between SE and NE transmitters, when SE is low, NE increases as a means to try to boost production of SE. When SE levels rise, NE production can drop off. In a brain in which SE production is impaired for some reason and when NE production cannot stimulate it sufficiently, the levels of SE rapidly become too low. That combination is postulated to cause symptoms of depression. An interesting adjunct to the hypotheses for NE causes of panic disorder is that if the increased NE cannot raise SE levels sufficiently, symptoms of anxiety and depression may both occur because the balance between these neurotransmitters is impaired, causing several systems in brain function to become disturbed.

Gamma Aminobutyric Acid

Another neurochemical involved with the etiology of PD is gamma aminobutyric acid (GABA). GABA is associated with relaxing the nervous system. Enhancing the effectiveness of GABA increases the sense of overall calmness and relaxation. If GABA is not working well, a person may manifest significant anxiety and paniclike symptoms.

Benzodiazepines are endogenous (internal) brain chemicals that affect GABA neurotransmitters. In a PD patient, the ability of the benzodiazepines to modulate GABA may be out of balance. Consequently, GABA may not calm the nervous system effectively. This imbalance may have several possible causes:

- The benzodiazepine receptor site on a GABA neurotransmitter may be insufficiently sensitive to the effects of the benzodiazepine neurochemical.
- The receptor site may have difficulty receiving the benzodiazepine.
- The brain may not be making enough endogenous benzodiazepine.
- The GABA receptor area may be dysregulated.

An additional aspect of the benzodiazepine-GABA connection relevant to the etiology of panic is that the brain may be producing too much anxiogenic inverse agonist (a substance that binds to a benzodiazepine receptor and causes a slowing down of chloride ion transmission). When chloride ions travel through the nerve cell they help relax the nervous tissue, slowing its activity. When the benzodiazepine receptor site is activated by a benzodiazepine, chloride (a negatively charged ion) is more available to flow through the nerve cell. In other words, chloride conductance is increased by a benzodiazepine at the receptor site.

If people with PD have too much inverse agonist binding to the benzodiazepine receptor site on the GABA-A receptor complex, this inverse agonist then acts opposite to the benzodiazepine. It causes a *decrease* in the chloride ion conductance in the nervous tissue. This results in heightened anxiety.

In PD patients a dysregulation of this chloride channel receptor complex may be caused by a problem at the benzodiazepine receptor. In these cases, benzodiazepine medications may help readjust the chloride channel conductance in the GABA-A complex and thus enhance relaxation of the nervous system.

Certain medications, including Xanax (alprazolam), Serax (oxazepam), Ativan (lorazepam), Valium (diazepam), and Klonopin (clonazepam), affect the benzodiazepine receptor site, enhancing the effects of GABA.

Neuroanatomical Structures Implicated in Panic Disorder

Neuroanatomic findings suggest other etiologic causes of panic. These may include structural abnormalities such as excessive or insufficient neurons in a region of the brain, abnormal blood flow, or problems in the connections of one region to another.

Dysregulation in Basal Ganglia Function

Basal ganglia (BG) dysfunction is a possible cause of PD. As noted earlier, the BG are a group of dense clusters of neurons that have several functions related to fine-motor movement (coordinated with emotion), general nervous system arousal, feelings of reward, and the modulation of anxiety. Many people with PD show increased activity in the BG, as visibly demonstrated by single positron emission computer tomography (SPECT) scans.

The Peripheral Nervous System

In the peripheral nervous system (PNS), NE acts on the nerves that affect physical functioning outside of the brain, and its impact on the muscles is relevant in anxiety disorders. NE can cause tremor and sweating, especially as seen in acute anxiety. Acute anxiety is a strongly aversive sensation that something is very wrong and it may go on at length. In response, the physical stress of heightened arousal in muscles, heart rate, and vascular system can create exhaustion and fatigue. At lower levels of activity the NE impact on the PNS causes the tension and irritability that mark GAD. Drugs called *beta-blockers* have their biggest impact on the peripheral neurons that affect heart rate, muscle nerves, sweating, and so on.

Lactate Sensitivity

Lactate sensitivity results in respiration increase and can trigger panic symptoms. There is some evidence that lactate-sensitive patients with PD have abnormal asymmetry of the parahippocampal blood flow on positron emission tomography (PET) scans.

Locus Coeruleus

There may be dysregulation in the locus coeruleus—a part of the pons, the area of the brain holding the majority of NE nerve cells. The locus coeruleus has NE projections connecting it to the hippocampus. Dysregulation of these projections may account for the problems with NE transmission hypothesized to cause panic attacks.

Seizurelike Activity

Patients who have epilepsy in their temporal lobe have a heightened likelihood for symptoms of panic. In seizures there is a phenomenon called *kindling,* in which nerve cells exponentially fire out of control. Just as the logs in a fire being started will, after kindling, catch on fire suddenly, so too nerve cells achieve a certain level of firing, whereupon a cluster of them will suddenly and randomly begin firing out of control. The kindling process occurs during epileptic seizure. Seizurelike activity may underlie some PD as well. A panic attack may represent the kindling effect of NE nerve cells firing rapidly out of control. This seizurelike activity may occur in the BG or possibly other regions of the brain to trigger panic attack.

MEDICATIONS USED IN TREATING PANIC DISORDER

If neurotransmitter systems are involved in causing PD, medications that ameliorate the impact of any imbalance will decrease the rate and frequency of panic attacks. By identifying symptoms and noting triggers, physicians and their patients can identify the medications that are most likely to have a positive impact on decreasing panic. Table 5.1 summarizes the neurotransmitter and neuroanatomical contributions to PD and the medications used to treat those problems.

TABLE 5.1 Etiologies of Panic and Medication Choices

Etiology of Panic	Symptoms	Medications
Increased NE at peripheral nerve receptors	Tremor Increased heart rate Sweating and flushing	Beta-blockers: Inderal (propranolol) Tenormin (atenolol)
Increased release of NE from presynaptic nerve cell	Increased triggering of panic symptoms Heightened arousal	Alpha-2 auto-receptor agonists: Catapres (clonidine hydrochloride)
Dysregulation of GABA receptor area	Increased frequency of panic attacks Higher tension	Benzodiazepines: Xanax (alprazolam) Klonopin (clonazepam) Ativan (lorazepam) Serax (oxazepam) Valium (diazepam)
Deficient chloride channel transmission	Increased tension Nervousness	Benzodiazepines (see above)
Kindling (increased firing of nerve cells)	Increased panic attacks	Anticonvulsants: Neurontin (gabapentin) is the most studied; more often used when PD is comorbid with social anxiety (see Chapter 11)
Dysregulation of basal ganglia	Increased panic attacks Increased physical symptoms of shaking, tremors, muscle tension	No known medication that absolutely works on this area
Comorbid depression (anxiety is part of the depression)	Depressed mood Negativity Lethargy	SSRIs, SSNRIs, and Atypical SSRIs (see Table 5.3) Tricyclics (see Table 5.4) MAOIs (see Table 5.5)

Medications to Decrease Release of Norepinpehrine

Different medications can decrease the release of norepinephrine (NE), and the choice depends on the most likely cause of the excess. When palpitating heart rate and vascular symptoms are prominent features of the panic, the beta-blockers Inderal (propranolol) or Tenormin (atenolol) may be the first choice. These medications block the effects of NE on the beta receptor on the postsynaptic nerve cell, meaning they stop the impact of excess NE. Beta-blockers are cardiac medications that slow down the effects of NE not only on the heart but also on the peripheral nervous system.

When irritability and impulsivity are significant features, the alpha-2 auto-receptor agonist Catapres (clonidine hydrochloride) may be the first choice. With this entire category of medications, side effects may include slowed heart rate or possible hypotension, which should be carefully monitored in all age groups. Discontinuation of these medications, if they are being used on a regular basis, should be tapered because anxiety symptoms may increase on withdrawal of the medication. Table 5.2 highlights the features of prescribing these medications.

Medications to Raise Serotonin and Create Balance with Norepinephrine

The feedback mechanisms between the neurotransmitters involved in mood regulation are complex and not completely understood. Research will continue to improve our understanding of the ways in which these neural chemicals affect each other, but at this time norepinephrine (NE) is understood to serve as both a brake and a stimulator of serotonin (SE) levels, depending on the type of imbalance in the system. Thus, raising NE levels may raise SE as well. And increasing SE may allow NE release to slow and thereby diminish anxiety stimulated by excess NE in the brain.

Several types of medications raise SE levels. Medications that affect SE are called "antidepressants," but are often good choices to treat PD. People who are prescribed these medications for anxiety should be told they are effective for both panic and anxiety, despite being labeled for depression.

The most popular antidepressants are the SSRIs because of their comparatively low side effect profile. Some antidepressants, such as Effexor (venlafaxine), combine selective action on both NE and SE; these are called *dual-action* SSRIs or SSNRIs. Some are atypical SSRIs, like Remeron (mirtazepine), which is selective for SE but uses a different action than reuptake-inhibiting alone. Two additional types of antidepressants, tricyclics and monoamine oxidase inhibitors, are used less often. The tricyclic antidepressants (TCAs) have higher side effect profiles and overdose risks because

TABLE 5.2 Beta-Blockers and Alpha-2 Auto-Receptor Agonists

Drug Name	Main Effect	Side Effects	Dose Range and Duration	Considerations for Use
Inderal (propranolol)	Blocks NE effects on peripheral nerve receptors, slowing shaking, sweating, and heart rate	Slowed heart rate, drowsiness	10–20mg 3–4 times per day May be used on an as-needed basis	2 weeks to see significant results
Tenormin (atenolol)	Blocks NE effects on peripheral nerve receptors, as above	Slowed heart rate, drowsiness	Dose range not yet established	2 weeks to see significant results
Catapres (clonidine hydrochloride)	Alpha-2 agonist, slows release of NE, increases relaxation of cells and diminishes tension and irritability	Dry mouth, sedation, constipation, possibly depressed mood	0.2–0.6mg per day in divided dose Available in patch form, useful with children	Used most often with panic symptoms in SAD and PTSD

they affect SE, NE, and dopamine (DA) less selectively. MAOIs improve SE levels by diminishing the rate of its destruction in the synapse.

SSRIs, SSNRIs, and Atypical SSRIs

The selective serotonin reuptake inhibitors (SSRIs) have been found to be very effective in treating PD. Medications in this category are considered first-line treatments for PD for a couple of reasons. First, pharmacological research has indicated that PD patients respond to this category of medication. Second, there is a high comorbidity between PD and depression. The SSRIs are useful because they treat symptoms of both the depression and the PD simultaneously.

When SSRIs are used to treat panic, they are generally started at a much lower dose than when treating depression. The onset of action of the SSRIs in treating PD usually is similar to that of their use in treating depression; however, it may take slightly longer (sometimes 3 to 8 weeks) before the effects are noticeable. Many PD patients have a hypersensitivity to the SSRIs. This hypersensitivity often results in a sense of internal restlessness and external jitteriness. Therefore, patients may notice that their anxiety or panic increases before it gets better. This is an important point to mention to patients, as they often get very frustrated when initiating treatment for PD. They should get a typical response of a 50% reduction of the intensity and severity of panic symptoms.

The choice of which SSRI to use for panic depends first on whether a patient has a history of success or failure with one or more of them. In the absence of prior experience using these drugs, Lexapro (escitalopram) has the fewest side effects, but Zoloft (sertraline) and Paxil (paroxetine) have excellent research results for reducing panic. Prozac (fluoxetine), in my opinion, is the most likely to cause agitation as a side effect, so it would be a secondary choice among SSRIs for panic and anxiety. The most frequent side effects for this category of medication include gastrointestinal discomfort, headache, weight gain, loss of libido or anorgasmia, and possible drowsiness. With all these medications, one should slowly taper down the dosage, otherwise flulike symptoms may occur. Table 5.3 highlights typical usage for the most frequently prescribed antidepressants of this type, all of which have a main effect of increasing SE and regulating SE transmission in the neuron.

Tricyclics

The tricyclic antidepressants can also be helpful for treating PD. Before the introduction of the SSRIs, which do not have many of the anticholinergic side effects of the tricyclics, these drugs (especially Tofranil/imipramine) were considered first-line medications for PD. Their main effect is to block

TABLE 5.3   SSRIs, SSNRIs, and Atypical SSRIs

Drug Name	Dose Range and Duration	Considerations for Use	Withdrawal Pattern
Prozac (fluoxetine)	10–40mg per day	Tends to have more agitation in first 3 weeks, fewer problems with weight gain and libido; may combine with a benzodiapine in first 3–4 weeks	Least amount of withdrawal because it has longest half-life
Zoloft (sertraline)	25–150mg per day	Short half-life; probably the highest incidence of sexual side effects	Like all SSRI's, it is best to taper gradually, e.g., decrease by half the dose every 5 half-lives
Paxil/Paxil CR (paroxetine)	10–60mg per day CR: 12.5–75mg	Has most FDA indications for anxiety disorders	Paxil CR is easier to wean off of than Paxil
Luvox (fluvoxamine)	50–200mg per day	Mostly used to treat obsessive compulsive disorders; sedating	Similar to Zoloft, Luvox should be tapered gradually, every 5 half-lives
Celexa (citalopram)	20–40mg per day	Has a lower side effect profile than others	Like most SSRI's taper gradually
Lexapro (escitalopram)	10–20mg per day	Perhaps the cleanest of all the SSRIs in terms of side effects	Typical SSRI withdrawal pattern

(continued)

TABLE 5.3 SSRIs, SSNRIs, and Atypical SSRIs (continued)

Drug Name	Dose Range and Duration	Considerations for Use	Withdrawal Pattern
Remeron (mirtazepine)	15–45mg per day	Weight gain/sedating; often used after others have proven ineffective or when sedation is desired; this medication may be used to augment other SSRIs	May experience increased drowsiness as dosage is lowered (Remeron is more sedating at lower doses)
Serzone (nefazodone)	300–600mg per day	Not FDA-approved, but often used, for PTSD or panic; has warning for potentially harming the liver	Use dosage tapering similar to other SSRIs
Effexor (venlafaxine)	75–375mg per day	Good for treating somatic symptoms of fatigue and pain due to dual mechanism NE/5HT. Starting dose of 37.5 mg is common for those with high levels of anxiety	Needs more careful tapering down patterns than the SSRIs; many require small, gradual reduction over weeks
Cymbalta (duloxetine)	20–60mg per day; higher doses currently being researched.	Good for treating somatic symptoms of fatigue and pain due to dual mechanism NE/5HT	Newer medication, withdrawal pattern not well established; likely to need tapering down similar to Effexor

reuptake of NE and SE, thereby increasing availability of both. The most important concern with tricyclics is the heightened side effect profile, which often includes lightheadedness or dizziness (as a result of a change in blood pressure between sitting and standing) and weight gain. Other side effects include gastrointestinal difficulties such as constipation, dry mouth, and dryness of mucous membranes. They also pose a much higher risk of lethal overdose than other antidepressants due to cardiotoxic effects at overdose levels. The cessation of use from these, as all antidepressants, should be tapering off, so as not to induce withdrawal that has flulike symptoms. Table 5.4 reviews these medications and their use in treating PD.

TABLE 5.4 Tricyclics

Drug Name	Side Effects	Dose Range and Duration
Elavil (amytriptyline)	Anticholinergic side effects (blurred vision, dry mouth, memory loss) Alpha-adrenergic side effects (postural hypotension, dizziness, sedation)	100–300mg per day (dose range same as in depression) Beneficial effects in 1–3 weeks, start low dose and make increase every 5–7 days, remain on meds at least 6 months, maintenance dose may be lower than acute dose
Pamelor (nortriptyline)	Anticholinergic side effects (see above) Alpha-adrenergic side effects (see above)	75–150mg per day (see above comments)
Tofranil (imipramine)	Anticholinergic side effects (see above) Alpha-adrenergic side effects (see above)	150–300mg per day (see above comments)
Norpramin (desipramine)	Anticholinergic side effects (see above) Alpha-adrenergic side effects (see above)	150–300mg per day (see above comments)

MAOIs

Monoamine oxidase inhibitors (MAOIs) are often considered a second- or third-line medication because they have an even greater side effect profile than the tricyclics, including lightheadedness and dizziness, weight gain, decreased libido, decreased sexual performance, and significant dietary restrictions. Foods that contains tyramine (such as aged meats and cheeses, pickled foods, smoked foods, and alcoholic beverages, especially red wine) must be avoided. Over-the-counter medications that have a decongestant must also be avoided, as the combination of the decongestant and MAOI may cause seriously elevated blood pressure (in some cases stroke has been reported). Hence, MAOIs must be used with caution. They may be very useful, however, due to their unique action for making SE more available in the brain. They act by slowing the destruction of available SE in the synapse. Table 5.5 reviews these medications and their use in treating panic disorder.

Medications to Enhance GABA and Chloride Conductance: Benzodiazepines

There are at least five known benzodiazepine receptor subsites of nerve cells. The benzodiazepine-1 (Omega-1) receptor area is responsible for the anxiolytic effect and sedative hypnotic effect of these medications. Benzodiazepines (Xanax/alprazolam, Ativan/lorazepam, Klonopin/clonazepam, Valium/diazepam) are often used as adjunctive treatment to the SSRIs, especially when initiating treatment of PD. They have the advantage of working immediately on the panic symptoms. Rapidly absorbed through the

TABLE 5.5 MAOIs			
Drug Name	**Dose Range and Duration**	**Considerations for Use**	**Withdrawal Pattern**
Nardil (phenelzine)	45–90mg per day	Most commonly used MAOI, must be careful of diet restrictions	Similar to tricyclics; wean off slowly
Parnate (tranylcy-promine)	10–60mg per day	Must be careful of diet restrictions	Similar to tricyclics; wean off slowly

gastrointestinal system, they have a very quick onset of action and they often have an excellent reduction of the panic symptoms. They act by increasing the effects of gamma aminobutyric acid (GABA) and by enhancing chloride conductance, which relaxes the neuron.

Xanax (alprazolam) has been researched the most extensively for treatment of PD (Verster & Volkerts, 2004). It is often regarded as the benzodiazepine medication of choice. Although its onset of action is very quick, its duration of action is short. This means that one may need to take Xanax frequently—up to three or four times a day. The quick onset and short duration of action also make it more abusable than other benzodiazepine medications. A medication like Klonopin (clonazepam) may have less abuse potential due to the fact that it has longer onset of action and a longer half-life (lasts longer) than Xanax.

The benzodiazepine medications have several other benefits in treating panic. They enhance the conductance of chloride, which allows a decrease in anxiety symptoms. Also, benzodiazepines help with the adjustment to SSRI medications because the PD patient is much more sensitive to feeling the internal restlessness and jitteriness associated with the side effects of SSRIs. Benzodiazepines help patients tolerate the SSRIs so that they can be adjusted appropriately or used at levels that would otherwise produce intolerable side effects. Finally, heightened stressors can trigger panic. The benzodiazepines can be used for quick relief on a short-term basis to help with these psychosocial stressors.

The major concern with benzodiazepines is that they are potentially addictive. Their side effects may include sedation, cognitive slowing, and slowing of reflexes. They also have a potentially dangerous synergistic effect with alcohol; one drink may become the equivalent of two or three drinks when combined with a benzodiazepine. It is also possible to develop physiologic dependence on the benzodiazepine medications, which can lead to withdrawal symptoms and increased panic attacks during withdrawal. Table 5.6 lists the primary benzodiazepines and their use in treating panic disorder.

Sleeping Medications

The sedative/hypnotic component of sleeping aids such as Ambien (zolpidem tartrate), Sonata (zaleplon), and Lunesta (eszopiclone) can also help treat the initial side effects of the SSRIs, which may include insomnia. Sleeping aids thus allow patients to adjust to the SSRI more rapidly. (See Chapter 8 for a more full discussion of these medications.)

TABLE 5.6 Benzodiazepines

Drug Name	Side Effects	Dose Range and Duration	Considerations for Use
Xanax (alprazolam)	Drowsiness Slowed reflexes	1–5mg (usually 3mg or more) per day in divided dose	Start at .25mg 3–4 times per day
Klonopin (clonazepam)	Drowsiness Slowed reflexes May elevate liver enzymes	1.5–2.5mg per day in divided dose	Longer half-life than Xanax, thus it can be taken two times per day Very sedating—give most of medication at bed
Ativan (lorazepam)	Drowsiness Slowed reflexes	2–6mg per day in divided dose	Onset of action slower than Xanax Easily metabolized in the liver
Valium (diazepam)	Drowsiness Slowed reflexes	4–30mg per day in divided dose	Rapid onset, long elimination time
Serax (oxazepam)	Drowsiness Slowed reflexes	30–120mg per day in divided dose	Shorter half-life than Ativan Easily metabolized in the liver

ENHANCING STRATEGIES FOR MEDICATIONS

Especially when PD is comorbid with other psychiatric complaints, it is often a helpful to look at ways of enhancing an SSRI or prescribing a combination of medications to best treat the PD symptoms. There are several enhancing strategies in treating PD. One is to combine the effects of an atypical SSRI, such as Remeron (mirtazepine), with an SSRI, which allows for a more rapid discharge of serotonin, thereby enhancing the effects of the SSRI. Remeron has two mechanisms of action that enhance serotonin availability. It acts as an alpha-2 norepinephrine (NE) autoreceptor, similar to Desyrel (trazodone hydrochloride). When it blocks the presynaptic alpha-2 NE auto-receptor site, it interferes with the autoregulatory mechanism of the nerve cell, causing NE to continue to be released. The NE activates alpha-I receptor areas on postsynaptic neurons. When NE is received at the alpha-1 receptor site, it activates a serotonin accelerator in the nerve cell and allows serotonin release to be enhanced. Hence, increasing NE is related to increasing the serotonin.

Another common combination is an atypical SSRI with a benzodiazepine. Serzone (nefazodone) acts very much like Desyrel (trazodone hydrochloride) as a serotonin *and* NE reuptake inhibitor. It also blocks the serotonin 2-A receptor (a postsynaptic receptor area, which, if activated, causes increased anxiety), which means that some of the SSRI-induced side effect of anxiety is diminished.

For people who respond well to the SSNRI antidepressants Effexor (venlafaxine) and Cymbalta (duloxetine), it is also possible to combine these with a benzodiazepine. Effexor and Cymbalta are reuptake inhibitors for both SE and NE, increasing the availability of both neurochemicals.

Although they are less frequently used due to problematic side effects, tricyclics or MAOIs may be used in combination with benzodiazepines.

RELAPSE RATES

When using medication alone to treat PD, it appears that, once medications have stopped, the relapse rate is much higher than that of depression once medications have stopped. If a patient has been in remission after using the benzodiazepines for 6 months to a year, tapering off on the benzodiazepines very slowly is required. Decreasing the dose too quickly may result in withdrawal symptoms, which could trigger a relapse of the anxiety. It generally takes 2–6 months to wean off of a benzodiazepine. If a patient is using a short half-life SSRI or a medication such as Effexor (venlafaxine), slow tapering is also important, as reducing the dosage too quickly may induce a type of withdrawal (though not a true withdrawal, as there is no dependence developed). The short half-life medications are much more difficult to wean off of and often require a wean-down of 3–4 weeks.

PEARLS ABOUT MEDICATING FOR PANIC DISORDER

Important ideas to take away regarding the use of medication with PD include:

• The starting dose of an SSRI in treating PD is usually lower than for treating depression due to PD patients' heightened sensitivity to SSRI side effects.

- Panic and other symptoms may get worse before they get better.
- Maintenance doses for treating PD are often higher than for treating depression.
- The onset of action for SSRIs in treating PD may be slightly longer than that for treating depression.
- Patients taking SSRIs typically experience a 50% reduction of panic symptoms.

The case of Sara, introduced in Chapter 4, is an excellent example of the integration of medication and psychotherapy for a case of PD. Sara was referred to me by her therapist. After an extensive medical workup had produced no positive results, Sara had finally sought therapy to treat her symptoms. As mentioned earlier, Sara had experienced serious side effects to steroids, which had triggered intense panic, and she was not very trusting of physicians. After thoroughly reviewing her history, I concluded that Sara seemed to have PD.

Her symptoms had been intense and of long duration, starting with her severe physiological (allergic) reactions to medications, suggesting the neurochemical balance between NE and SE could have been altered by a medical event. I described how SSRIs worked, and I suggested a trial of one of these medications. She agreed—her panic was so debilitating that she felt she must give medication a try.

Because Sara had a poor experience with medication side effects in the past, I put her on Lexapro (escitalopram), a short half-life medication with a minimal side effect profile. Although it was not FDA-approved for PD at the time, I did this because I believe all the SSRIs are likely to reduce panic symptoms. I started Sara on a low dose (5mg/day for 1 week). I increased her to 20mg over the next 3 weeks. I started at a low dose because people who have PD tend to be more sensitive to side effects of the SSRIs.

Sara also needed some immediate relief of her panic symptoms. I prescribed a dose of Xanax (alprazolam) at 0.5mg 3 times per day and cautioned her about the side effects of drowsiness and slowed reflexes. This allowed Sara to participate in psychotherapy with more attention and use her methods of breathing and relaxation to interrupt the onset of panic with more reliable results. As she gained confidence in her ability to slow or stop the panic, she was able to wean off of the Xanax.

Sara's response to psychotherapy and medication was prompt. (This may well have been due to her history without premorbid anxiety or depression.) Once the Lexapro started to take effect after about 3 weeks, I weaned Sara off of the Xanax and prescribed it for her to use only as needed and in coordination with her psychotherapy. She continued to do well with the Lexapro and was able to discontinue use altogether at 6 months, without relapse.

Sara's treatment was brief, but she was a clear example of a person with PD who needed to reregulate her serotonergic system to gain relief from symptoms.

CONCLUSION

Panic disorder is an illness that involves spontaneous panic attacks. There is often an association between the physical symptoms and the cognitive symptoms, where heightened autonomic arousability and its numerous somatic worries trigger the condition of anticipatory anxiety. Anticipating panic attacks makes it more likely that they will occur. Theories about the etiology of PD include the dysregulation of norepinephrine (NE) and gamma aminobutyric acid (GABA), as well as neuroanatomic abnormalities seen on PET and SPECT scans.

Pharmacologic treatments target these various biological causes. The main treatment for long-term correction of neurotransmitter dysfunction involves increasing serotonin (SE) through the selective serotonin reuptake inhibitors (SSRIs). Benzodiazepine medications are typically used to treat the immediate symptoms of panic attacks. Combinations of benzodiazepines and the SSRIs, tricyclic antidepressants, or atypical SSRIs are often used to produce the greatest positive effect on the combined problems of PD.

Panic disorder must be considered a potential chronic disorder. As such, it may be appropriate to keep patients on medications for longer periods of time—possibly several years to the duration of their life. More studies need to be done to further establish good guidelines for duration of treatment.

CHAPTER SIX

GENERALIZED ANXIETY DISORDER: WORRY WITHOUT REASON

Generalized anxiety disorder (GAD) can be typified as worry without reason. No amount of rationalizing relieves the inner sense of dread; no amount of reassurance relieves the worry. Although kernels of truth exist as the seeds of worry, there is often no significant cause for the worry in the first place. People with GAD become experts at worrying about things that may never happen and over which they have no control.

Typically, the discomfort of GAD is not just the exaggeration of cause but also the intensity of the anxiety, which is entirely out of proportion to any actual need for concern. No matter how insignificant the possible cause for worry, constant reviewing, fretting, or rehashing preoccupies the GAD sufferer. Concentration and attention both suffer when worry preoccupies the mind. The experience is thoroughly unpleasant, and escape from it is nearly impossible when GAD has taken root. When worry preoccupies, inattentiveness follows, and inattentiveness can lead to making mistakes that create more cause for worry. People I have treated have described GAD variously as "the voice of a devil, urging me to worry now," or a "third person in my inner dialogue, butting in with worry," or "another part of me that cannot let go of worry." The intensity of the urge to worry is experienced as "not me" or not a part of the *real* self. And all agree it is nearly impossible to banish this voice.

Generalized anxiety disorder affects about 3.1% of the U.S. population at any given time (National Institute of Mental Health, 2006) and is comorbid with depression about 50% of the time (Middeldorp, Cath, Van Dyck,

116

& Boomsma, 2005). It appears that more women than men have GAD; however, the disproportion is small, and it may be a cultural factor that is preventing men from seeking help for this disorder. Generalized anxiety disorder may underlie other behavioral problems including abuse of alcohol and "workaholism," a behavior that is usually rewarded in this culture.

GAD may appear at any age, striking children as often as adults. Children go through a natural stage of fearfulness between 2 and 4 years of age, when they fear monsters and the dark and have other kinds of worries. Children with GAD, however, tend to be more alert to potential threats and to interpret the risk of threat more often than other children (Rapee, 2001; Lonegan & Phillips, 2001). These children may be clingy and do more reassurance-seeking than children without anxiety. Generalized anxiety disorder in children can be evident in some settings but not in others, so that the child may seem fine at school but very tense at home or vice versa. Like adults, GAD children can be highly active and appear to be in control, but their cognitive distress is a key feature to note. Children can become worriers at any age, and adults with GAD often report worrying excessively for their entire lives.

Bright children seem at special risk for GAD. They are able at young ages to take in and retain information about the world that they are not yet prepared to understand. For example, a bright 8-year-old may be able to read a newspaper or listen to a news report about conditions of war or disease in another country. However, he does not yet have the capacity to appraise the actual risk to himself or his family. His brain development does not let him grasp distance or put such a report into context with other worry-mitigating information. Often teachers and parents just dismiss these worries, responding to questions such as "Will the war come here?" or "How many people can die of bird flu?" with "Don't worry, that can't happen." This type of response will not reassure a bright GAD child. What he really needs is help learning how to discern from his reading and listening what is worth worrying about.

DIAGNOSTIC CRITERIA

According to the *DSM-IV-TR,* a diagnosis of GAD requires that, for the last 6 months, a person has spent "more days than not":

- Worrying excessively about common life events or concerns
- Experiencing signs of physical tension

- Experiencing problems with attention and concentration
- Suffering from a depressed mood

Three Clusters of Symptoms

Like all the anxiety disorders, the symptoms of GAD show themselves in three clusters: physiological, cognitive, and behavioral. The common experience of worrying about someone who is late in arriving home demonstrates how GAD develops in the three clusters of symptoms. If you did not know where that person was or what was causing the delay, you have experienced the three clusters of GAD symptoms. The "waiting anxiety" looks like this: You are waiting after midnight for your teenager to come home. Your initial irritation soon turns to worry and then turns to outright fear about what may have befallen the child. You cannot think of anything else but this worry until it is resolved. Your *cognitions* include rational and irrational fears, and planning and replanning what to do and whom to call, but all *thoughts* are about the worry. Your initial *physical sensations* of slight arousal turn to agitation and then quickly to feeling sick to the stomach with a rapid heart rate. Your *behavior* becomes focused on your problem. You might do some activity that allows you to worry while you "work"—clean the refrigerator out, balance a checkbook, play a video game—but soon all you can do is pace around the room and wait for signs of a return: footsteps on the staircase, headlights in the drive. This physical arousal can, in fact, go on for hours. Such a state of high anxiety is common to those who have severe GAD (although with GAD there is usually no good reason for the worry) and typifies the symptom picture. The primary complaint that brings people with GAD to therapy is usually the cognitive distress of being unable to shake off worry, but all three arenas of symptoms need attention.

As noted earlier, depression is comorbid with GAD about 50% of the time. Depression stems from similar neurobiological conditions, so there is a strong connection between these two disorders. When clients present with comorbid depression, it is important to find out whether the depression preexisted the anxiety. If the depression did not preexist the anxiety, therapists should consider this simple explanation for it: It is pretty darned depressing to be so anxious! Many clients who suffer from GAD state, in these words: "If I have to live like this for the rest of my life, I would rather be dead." These clients are not expressing suicidal ideation. Rather, they cannot envision any reason to be in a life in which they feel this level of dread every day. Although we must *always* evaluate suicide risk when a client is depressed, we also need to remember that this type of statement is quite typical of the GAD client, who may feel quite good on days when the dread and worry are at low levels or gone altogether.

Physiological Symptoms

Symptoms of GAD show themselves in a variety of physical conditions that are exacerbated by stress and are often the result of prolonged physical tension. They include:

- Headaches
- Ulcers
- Colitis
- TMJ
- Fibromyalgia
- Fatigue
- Backaches
- Chronic fatigue syndrome
- Muscles weakness
- Muscle tension
- Weight gain
- Sleep disturbance

In listening to clients describe how they feel physically, I have come to regard statements such as "I don't know—I just feel bad" as a diagnostic indicator of GAD. When one considers the biology of this disorder, the description is apt: The result of the neurobiological hyperarousal that causes GAD is a low-grade physical, mental, and emotional state that just "feels bad."

Physical tension. The client with GAD suffers constant physical tension. This tension results in headache, jaw ache, backache, and aches anywhere one can get an ache. Holding the body tightly is a less-than-conscious bracing against possible disaster, and it creates a very sore body over time. This "armoring" of the body against approaching danger is not as physically dramatic and frightening as panic is; rather, it is a constant, low-grade state of physical defensiveness. Never knowing when or where the danger might emerge, the person with GAD is vigilant to all possibilities.

This type of tension originates in heightened arousal. Two reasons for the arousal may be:

- Excessive amounts or release of norepinephrine (NE)
- A chronic state of stress response, which could be caused by excessive neurons for or release of corticotrophin release factor (CRF) to stressors

There are physical results of dysregulation in those systems: upset stomach, fatigue, muscle weakness, and other sensations of being drained.

Physiological differences between GAD and other anxiety disorders. Ruling out acute anxiety from panic is important to a differential diagnosis between GAD and other forms of anxiety. Some clients with GAD state emphatically that they panic for hours at a time. In the absence of adrenal gland dysfunction or clear, ongoing, physical danger, no one panics for hours without interruption. As people with this complaint describe what they mean by "panicking for hours," you will hear symptoms of distressingly heightened arousal but not the full-blown "fight or flight" of panic. However, although acute anxiety states are less intense than panic, they are still exceedingly uncomfortable. One person described the constant acute anxiety of GAD as the feeling one has "when you are standing on a chair to reach something and the chair starts to tip over. It is that moment when you gasp—except I feel that moment all day long." Discomforting as such a feeling may be, however, the physiology of GAD is rarely enough, by itself, to cause people to seek treatment.

Cognitive Symptoms

Always self-reinforcing and always negative, worry is the primary cognitive symptom of GAD. There are several varieties of these worries, and they must be distinguished from social anxiety and PD because they need to be handled differently. People with GAD experience worry differently than people who do not have GAD (Ruscio, 2004). GAD worry can show itself as:

- Simple worries that are distressingly ruminative
- Fears about health or other things that seem irrational to the point of delusional
- Rehashing possible social mistakes
- Mental hypervigilance about responsibility
- Perfectionistic carefulness about job, home, or school performance
- Intolerance of ambiguity

Worry and negative arousal reinforce each other (Figure 6.1). There is a circular reinforcement pattern in GAD that is similar to PD, but the function of the worry is different. In PD the irrational cognitions (e.g., "I am dying") intensify the symptoms and make the panic attack even more aversive. The fear becomes a fear of having another attack. In GAD, worry serves a different purpose in that it is an attempt to gain control over the symptoms. The persistent, low-key sense of dread is unpleasant. The brain does not like to have physical sensations without explanation, so the anxious brain of the GAD sufferer goes on a hunt to figure out why the dread is present. It looks for something to worry about and always finds it. Finding a real worry is a relief in a way ("At least I know why I feel this way!"), but the

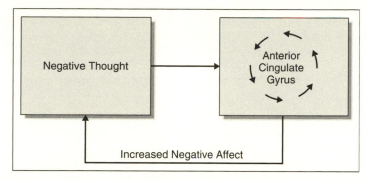

FIGURE 6.1.   Rumination reinforces negative affect.

neurobiological act of worrying enhances the tendency of the brain to worry. Once a worry is identified, the GAD brain believes that if it can just get rid of the worry somehow (through reassurance-seeking or solving the problem), the sensation of dread and doom will go away. However, the physiology does not go away even if these attempts to relieve the worry are successful. So the brain then goes looking for another worry, which it will, of course, find. Thus, the worry of GAD is an attempt to solve and remove the physical sensations, even while it keeps them in place. This is what makes GAD worry so different from the cognitive distortions of PD.

Rumination. People with GAD may be beset by ruminative thoughts about almost any type of worry. No matter which type of symptom predominates, the worries are hard to turn off, even in sleep. Rumination can be so intense that it is mistaken for OCD. When worry takes center stage, it is preoccupying. Concentration and attention fail in the face of the intense worried thoughts. Figure 6.2 shows how rumination reinforces negative affect.

Irrational cognitions. People with GAD usually worry about irrational things that have only a tiny kernel of truth. Although they know they are "making a mountain out of a mole hill," the worry still *feels real*. The need for reassurance often compels people with GAD to reveal their irrational thoughts to others, but they simultaneously fear they will be seen as crazy. Indeed, they themselves may worry they are crazy for having the thoughts, even when they are *sure* it is the thought that is crazy and that they simply have problems turning the thoughts off.

A common way of checking out how someone will respond to their thoughts is to drop clues into the conversation to test the listener. For example, one of my clients, Pattie, did this when she smiled and said at the end of a diagnostic session, "Well, I guess that is all I have to work on, un-

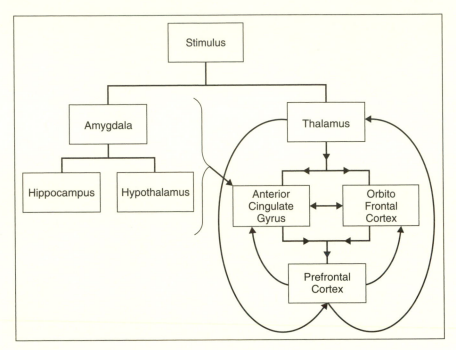

FIGURE 6.2. The path of a stimulus, with the anterior cingulate gyrus conveying limbic information to the cortex.

less you count how I am going to handle my responsibility for potentially introducing plague to the United States when I came back from my international trip." (It turned out Pattie actually had an irrational fear that she had done this. She had returned from an African visit with a bad cold and was wondering if she could have brought back a terrible virus similar to what she had read about in a novel about bioterrorism. She knew it was irrational, but she could not shake off the dread that it might be true.)

There is actually nothing delusional about this kind of worry. It is the runaway nature of a brief intrusive thought ("What if I don't have just a bad cold?") causing a spike of fear ("What if I caught a horrific, contagious virus in Africa?") and then building up without intervention of logic ("Now I could be carrying the contagion back with me to infect the whole country!"). The prefrontal cortex (PFC) of the GAD brain has trouble stopping that kind of buildup and bombardment of worry.

Worrying about social errors. Distinguishing the social worries of GAD clients from those of social anxiety clients is fairly easy. People with GAD may be gregarious and comfortable socially, and they don't expect to be rejected. However, they may worry intensely if they suspect they made a social gaff. Then they may obsessively review the comments they made or worry about whether they were likeable enough or talked too much.

Perfectionism and mistakes. Mistakes are dreadful causes of anxiety. Not wanting to feel the anxiety of making a mistake causes people with GAD to be perfectionistic in whatever they do. Whether they are office managers, cashiers, or homemakers, whether they are worrying about a million-dollar decimal point misprint in a report or a birthday party, they worry with equal discomfort about errors.

Ambiguity. Ambiguity in any situation puts GAD clients on a cognitive see-saw. They worry about their physical health, noting a vague symptom, and they have trouble waiting to see if it disappears or worsens before they evaluate it. They may seek a medical opinion or just remain preoccupied with it, but the symptom dominates their thoughts until they resolve it. This characteristic intolerance of ambiguity is particularly destructive in relationships. Friendships and romances often involve periods of ambiguity. People with GAD cannot tolerate letting small things rest. They want to know what is wrong, and they want to know it now! This hallmark of GAD, difficulty with ambiguity, may be of psychological origin or be determined by low brain energy (Hsu, Bhatt, Adolphs, Tranel, & Camerer, 2005; Bouton, 2002), as is discussed later.

Paul was a classic GAD case. An electrical engineer, he frequently became beset by worry, uncertain about whether he double-checked the numbers on his work before sending it to his project group to review. His worry made him inattentive, and that increased the likelihood of more worry—even though he had never failed to produce accurate, double-checked work in the past.

He knew that incorrect figures would present a problem and cause additional work, but the kernel of worry "Did I double-check?" grew into "I made a terrible mistake and no one will catch it. The whole project will be done badly. I will be fired and never get a job again!" The true part of the worry—that it would be a problem if he made an error—was completely distorted by the time GAD was done with it. It would have been reasonable for Paul to resolve to check out the problem at the next opportunity, and then let go of the worried thoughts. However, the thoughts of ruination pursued him and were hard to shake off.

While worrying about whether the plans went forward with an error, Paul neglected to attend to personal concerns. His preoccupation with work-related errors caused him to forget to pick up his kids after school. He also forgot to record several checks he'd written to pay bills. These errors understandably increased his upset and worry. In short, Paul felt as if every part of his life created something to worry about, and his constant internal drive to worry was palpable. Paul's wife was becoming frustrated with his unrelenting restlessness, worry, and inability to be in the moment. He, in turn, was irritated with her assumption that what he had on his mind was no big deal. In truth, Paul also knew it was no big deal, but he could not stop the thoughts, and he could not work hard enough to feel safe. His mind always found something to get carried away with.

Behavioral Symptoms

Behaviorally, clients with GAD show marked avoidance—as in all anxiety disorders. Avoidance is always an active strategy even though it may not appear to be. Symptom management depends on identifying not only what clients are avoiding but also how they avoid it. The types of avoidance include:

- *Working extra hours and with great care to prevent mistakes.* This demonstration of energy and effort may not look like anxiety as much as good work ethic.
- *Cognitive exertion.* It takes a great deal of swift and clever mental activity to avoid listening to newscasts that could trigger fear, to read a newspaper but avoid stories that heighten anxiety (like medical reports or murders), or to anticipate and manipulate conversational topics that might lead to anxiety.
- *Checking things over.* Double-checking things like turning off the lights, washing the counter, examining the tire pressure on cars, or asking someone one more time about whether they finished an important task has the quality of OCD, but it differs from OCD in that it is easy to reassure the GAD client that the lights are indeed off or the tire pressure is fine.

NEUROBIOLOGICAL CAUSES OF GENERALIZED ANXIETY DISORDER

What is going on in the brain of the GAD client? Plenty—and constantly. There are several aspects of brain function that may underlie this disorder. Important features of GAD are determined by neurobiological biological makeup:

- Ruminating worry or mentally getting "stuck" stems from anterior cingulate gyrus (ACG) overactivity.
- Hypervigilance (to the point of paranoia) is probably the result of elevated norepinephrine (NE) or overactivity in the basal ganglia (BG).

- Rumination, despair, and a predisposition to feeling anxious may be caused by serotonin (SE) deficits, which affect the limbic system and the prefrontal cortex (PFC).
- Heightened worry and feelings of dread may be caused by insufficient or ineffective GABA.
- Overreactivity to stress may be caused by an overreactive HPA axis. This overreactivity may be due to biological predisposition (like too many CRF neurons), prolonged stress, or trauma. An overreactive HPA axis makes small things seem big—and they *are* big neurobiologically, stressing the system even more.

Overactive Anterior Cingulate Gyrus

The first brain region to consider when people present with GAD is the anterior cingulate gyrus (ACG). The ACG transfers information, amplifying and filtering emotional information passing from the amygdala to the prefrontal cortex (PFC) and back again. The amygdala assigns significance to sensory stimuli. When the amygdala recognizes a stimulus from a previous negative experience, it attaches negative significance to it. The PFC examines it, using information from the hippocampus about the details of the current situation, and sends back modulating information that will either confirm that the situation is negative or tell the amygdala to let it go.

To understand how this loop functions, consider a typical worry scene: A student comes in for a Monday morning class and the professor hands out a pop quiz, sarcastically saying that she "is sure that everyone is fully prepared after a weekend of study." The student may suddenly feel intensely anxious. Her amygdala hears the mild threat in the sarcasm and flashes to anxiety, revving the body to immediately increase respiration, produce more NE, and activate the hypothalamus for stress response. While the ACG bombards it, the PFC must respond to the anxiety, sorting out the intense emotionality of the anxiety and determining whether there is merit to it. The ACG is so overactive that it cannot easily relay soothing cognitions back from the PFC that would calm the amygdala, such as "This professor is always sarcastic and that doesn't mean the quiz is hard," or "You are prepared, and you have never failed her quizzes." Figure 6.3 demonstrates the role of the ACG in processing incoming information.

When serotonin levels are low, the ACG cannot suppress the limbic system. It therefore gives too much consideration to a single thought, making it into a worry, and then reviews it repetitively. This is the most frequent cause of intense distress in GAD. Everyone experiences small moments of unnecessary concern or momentary intrusions of irrational worry. Once

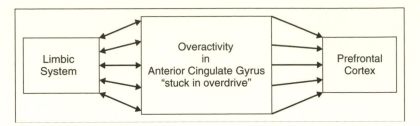

FIGURE 6.3.   Worry bombards the prefrontal cortex.

that kind of thought gets stuck in the ACG, it leads to fretting, illustrated in Figure 6.4.

Hypervigilance and Neurotransmitter Levels

High levels of norepinephrine (NE) or low levels of serotonin (SE) contribute to the imbalanced levels of activity in the limbic system, basal ganglia (BG), and cortex, as well as in the anterior cingulate gyrus (ACG). This imbalance creates the negative, worrying mind that is so distressing to clients. These neurochemicals interact in complex feedback loops with each other; when they are out of balance, physical and cognitive symptoms result.

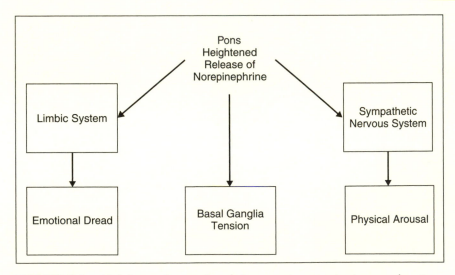

FIGURE 6.4.   Heightened norepinephrine creates constant arousal or tension

When the limbic system is short on SE, it becomes overactive and generates negativity. Thus, the limbic system shortage of SE readily contributes to worry in the anxious brain, with focus on what is wrong, difficult, or bad. When NE is too high, people feel physically agitated and tense.

The primary cognitive symptom of high NE levels is hypervigilance, which can be so intense that people with GAD may appear paranoid. It is as if the brain has gone into a radarlike scanning mode, examining all incoming stimuli for signs of a problem. High NE levels may contribute to overactivity in the basal ganglia (BG), which play a big role in maintaining general levels of arousal in the brain and body. When there is too much activity in this region, hypervigilance may result.

Rumination

The neurotransmitter serotonin (SE) may play a role in the rumination caused by overactivity of the ACG. Low numbers of SE neurons are found in people with anxiety disorders, and there is evidence that poor transmission of SE across the synaptic space may also result in low SE. Serotonin is involved in regulating many types of activity in the brain, and insufficient SE levels may not only exacerbate the overactivity of the ACG but also cause increased negativity from the limbic system, so there is more to worry about and less energy in the PFC to suppress the negativity. Serotonin neurons in the raphe extend to the ACG and to the cortex. Because of their regulatory impact, insufficient SE neurotransmitters may affect BG sensitivity. When there are not enough SE neurons, or when the transmission of the SE neurotransmitters is insufficient, SE transmission becomes a factor in the difficulty controlling worry and negativity. Medications that rebalance NE and SE help restore healthy brain function.

Negativity. Why does the brain resort to worry when it has difficulty shifting thoughts? Why don't we think ruminatively about positive things? This is primarily because the amygdala is specialized to pay attention to any stimulus that presents a potential of danger or threat. The body needs to respond efficiently to threat to stay alive, and to that end it is watchful against anything that may harm it. Sadly for our emotional state, our survival does not depend on alertness for approaching joy! Living well might require that, but survival does not.

Insufficient or Ineffective GABA in the Basal Ganglia

The BG also play a role in the worrying of GAD. GABA is an important neurochemical in the BG, which, as noted earlier, set the overall level of mental energy or tone. GABA slows down the rate of firing of neurons. In the BG of a client with GAD, it is likely that GABA is insufficient or not allowing the relaxation of the neurons, leading to excessive firing of the neurons in the BG. That sets an overall energy tone that is tense or high-strung. The concept of being tightly strung—like a piano wire—is a good metaphor for the tone of the GAD client. Already "wired," GAD clients need only a small tweak of stress to get them vibrating with tension. The relaxed piano wire cannot produce a vibration, but a tightly strung wire will respond with tone to a firm strike. Although tightly strung people may just be high-energy types who are physically active and get a lot done, they might also begin to suffer from GAD if the output of energy is blocked or the outcome of a project fails. This was the case with Sheila.

Sheila was a marathon runner who trained other runners, managed her household, and acted as president of a major community organization. When she broke her ankle, everything came to a standstill. Within weeks Sheila felt as if she would jump out of her skin, and a previous tendency to be a "worry wart" burgeoned into full-blown GAD. She had no outlet for that high degree of tense energy, and thoughts about problems in her life now caused reverberations of worry throughout her whole being. With an ACG that tended to ruminate, Sheila became stuck on worries she had previously pushed out of her mind by focusing on her projects. The high energy generated by her BG tone translated into overreactivity to minor stresses.

Having a heightened BG tone also means that people with GAD can easily feel mentally frozen when faced with emergencies. (Amen, 2003) Even though they may have the energy and competence to deal with the sequelae of an emergency (such as remaining calm and strong while sitting with a child in need of stitches and competently questioning the staff in an emergency room), it is the moment of emergency—facing the need to staunch the blood from that cut needing stitches—that leaves them frozen. One client with GAD recounted an occasion when he witnessed a car accident in front of his window. While he gazed at the scene, taking in how crumpled the car was, he could not move for a minute. When his wife called out to him, asking if he'd dialed 911 yet, he came to and picked up the phone. He was then able to mobilize himself to get some blankets and go out to see what assistance he could offer. He felt deeply ashamed of his lack of response and described how this was typical of his responses to other emergencies. He was relieved to know that this is common for people who have high-tone BGs.

Overreactivity to Stress

Another major underlying cause of GAD is stress. Stress can generate this disorder if it is chronic and unremitting—and if the client is not diminishing the impact of chronic stress with good self-care. Ongoing stress creates problems with sleep and the depletion of neurochemicals, setting the stage for the brain to become anxious. GAD clients are more willing to take care of themselves with nutrition, exercise, and better sleep hygiene if they understand that their stress depletes their ability to respond to further stress, causing all subsequent stress to be harder on them. People with GAD tend to feel guilty that they "can't handle what they used to handle"—until they learn that they have exhausted their supplies of energy, neurotransmitters, and immune function though chronic stress.

Healthy balance in the stress response system can be restored, but not without changing the stress level and the self-care routine. A full description of the action of the HPA axis and stress is given in Chapter 1. The contribution of the HPA axis to GAD is similar. The HPA axis may malfunction even when the objective level of stress is not intense (Talbott, 2002; Yehuda, 1997). When early life trauma resets the HPA system to fire too intensely in response to small stressors, clients constantly feel "stressed" (Rothschild, 2000). They thus undergo the same kinds of physical damage that significant stress causes.

BRAIN FUNCTION, IMPULSE CONTROL, AND GENERALIZED ANXIETY DISORDER

Low energy in the orbitofrontal cortex (OFC) means problems with suppressing inappropriate behaviors and impulse control. The activity in the OFC generates automatic kinds of behavior. The cognitive process there is less internally verbal, less intentional or conscious, than the analyzing quality of the prefrontal cortex (PFC). The activity in the OFC can suppress inappropriate social actions and impulses.

When driven by anxiety, a person with GAD might have an impulse to get rid of the anxiety: to confront someone, be aggressive when it is not necessary, or behave in a socially inappropriate way. For example, a worker anxious about downsizing may decide she has to confront the boss to demand a list of who is being considered for retirement. Or someone anxious about the ambiguity of whether he will need to book a hotel room may aggressively demand to know if the delayed flight is going to leave or be cancelled. These kinds of behavior can offend others and create interpersonal tension even though they eliminate the anxiety.

Low OFC energy may also fail to suppress impulses that are not aggressive. The impulse might be to run away (like quit a job) without waiting to see if another option emerges. This is where the anterior cingulate gyrus (ACG) comes into the picture as well. The ACG helps create cognitive images of new options to solve problems. When that part of the brain is stuck on the first thing that comes to mind, usually a negative option, and the higher structures of the brain are low on energy to stop it, the impulse to escape gets stronger. This system failure from limbic to ACG to OFC to PFC and back again is largely the result of low levels of serotonin (SE) that contribute to the negativity and rumination of GAD, as well as to cognitive slowness or low energy in the cortex.

CHILDHOOD DEVELOPMENT
AND GENERALIZED ANXIETY DISORDER

What life issues play into brain function? How the amygdala registers emotional tone from infancy is discussed in Chapter 3. The amygdala may start causing problems for worriers early in their lives and shape its own tendency to screen for the worst (by noticing that there are worrisome events). When parents reinforce this tendency with overprotective reassurance, child worriers are set on a path that encourages them to continue reacting fearfully to what is novel. The amygdala's primary job is to screen for novelty (changes in the environment) and if the young person interprets novelty as frightening, he or she is on the path to GAD. In addition to neuroanatomical problems of heredity or genetics, specific emotional factors that emerge from problems in early attachment can have a dramatic impact on brain function in GAD.

Anxious Attachment Experience

The children of parents whose affection and attention are present at times but dramatically absent at other times will develop a state of hypervigilance. The child must be alert to cues of parental availability to know if it is safe to approach the parent. This can happen in nonverbal ways during the first 3 years of life, when emotional safety and security is essential to survival and to developing a healthy brain. When safety and security are undermined by the parent's unpredictable availability, the child becomes tense and hard to soothe or even rejecting of soothing when tense (Schore, 2003; Siegel & Hartzell, 2003).

This kind of unpredictability may occur with drug-addicted parents who are attentive when straight but mentally absent when under the influence of the drug. It might also occur when parents have severe anxiety or depression and cannot always escape their own preoccupation with their problems to connect emotionally with their child. Parents may be physically present but emotionally detached, which is distressing to a child. Obviously, parents with more serious psychological disturbances such a psychosis or personality disorder have problems establishing the emotional bond that is the lifeline for the child's psychological development.

It is the uncertainty of the supply of attention that is anxiety-provoking for children. When they experience it too often, they develop a persistent anxiety about the relationship with the parent. The child's temperament is also relevant to how the child responds to parental unpredictability. A child who is temperamentally tense and slow to warm up and who relies excessively on the safety of a consistent parent will be more susceptible to tension from the ambiguity of whether the parent will be available or not.

These qualities of attachment experience are not present for all people with GAD but do represent the kind of underlying early life experience that can cause psychologically based anxiety. The attachment process is necessary to brain development, and when there are serious disruptions in the close attachment, the brain does not develop as it ought to. (Although the impact of poor attachment outcome must be addressed in long-term therapy, the symptoms of GAD can be managed with short-term treatment.) Poor attachment outcomes are seen in adult clients who have relationship problems with excessive dependency or intolerance of emotional attachments. They may have difficulty tolerating ambiguity in general.

Ambiguity intolerance can result from this anxious attachment. Being vigilant to watch for what might happen next is exhausting. It creates an intolerance for ambiguity in life. In adulthood, the origins of ambiguity intolerance caused by anxious attachment may be lost, but the behavior and cognitions that reflect this early life problem are manifest in people with GAD.

Ambiguity hits a major cognitive "fault line" for people with GAD. Ambiguous situations abound in life, and many people do not feel distressed or even notice that they are surrounded by problems waiting to be solved, by situations about which they need more information before they can decide, or by circumstances that might never be fully resolved. This is life. People have to live with work rumors about downsizing and be able to handle being in relationships without knowing "where it is going." We go on vacations without knowing exactly what we will see or what the hotel will look like, we try new restaurants in spite of not knowing if we will like the food, and we start projects at work without being certain of their outcome.

Daily life ambiguities are very hard on the person with GAD. These clients have difficulty maintaining their cool at the office, fret about losing the job and start hunting for a new job, or quit precipitously over fear of being fired. A GAD sufferer who appears controlling may actually be demonstrating an intolerance for ambiguity—a mother who wants every detail of a vacation trip nailed down months before she leaves may not be controlling as much as she is anxious about ambiguity. She may not really care what the family will do on the vacation, but she needs to have it planned so she can relax her mind about it. If no one else will do it soon enough to make her feel comfortable, she will do it all. She might be cheerful about controlling the details or resentful about all the work she has to do, but the details need to be managed before she can lower her tension level. The typical micromanager at work might be another good example of ambiguity intolerance.

Ambiguity intolerance complicated by brain function. A child may be born with the genetics or brain heredity to develop anxiety and then also experience problematic attachment. Then problems in brain function complicate psychologically-generated ambiguity intolerance. The inability to tolerate life's ambiguities without rumination and controlling responses represents a sort of "system failure." The prefrontal cortex (PFC), orbitofrontal cortex (OFC), and anterior cingulate gyrus (ACG) fail to manage subcortical activity that has created a tendency to worry and be negative. It is a failure to modulate negative input from the limbic system. Low energy in the left PFC causes difficulty generating a positive attitude when negative thoughts about a situation arise. When high activity in the limbic system is generating negativity, and overactivity in the neuronal connections of the ACG cause rumination, it takes high energy in the PFC to take control, generate positive thoughts to suppress the negativity of the limbic system, and override the rumination of the ACG. Tolerating the normal ambiguity of life requires both the ability to wait (suppress impulse for action) and to think (PFC) about several possible acceptable outcomes (ACG and limbic system).

CONCLUSION

Although many people with GAD function at high levels in their lives, they often do so while feeling miserable. The great damage of this disorder is to the mood and resilience of the person who suffers it. The loss of joy and relaxation and the physical damages from stress reveal themselves cumulatively. Some people may be biologically predisposed for GAD, and anxiety-producing life events that cannot be controlled can exacerbate symptoms. When children suffer from GAD, it shapes not only their achievements but also their mood and personality.

Generally people have more control over their choices as they move from childhood to adulthood. They may be more able to direct where they live and work, but they also recognize how much they cannot control about life. People cannot control other people's emotions or choices. They cannot control when accidents happen or whether they get sick. And they certainly cannot control how they age and eventually die. Those aspects of living that all people must cope with are harder for those with GAD. Becoming calm and accepting of the things over which we have no control is a major treatment goal with GAD.

CHAPTER SEVEN

TREATING GENERALIZED ANXIETY DISORDER

Debbie could have been the poster child for GAD. In her late thirties, she was a homemaker and the busy mother of three children who caused the normal amount of problems in school and at home. Debbie was also active on several church and community committees.

Debbie stated that she had been a worrier all her life and that it ran in her family on both sides. But it was not until injuries from a car accident prevented her from leaving the house for an extended period of time that she began to have trouble with worry she could not control. Debbie explained that she felt she was going "out of her mind" with worry, feeling frantic physically and emotionally. She had become unable to stop thoughts that were bombarding her to the point of distraction. She was worrying constantly that she might have a recurrence of breast cancer that had been in remission for 7 years and of which she had been pronounced cured. She had fears about whether her daughter was getting involved with drugs because she was dating a boy with a bad reputation. She could not sleep well. She was in a perpetually irritable mood and snapped at her husband's foibles, which she previously could ignore with humor.

Debbie came to therapy when she realized she was getting out of bed more tired each day after a bad night's sleep. She felt exhausted and wished that she would "just die if it was going to go on this way." She could feel her heart pounding and her stomach was nauseated. The acute anxiety was almost more than she could bear.

Debbie's symptoms were garden-variety GAD. What made her situation dramatic and urgent was that she had them *all* and so strongly. It was necessary to rule out medical concerns immediately, so she got a physical, which yielded negative results for heart, sleep, and gastrointestinal problems. She made an appointment for a medication consult with a psychiatrist, but she chose to schedule it a month after we began therapy so that she could see if she could manage her symptoms on her own first. (This is typical of GAD clients who start psychotherapy before they see a psychiatrist.)

Debbie was a prime example of someone with GAD who comes for treatment after years of annoying but manageable low-grade anxiety. With the onset of GAD's relentless worry, irritability, and sleeplessness, however, Debbie needed symptom management and she needed it fast. For GAD clients, the beginning of effective symptom management is learning that their brain generates worry without a good reason and that therapy can teach them how to control the anxious brain. Clients must intellectually believe that worry is an unnecessary byproduct of overactive brain cells. That belief will help them apply the methods that interrupt worry and slow down the brain.

Long-term therapy is often necessary. Long-standing GAD symptoms shape clients' personalities and interactional styles. Anxiety will have disrupted relationships, molded patterns of work and play, and altered clients' view of the world so pervasively that longer-term psychotherapy is necessary to undo false beliefs and maladaptive patterns of interaction. Life experience also shapes the symptom expression and longer-term therapy may be necessary to resolve those issues. But immediate change can begin with the symptom-management techniques discussed in this chapter.

Our goal is to make changes in physiology, behavior, and cognition that will help the anxious brain learn to control itself. Symptom relief depends on changes involving:

- Lifestyle factors including overwork and perfectionism, sleep and nutrition, and relaxation and leisure
- Anger management
- Spiritual life assessment and development
- Cognitive control (managing thoughts run amok)

As with PD, the first step of treatment is to address the physiology. The second and third steps focus on changing behaviors and cognitions.

Step 1. Address Physiology. This involves teaching clients to:

- Use relaxation techniques to calm down and reduce physical tension and the pain it causes.
- Improve sleep.

Step 2. Address Behavior. This involves making basic changes in lifestyle:

- Altering work style and developing a lifestyle that reflects personal values about life.
- Planning fun or relaxing activities to reduce physical tension.
- Remembering to laugh.

Step 3. Address Cognitions. This involves:

- Taking control of ruminative thoughts
- Dispensing with irrational guilt and building positives.
- Calming anger and irritability.

STEP 1. ADDRESS PHYSIOLOGY

The description of stressed people as "uptight" is apt: Most people react to stress by tightening up physically. And they don't notice it until they have headaches or knots in their backs. Physical relaxation does not come naturally if a person is stressed out. Most people with GAD don't notice how they have tightened up in the neck or shoulders, lower back, buttocks, or legs until they have pain somewhere. Tension headaches are born of tense muscles in the head and neck that restrict blood flow or affect nerves.

Relaxation Techniques: Relax the Body
(and the Mind Will Follow)

Teaching relaxation and tension release is a first-line treatment. Deep relaxation not only eliminates the negative outcome of muscle tension but also reduces high blood pressure, fosters heart health, and promotes emotional calm. Yoga, meditation, and even some of the martial arts are good ways to learn this kind of deep relaxation. These methods typically require specific training from practitioners of these arts, but anyone can learn how to use the technique of progressive muscle relaxation to great benefit in a single therapy session.

Progressive Muscle Relaxation
The progressive muscle relaxation script has many variations, but the basic plan in all of them is to relax the muscle groups in a systematic manner. The muscle relaxation usually takes 10–15 minutes.

THE PROGRESSIVE MUSCLE RELAXATION TECHNIQUE

Use this script to learn the progressive muscle relaxation exercise. You can begin at either the head or the toes—this script begins with the toes. Instruct your clients to:

1. Make sure you are in a relaxed position, but not in a bent position, sitting with your neck upright or lying flat.
2. Close your eyes if you are comfortable doing so and then allow your focus to rest entirely on the sensations of each muscle group.
3. Now focus your attention on your toes. Tense your toes—curl them tight, tight, tight or imagine pushing your foot into the earth. Now release. Feel the warmth flood into them. Feel the energy and warmth suffuse those muscles. With each exhalation of breath, feel how warmth flows into the toes. (Repeat the tense, hold, and release three times before moving to the next muscle group. It is amazing how much tension remains after just one or two tightenings.)
4. Now focus on your calves and shins. Tighten them by pointing your toes and feel the stretch down your shin and the contraction in your calf. Then reverse by pulling your toe up and pushing the heel forward. Feel the stretch down your calf and the contraction in your shin. (Again, repeat the tense, hold, and release three times, and each time notice the warmth and energy that suffuses the muscles as tension is released.)
5. Now focus on your thighs, tightening them by using the muscles above the knees and using the buttocks as little as possible. (Repeat three times, noticing warmth and energy.)
6. Now focus on your buttocks. Tighten them by squeezing them together. (Repeat three times, noticing warmth and energy.)
7. Now focus on your back and abdomen. Tighten this area by imagining a string pulling your belly button toward your spine. (Repeat three times, noticing warmth and energy.)
8. Now focus on your arms. Tighten your forearm, wrist, and hand by clenching your fist. (Repeat three times, noticing warmth and energy.)
9. Now focus on your shoulders. Raise your shoulders up, hunching them. (Repeat three times, noticing warmth and energy.)

10. Now focus on your neck. Do not make neck circles, because those are hard on the spine, but rather let your head drop forward with the weight of it pulling your chin toward your chest. You will feel the stretch down your back, even as far as your lower back if you are very tight. Then return your head to a full upright position before leaning it back in the opposite direction. Then tilt it to one side, with your ear moving directly toward your shoulder. You will feel the stretch as far down as the shoulder blade. When your head returns upright, feel the warmth flow in where the stretching was. (Repeat three times, noticing warmth and energy.)
11. Now focus on your face. Squint your eyes and purse your mouth to tighten your face. (Repeat three times, noticing warmth and energy.)
12. Now focus on your forehead. Wrinkle your brow. (Repeat three times, noticing warmth and energy.)
13. Now focus on your scalp. Raise your eyebrows to tighten your scalp. (Repeat three times, noticing warmth and energy.)
14. Feel the energy flowing in with each breath and coursing down through your body with each exhalation. (If you began your script with the head rather than the toes, notice the energy flowing down through the relaxed muscles and end with the awareness of the soles of your feet feeling connected to the earth through the floor.)

Progressive muscle relaxation can be fun at even very young ages. For smaller children, use images of animals they can relate to (a cat stretching out in the sun, a lion opening its mouth to yawn) to lead them through. "Stretch and release" instead of "tense and release" works very well. Adolescents can benefit with the adult ways of doing relaxation but are sensitive to not appearing foolish. Also note that many children do not like being singled out to do this, so stretching as a group exercise can be beneficial to helping them learn.

Diaphragmatic Breathing
Diaphragmatic breathing is the necessary foundation for relaxation or meditation. It is also important for cuing the relaxed state discussed in the following section. See Chapter 4 for a full description of this technique.

Cued Relaxation
Because it results from high basal ganglia (BG) tone, physical tension is not going to disappear with one session of relaxation. Rather, it will reappear

constantly, even without overt stress. People with GAD must use muscle relaxation as a lifelong tool. Consequently, it is necessary to pair muscle relaxation with diaphragmatic breathing to produce what can be called "cued relaxation." This pairing of breath and muscle relaxation has several purposes.

- Deep breathing encourages parasympathetic calming of the stress response. The overactivity of the stress response system is addressed by encouraging the brain to calm itself.
- Muscle relaxation interrupts the tension level caused by high tone in the basal ganglia (BG).
- The pairing of breathing and deep muscle relaxation is needed to form an association between one or two full diaphragmatic breaths and total relaxation. Once that association is made it will allow a person, at any time and in any place, to induce cued relaxation by taking a controlled deep breath.

Suggest diaphragmatic breathing for a few minutes before beginning the relaxation technique. This will help connect breathing with relaxation and will deepen regular breathing during the relaxation when attention is not specifically given to breathing.

Debbie became adept at pairing breathing and relaxation very quickly. Before teaching Debbie relaxation techniques, I briefly described the brain-driven nature of tension and rumination. (Generally GAD clients will be more compliant with practicing techniques if they know the reason behind using them.) Debbie understood why she needed to work first on symptom management, starting with learning to relax her body. She was in a constant state of high tension and, although she was not panicking, she felt acute anxiety when she started to worry about cancer or her kids. She needed to be able to stop the physical stress response when the anxiety grabbed her, and she needed to loosen the grip of tension.

I then taught Debbie diaphragmatic breathing and progressive muscle relaxation, and she practiced both until she developed the ability to cue relaxation. She benefited from these techniques immediately and quickly forged a link between her breath and a state of relaxation.

She then began to use cued relaxation several times during the day to diminish her physical tension, which helped with sore muscles and her general feeling of being "wired." She liked the image of "plugging into the earth" with her feet and discharging her extra (tense) energy into the earth. We used the reminder phrase "I am sending energy into the earth, which absorbs all energy, negative or positive, and transforms it into life."

Relaxation Imagery

Imagery that can assist in muscle relaxation is very helpful for some clients. Following is one version of imagery that is commonly used.

IMAGERY OF ENERGY AND LIGHT

If you read this imagery aloud, elaborate as you speak, but follow this general outline:

1. Imagine that a sphere of light is above your head.
2. The light is the color you most associate with [peace, calm, healing, energy, etc.].
3. As you inhale, you draw this light into your body through your breath or through your crown chakra.
4. As you exhale, the flow of energy streams through your body.
5. Become aware of each body part feeling the flow. (As in muscle relaxation, go through each part separately.)
6. Imagine sending energy flowing through your spine as roots into the earth.
7. Imagine sending energy flowing through the soles of your feet (when you reach that part of the body).
8. Experience the energy flowing through your pores to form an envelope around your body.
9. Find a word that you associate with this sensation of total relaxation, such as *calm,* or even a sound such as *ah* or *mmm.*
10. This energy provides a barrier to negativity for the day, preventing all criticism, disapproval, harsh words, or ill treatment from penetrating to your heart. It is permeable to all positive energy, so that words of praise, approval, and affection can immediately be received in the heart.
11. As the envelope of energy fades through the day it can be renewed with a deep breath, imagining light and saying or hearing the sound you chose.

Exercise

Believe it or not, physical activities are better sources of physical relaxation than sitting still. Aerobic exercise is the best because it is a great long-term relaxer, and it may help out at the moments when stress is high. Also, exercise increases blood flow to the brain and may help generate new neurons (DeAngelis, 2002). Aerobic or anaerobic workouts discharge pent-up energy and cause neurochemistry changes. The vigorous activity uses up the adrenalin of the stress response and helps to rid the body of toxic cortisol. It also counteracts the weight gain that constant stress can lead to. Additionally, muscles that are used in vigorous exercise are stretched and relaxed afterward. There is no downside to vigorous exercise. Remember the prescription from Chapter 4: Exercise 5–7 days a week for 25–45 minutes at 70% of your maximum heart rate.

Quick Stretching Techniques

These techniques promote muscle relaxation by loosening tensed muscles, increasing general blood flow, and readjusting tensed posture. Most can be done anywhere and at any time. Several of them can be done at work or school or while sitting in a confined place such as a car or airplane seat. They also take very little time—most only require a momentary pause.

QUICK STRETCHING TECHNIQUES

- Simply yawn, stretch your arms upward, and release. Repeat.
- For gentle back stretching, try torso relaxation. With feet comfortably spread apart for support, let your torso fall forward with your head gently leading the way down, bend at the waist, and come back into an upright position by literally reversing the motion. Imagine that you are a puppet being released and then drawn upright by a string.
- Continue the action of this simple stretch into an overhead stretch once you are upright. Lift up your arms, reaching high overhead, and gently tilt your head by lifting your chin until you gaze directly up. Make this and all releases gentle.
- If you get up to walk somewhere after you have been sitting too long or are too tight, pause for a moment and do some gentle leg lunges.
- If you have the opportunity to go up or down a few stairs, pause, and with the toes balanced on the edge of the stair, let your heel drop, stretching the back of your leg. Do this for 2 seconds of stretch and then pause. Repeat it a few times. You can do this one leg at a time with the other foot firmly planted on the stair if you are worried about your balance.
- Seated-at-desk head tilt. You can do this while on the phone or looking at the computer and not even lose time from work. *Do not rotate your head in a circle.* Let your ear fall toward your shoulder

---

as far as it can without hurting. Raise your head upright. Then let your chin drop slowly to your chest, feeling the stretch down your back, and raise your head upright. Then drop the other ear toward the other shoulder and, again, raise your head. Finally, let your head feel heavy and drop slowly backward. Return to the upright position before you go on to repeat this.

- Seated-at-desk arm stretch. Raise one arm straight overhead and then bend it at the elbow, reaching with that hand down and toward the other side of your body, as if you were going to scratch your other shoulder blade. Then relax. Take the same arm and reach across your chest and wrap your hand around the opposite shoulder. Using the unoccupied hand, grasp the elbow of the reaching arm and gently exert pressure to increase the stretch in the shoulder and upper arm.
- Seated posture change. Another way to prevent inadvertently tightening up is the seated posture change. This preventive measure can be practiced constantly if your job requires sitting all day. It involves regularly rotating through changed positions. Have a stool (or just a box) by your feet on which to rest them. For 15 minutes in each position, sit with one foot raised, then the other, then both, then neither. You can do the same thing with a back pillow or rolled towel. Put it behind your lower back, then behind your middle back, and then do without it.

There is one simple, general rule about stretching for release: Never do anything that hurts! If it hurts, stop immediately.

Cognition and Relaxation: The Willingness to Believe You Need Relaxation

There are four typical cognitions that interfere with relaxing the body. People with GAD may never have noticed that they think this way, but many have the following attitudes about relaxing that prevent them from loosening their bodies and minds.

- "No one can have a relaxed body while they are working."
- "I am just not a person who can have relaxed muscles."
- "I will relax at the end of the day, when I *deserve* it."
- "If I relax, I won't get enough work done."

This last attitude is the *pièce de résistance* for worrywarts. In a black-and-white kind of way, they equate relaxation with being completely unproductive. Most with GAD will not risk that. Productivity wards off anxiety.

Cognitive errors like these can interfere with taking time for or even with achieving physical relaxation. They also lead clients to make poor choices about how to use activities we equate with relaxation, such as sharing a meal, having a drink, or watching television.

Activities That Can Either Help or Hurt Relaxation

Examine with clients whether the following activities intended for relaxation are being used to their advantage and if they are not, encourage clients to correct their use of these activities.

Mealtimes

Are you a "relax with dinner" or "relax with eating" person? (These are not necessarily the same, except that food is involved.)

- Those who relax over a slow, lingering meal with conversation may be getting the most out of the evening meal with family or friends: slowing down, tasting their food, and engaging in social discourse. The end result might be to loosen up and relax the body tension level. If this sounds like you, you are getting the most out of the relaxation of the meal.
- However, if you *eat as a substitute for relaxation* and wait for a chance to eat as a treat, you may be eating *for* relaxation and not relaxing *while* eating. You will train yourself to use food as a reward for working and a trigger for feeling a moment of relaxation. When the food, not the mood, of the meal is used to take a break, eating can become a problem. Those who eat to relax tend to eat more than they need, and they end up increasing their stress by gaining weight.

Alcohol

Having a drink is a common and socially acceptable means of inducing a relaxed feeling. Especially when in a social context of sipping a drink while chatting, the ambiance combines with the relaxant effect of alcohol. But if you rely on drinking to relieve stress you run the risk of developing health problems or even addiction. The following typical patterns of using alcohol to relax can create more problems in the long run, even if they do not lead to alcohol abuse.

- Do you regularly relax after a busy day with a drink? Alcohol may be a very reliable way to start *feeling* loose, but it is not always associated with muscle relaxation.
- If one drink becomes two or three, especially before dinner, you may end up both drinking and then eating too much.
- If you relax with a couple of drinks before bedtime to settle down, you will probably accomplish your goal of getting drowsy, but you won't sleep as well. Just as you are getting to the deepest part of the night's sleep, the detoxification of the alcohol will physically make nerve endings jangle, and it will awaken the sleeper with a feeling of being tired but too jittery to fall back to sleep.

TV and Electronic Toys

Electronic activities are physically *passive* and thus give the impression of being relaxing, but they most often do not relieve physical tension, and they are only effective mental relaxers when used sparingly. Many people use video games, computer games, and television to distract themselves from anxiety. These are so good at "zoning you out" that you may not realize they ultimately increase stress.

- Do you watch television or play video or computer games for long stretches at the end of the day? These may prevent you from thinking, but they do not give you physical relaxation.
- The sensory bombardment of electronics can be overstimulating for your nervous system, even though you are not using your body at all.
- Many people who feel tired and want to lie in front of the television are actually more mentally tired than physically worn out. Using the body actively is often a better way of achieving relaxation, so physical activity followed by a pleasant distraction such as watching a television program is optimal for tension reduction.

With electronic methods of relaxation, as with eating and drinking for stress relief, moderation is called for.

Electronic activities and children. The American Academy of Pediatrics recommends no television or video games for children under the age of 2 and no more than an hour a day thereafter (Christakis, 2004; Elias, 2004). Learning to use and work on a computer is not the same. Computer and keyboard skills are necessary in this society, and learning to use the computer can be intellectually stimulating and interactive. Separate use of the computer to learn and expand knowledge from using it to play games. But minimize the amount of chatting, blogging, and instant messaging your child or young teenager is doing. There is significant evidence that social skills must be developed in fact-to-face interactions. In fact, communication on the computer not only fails to develop social skills but also appears to encourage cruelty and insensitivity because the person writing does not see the pain their remarks create via feedback of face or tone of voice. It is probably a good idea to limit computer use to areas of the home where the child (and the screen) can be observed.

Take Time for Relaxation

The high tone of the basal ganglia (BG) drives motivated people with GAD to be busier than most people, and they are often less likely to spend time in leisure. The cognitive side of this disorder may cause people to be perfectionistic, driven workers. Between the physical tension and the belief system that drives them to overwork, people with GAD may end every day feeling tense and needing to relax. But, like those who take power naps, these clients may be looking for "power relaxation." Regrettably, the high energy of the BG does not just turn itself off without some help. It is nearly impossible for clients to work at high speed all day long and then get quality relaxation in the space of the 30 minutes they may allow themselves for relaxation before collapsing into sleep. It would be like spending only 30 minutes a day with a child and expecting that time to be "quality time." For relaxation, as for kids, quantity usually is necessary to produce quality. Encourage clients to examine both their attitudes and practices of relaxation and plan immediate, small steps to improve the quality of their relaxation.

Sleep

Getting enough sleep should probably be the first recommendation for treating all physical and mental disorders because it is the very foundation of health. Good sleep improves physiology: In addition to simply feeling rested, the body, including the physical, anxious brain, heals itself during sleep. During sleep we:

- Learn, as the brain stores information and experiences in long-term memory
- Relieve stress and worry
- Heal from emotional trauma
- Heal from illness
- Renew our cells, including the ones that produce neurotransmitters

Sleep thus is the link between physical and psychological health. A healthy brain is necessary for a healthy mind.

The Worried Brain and Sleep

People with GAD commonly report poor quality of sleep, where they do not feel rested even after being in bed for 8 hours (Papadimitriou & Linkowski, 2005). They may not be having nightmares, but people with GAD frequently have "worry dreams." This is the type of dreaming in which brain is still processing the events of the day, but rarely are they the fun or enjoyable events. Rather, the dreams pick up on details that were challenging, potentially problematic, or frustrating.

Worry dreaming is not something you will read about on the Sleep Disorder Association website. We are not aware of formal research on this, but we have seen so much of it in our own professional practice that we believe it is common. A possible explanation for the occurrence of worry dreaming is that the brain stays too alert to sink into the very deep brainwave patterns that precede REM sleep. Rather, the sleeper is stuck in the hippocampal dreaming sleep stage. Preceding REM dreaming, the hippocampus sends the details of the day up to the left prefrontal cortex (PFC) where they are reviewed and discharged during REM. REM sleep is when most of the benefits of sleep activity seem to occur, although these processes are not fully understood. It appears that REM activity directs significant information and emotional context into long-term memory storage. Additionally, the cortex neurobiologically instructs the hippocampus and the amygdala to delete most of the irrelevant details and emotional upsets of the previous day, resulting in relief of worries and cares. If the dreamer never reaches the REM stage, the cortex has no opportunity to delete the irrelevant details and emotional upsets, and the dreamer stays stuck in the hippocampal stage.

There are some ways to bounce back from this kind of restless sleep, to increase the length of a night's sleep, and to improve the overall benefit of sleep in restless GAD sleepers. Sleep medications can be of great help in getting past the hippocampal sleep stage to deeper sleep; however, all sleep medications create some rebound insomnia and thus should be used with caution (see Chapter 8). Many GAD clients report that their regular antianxiety medication at bedtime helps eliminate this kind of restless sleep, but practicing good sleep hygiene is the best long-term answer.

Sleep Hygiene

There are specific practices that make sleep deeper and more regular.

Set a regular pattern. Go to sleep and get out of bed at the same time every day. This will take a while to work, so don't be discouraged by trouble falling asleep or trouble waking up. Just do it. Take no more than an hour's variance on weekend nights!

Get enough sleep. Most people need 7 1/2 to 8 hours. Teens need 9–10. Children need more, depending on their age. Go to bed early enough that you can sleep the full 8 hours, even if you wake sooner than that for a while. Stay in bed and rest for up to 8 hours while practicing the methods that will help you stay asleep (to follow). Once you are sleeping on a regular schedule and fairly well, you will find that you awaken when you are rested, and you will discover exactly how much sleep your body needs on an ongoing basis to feel rested.

Accommodate age and schedule. Teens are in a special category due to their circadian rhythms. They are often not ready for sleep until midnight (unless exhausted) and not ready to awaken until 9. School is at exactly the wrong time for the adolescent body! Teens must decide how to accommodate this problem, but most can sleep by 10 P.M. That will probably require time limits on using the computer, phone, or playing video games in the evening in order to finish homework and school activities in time to sleep.

Young children need more sleep. Children under the age of 6 generally need up to 12 hours; toddlers need even more. Depriving young children of sleep to accommodate a parent's schedule is a recipe for learning and behavior problems, in addition to the stress it creates.

Anxious teens and children are in particular need of enough sleep. They can repair some fatigue due to sleep deprivation by sleeping more hours on the weekend. But that will not provide the daily stress relief that is so necessary. Parental control may be needed to achieve a healthy sleep plan.

The elderly may sleep more restlessly because of needing to use the bathroom or because they are not producing sufficient melatonin. Their environment may be too noisy or too light. Look at how components of their environment and lifestyle can be made more conducive to sleep, and see if they are candidates for supplements such as melatonin or valerian before using medications.

Sleep in a room that is as cold and dark as possible. This is the best way to establish a good circadian rhythm that will promote a regular sleep cycle. People often say they *need* light or noise (like television or radio) to fall asleep, but these things are disruptive even though they are accustomed to them. This is because the amygdala functions in sleep as it does in waking—keeping us aware of the warning signals that danger might be near. It responds to and registers stimuli like sounds, smells, and sights, even during sleep. *Variances* in sound, smell, and so on are noted as important, so the brain wakes up when it notices a change. Television or radio may drown out other environmental noises that would otherwise keep a person awake. It is true that screening out environmental noise (like people talking in another room or noise from the street) is very important, but leaving the television on is not the best way to do it. A television changes pitch, pace, and volume, constantly causing too much alertness in the amygdala. Creating white noise, with a fan, for example, is a better choice. If you *must* use the television to fall asleep, remember that most of them have sleep timers. Use them!

Keep the brain calm before sleep. Introducing worry or stirring emotions shortly before sleeping makes it harder for a restless brain to calm down for sleep. That is also true for any activity or substance that stimulates the brain. The following suggestions will keep calm your brain before sleep.

- Eliminate violent or exciting television, including television news, for several hours before sleep. (Even better, don't *ever* watch it!). Television news comes complete with amygdala-jarring music, unexpected and often gruesome visuals, and overexcited voices. Its *sole purpose* is to keep you watching for the advertisers. The opening lines of news broadcasts are deliberately written to scare you enough that you will be forced to continue watching just to calm down. Get news from the radio, newspaper, and weekly news magazines instead.
- Take a warm bath for 20 minutes before sleep. This relaxes tight muscles and stimulates oxytocin, a hormone that soothes.
- Have a *small* high-carbohydrate snack. This boosts the insulin and blood sugar levels necessary to help the neurons receive proteins that build neurotransmitters during sleep.
- Don't use alcohol to get drowsy. Try herbal teas such as catnip or chamomile. Remember that herbal teas must be steeped in boiling water for 5–10 minutes to get the medicinal properties of the tea. A minute in a microwave won't do it.
- Keep caffeine as low as possible, especially after noon.
- Avoid napping during the day.
- Use mental calming routines before sleep (see the "clear your mind" exercise on page 167). Prayer, meditation, reading peaceful literature, and listening to quiet music may all help.

Interrupt worry dreams. It is generally recommended that restless sleepers stay in bed and try to go back to sleep if they awaken. Those who have worry dreams, however, may find that this results in the dream's continuing in its ruminative, never-ending kind of way. It works better to awaken fully for a few minutes and shake off the dream by consciously finishing the topic, dispelling its importance, and then focusing on something pleasant while falling back asleep.

Plan for awake times. Each night before sleeping, pick a topic to think about in case you awaken. Worry dreams and restless sleep may cause you to awaken with a sense of foreboding. It is best to refuse the urge to think about what might be wrong and instead immediately direct your thoughts to the topic you selected for the night and try to fall back asleep with the pleasing thought.

All of these sleep methods may not be needed in each case, but sleep is a top treatment priority. As the case of Debbie illustrates, poor-quality sleeps is distressing and blocks full recovery.

As described earlier, one of the symptoms Debbie presented with was poor quality of sleep. Indeed, Debbie had not been sleeping for more than 2 hours at a time, and she was restless all night. It was necessary for her to improve the length and the quality of her night's sleep.

Debbie decided to use sleep medications for a short period while learning better sleep hygiene. She reviewed the previously described methods for sleep hygiene and implemented most of them immediately. She particularly liked the idea of having a "room of peace" for her evenings. She kept the television and computer out and made her bedroom a place for quiet music, reading, meditating, and sleep. She also asked her family not to bother her during this quiet time with anything that might be upsetting. Because her sleep pattern was extremely disrupted, it took several weeks for Debbie's sleep routine to stabilize, but she was eventually able to discontinue the medication and achieve a full night's sleep on her own.

STEP 2. ADDRESS BEHAVIOR

Because high activity in the basal ganglia (BG) results in highly motivated, goal-directed behavior, people with GAD are the type who get a lot done in a day—regardless if whether that work is washing windows, writing computer programs, completing schoolwork, doing home repair, running a household, participating in volunteer work, or engaging in extracurricular activities. People with GAD almost always do more than is necessary, and they may end up paying for it. Others may see them as controlling or feel their own contributions are not valuable. Generalized anxiety disorder workaholics may push themselves to the point of exhaustion, which may negatively affect their health or relationships with family and friends.

When people with GAD are blocked from working, they feel agitated. Lifestyle assessment and changes are intended to immediately calm and slow their pace. Calming the activity of the BG is accomplished with a wide range of techniques as diverse as meditation and goal-setting.

Altering Work Style and Developing a Lifestyle That Reflects Personal Values

Generalized anxiety disorder clients tend to be perfectionists, because they see perfectionism as a way to ward off anxiety. They believe that the fewer mistakes they make, the less they will have to worry. What they do not realize is that they are going to worry no matter how hard they work. When starting therapy, perfectionists often fear that the therapist's unspoken goal is to turn them from an active type A personality into laid-back type B personality. Actually, the goal is to help them continue to be a productive type A. There are two kinds of type A: *type A-hardy* and *type A-hostile*. Type A-hostile personalities fly into rages and do not attempt to calm themselves. They are prone to high blood pressure and heart problems (Siegman & Smith, 1994). Type A-hardy personalities thrive on hard work and cope well with problems that come along. With GAD clients, a reasonable goal is to help them be productive type A-Hardy without anxiety.

When addressing work-style issues with GAD clients, question them about their perfectionism:

- What is the difference between good enough and perfect?
- In which situations is perfection necessary and in which situations is "good enough" okay? There is a difference, for example, between preparing for a competition like a sporting event or music recital and doing the critical calculations for the maximum weight load of a bridge you are designing—or between doing sensitive medical research and throwing a birthday party or mowing the lawn.
- Do you understand that absolute perfection is impossible?

Children get into the lock of perfectionism as well. A young child might insist on drawing a perfect picture, redoing it several times or taking a long time to make it just right. An adolescent might practice extra hours for music or sports activities. Perfectionist children get very tense when they feel they have to perform, such as take a test or play a game. They take over leadership of any group they are in. Although striving to do their best is a value you want to see in children, the GAD child cannot tell when it is okay to lighten up. Pointing out these differences at each developmental level is necessary, as responsibilities and activities change over the course of growing up.

The GAD sufferers' fear of moderating work effort and perfectionism may also stem from the all-or-nothing cognition that they won't be productive at all. But the lives of people with GAD are often out of balance in serious ways. You can help GAD clients loosen their psychological grip on work and perfectionism by asking them to look at their values about living a good life.

- What qualities of life make it worth living?
- What is the value of balancing work with leisure and family or social activity?

If they recognize balance as valuable, they will learn to value their leisure more. Also, if they begin to worry less, they may become less perfectionistic, and they won't need work to ward off fear. That said, GAD clients *will always remain motivated.* It is the way their brains are made. If they get a little less work done, it will be because they are adding other activities that create some balance in their lives. They may even discover what efficiency experts have proven—that taking breaks from work can help them be more productive than when they never took time off.

Planning Fun or Relaxing Activities

Worry is the antidote to fun. It is hard for people with GAD to have fun when they spend so much time preoccupied with preventing bad things from happening. They consequently do not enjoy the leisure time they do have, and they may avoid any leisure time at all.

Carol, a gregarious client in her mid-thirties, was a case in point. Carol's home had an open-door policy, and she and her husband were known for their lively parties. However, Carol spent most of the party time waiting for it to be over. She was so consumed with trying to be a perfect hostess that her only pleasure in the event was hearing how much her guests enjoyed themselves. Carol needed to find leisure activities that did not come with a burden to perform so she could have some fun and lighten her mental load.

The methods for getting people with GAD to have fun are simple. They ask clients to focus some attention on how they use leisure and help them see what aspects of leisure are pleasurable. Ask clients the following questions:

- What were you doing the last time you laughed a lot?
- What part of your time off work feels pleasurable? (When you ask clients this question, do not allow them to use caveats that rob activities of fun. For example, if a client played games with the family on a Friday night, he or she must not answer the pleasurable/unpleasurable question by saying, "It would have been fun if I had done better." The "if" changes the experience.)
- What did you do when you were a child that felt like fun? How can you replicate that as an adult? (For example, if a client liked basketball games in the neighborhood as a child, could he join a park district team for his age group?)

Children with GAD tend to be team captains or club presidents. When helping these clients plan fun activities, it is good to give them permission to participate in activities without being in charge and to encourage them to do activities that are not scored or rated, like bike-riding.

It is also a good idea to help clients feel that they *can* be slow and leisurely without feeling anxious. Some activities that are great for calming the body are also great for inducing genuine leisurely movement and activity. The person with GAD often needs a good reason to do something that seems lazy or unproductive. Following are some of the reasons behind doing these obviously relaxing activities:

- *Get a massage.* The therapeutic value of massage has been recorded in several studies. It has been shown to reduce stress and anxiety, relax muscles, reduce pain perception, and aid in circulation, digestion, and excretion. Being touched stimulates oxytocin, a hormone involved in feelings of being soothed (Kosfeld, Heinrichs, Zak, Fischbacher, & Fehr, 2005; Field, 2002). There are many different types of massage—effleurage, deep-tissue, and relaxation massage. Even the simplest massage from a family member may convey to the recipient a feeling of being cared for, which literally reduces the impact of stress. Field's study of postpartum mothers showed that massage corrected the effects of stress. The massage group had statistically significant changes in saliva cortisol levels after their sessions and was the only group to show decreases in anxiety scores.
- *Take a warm bath and use aromatherapy.* Warm baths also stimulate oxytocin and the warmth relaxes muscles. Aromatherapy is the practice of using essential oils to enhance relaxation or target symptoms. The oils are highly concentrated substances distilled from plants known to have therapeutic benefit. The mechanism of action of topically applied essential oils is not clear, although they may work through absorption or inhalation of airborne physiologically active compounds. The oils most consistently used for depression and anxiety are lavender, jasmine, ylang-ylang, sandalwood, bergamot, and rose. Several of these oils have been shown to have muscle-relaxant and sedative properties.
- *Acupuncture* has been used in China and other Asian countries for thousands of years. As with several other complementary and alternative medicine modalities, acupuncturists make a diagnosis based on the pattern of symptoms expressed in each particular patient. In acupuncture, hair-thin needles are inserted at certain points along meridians of energy, or Qi (chi), to stimulate sluggish energy or correct imbalances. In acupuncture theory, anxiety is characterized by an overactive sympathoadrenal system that may be relieved by endorphins; acupuncture has been shown to decrease sympathetic nervous system arousal and increase the level of endorphins.
- *Stroll in the sun.* The skin should be protected from UV but our brains need the stimulation of light to develop good circadian rhythms (pro-

moting sleep) and to prevent depressed and anxious states. A 30-minute walk outside provides enough light stimulation help prevent loss of serotonin in gray weather seasons. Being in the warmth of the sun is also a good muscle relaxer.

- *Spend time near lapping or running water*—a lake, a river, an ocean— *and breathe.* The ionization of the air near bodies of water allows for greater relaxation.

These methods can be successful with clients of all ages. Children can typically enjoy relaxation without worrying that they should be doing something else. If they do not seem able to relax, explore whether they are staying mentally on guard because of a problem in the home—abuse from parent, a family member using alcohol or drugs, family tension due to illness or financial or legal problems, and so on.

Despite all the great techniques for calming the brain, GAD clients probably will still have a high BG tone, so they will not be likely to find fun in slow-moving, lie-in-the-hammock-type leisure activities. Remember that their need for activity is a positive in most ways and should be accommodated in their plans for leisure time. Listen to their urge to be active, and make sure the activity is not being done because they would feel anxious if they did not do it. Listen for statements that the high activity was experienced as fun. Whether it is a day of gardening, a 40-mile bike ride, or hitting every garage sale in town on a Saturday morning, GAD clients probably want their fun time to be busy, not leisurely. Discharging energy is good for anxiety relief and calming the stress response.

Laughing

Laughing is a great way to increase good feelings while discharging tension. Fun and laughter are vital to building a life that is worth living (Sobel & Ornstein, 1996; Berk & Tan, 1989). The problem for anxious clients is that they gradually take life so seriously that they stop experiencing the humor in everyday life. They spend their time watching for potential problems rather than for potential delight. Stopping patterns of worrying entails thinking about other possible attitudes. People with GAD need to remember what life was like before they were consumed with worry. Recreating fun and getting the relief of laughing is serious therapy for these clients.

Give clients an assignment to do something they know will be good for a laugh and come back and report on it. When someone cannot come up with idea, I urge them to spend some time with small children, who can almost always guarantee a laugh with their wonder and enthusiasm. (If there are no small children in the house, ask clients whether they have a relative, neighbor, or friend who has children—most parents are happy to let someone take care of their kids for a few hours.) Writing about how the fun felt and talking about what was fun in therapy will expand the experience of pleasure and make it easier to find similar opportunities to have fun.

All these methods for changing behavior can help sufferers of GAD rebalance their lives and discharge their tension. For Debbie, introduced at the beginning of this chapter, changing behaviors was a vital part of treatment. Debbie was very involved with her children, participating in their athletic and dance events. Although this appeared to be social time, Debbie was always organizing these events rather than just being there. She was having fun in the eyes of others, but she was actually working whenever she went out—bringing the Gatorade and snacks, acting as the Band Booster president, decorating the hall, ordering the pizza party for the soccer moms, and so on. When I asked her to make a list of fun activities, she was stymied. Other than having an occasional lunch with a friend, her list was pretty brief. Getting in touch with fun and play is not easy for the serious, tense worrier, so I encouraged her to watch for any impulse she felt to do something just because she felt like it in the moment. I asked her to do one thing over the weekend on that impulse.

When I saw her next she seemed transformed. She said, "I had an impulse to stop for an ice cream cone, so I just went out and got it. I can't remember the last time I felt like doing something and just did it—with no worries about whether I should bring some home for everyone or whether I should wait until later and bring the kids along. It was fun!" Over time, listening to her inner wishes helped her feel as if life held some fun, and she became more able to value fun time without having to be the organizer.

STEP 3. ADDRESS COGNITIONS

Most of the cognitive symptoms of GAD are related to worry—repetitive, depressing, hard-to-shake-off worry. Generalized anxiety disorder worry is an art form, and it may achieve paranoid or delusional proportions. People with GAD worry about anything and everything: breaking laws, germs and contagion, poisoning, hurting others by accident. Worries about normal things are out of proportion to reality. People with GAD know their worries are irrational, but they cannot stop them. And they often seek reassurance while simultaneously trying to cover up just how odd their worry is. Treatment involves avoiding reassurance and learning to stop worry in its tracks. Not an easy task for the therapist or the client with GAD!

Reassurance and GAD

Reassurance is a major need for those with GAD. People who have a ruminative worry always try to get rid of it by seeking reassurance that their worry is unfounded. They believe that if they get the right kind of solution to their problem or the right piece of information, they will feel reassured and will be rid of the worry once and for all. In reality, however, their anxious brains will simply find some flaw in the reassurance, which prompts them to seek better reassurance.

Additionally, GAD worries are often bizarre, and worriers know this. But they cannot get reassurance unless they mention these odd thoughts in some way. They may make quips about the topic of their anxious thoughts, seeing how others (including the therapist) will react. Joking about a topic that scares them is a subtle way of getting reassurance. And getting reassurance can be difficult, because to really relax and accept the reassurance, they must know they have been *perfectly* understood. This was the case with Courtney.

Courtney was worried that she had caused a problem by using her sister's credit card. Even though she used it with permission, she had signed her sister's name, and she was now concerned that she had committed fraud. She worried that the credit card company would charge her sister with a crime for misusing the card. When Courtney mentioned this concern to her sister, her sister just laughed it off with, "Oh, everybody does it." But Courtney knew she had not explained all the potential ways this could be a problem, and she did not feel reassured by her sister's flip response. When Courtney brought the problem to therapy, her therapist also thought the problem was minor, but this did not comfort her. It was not until she had presented every little detail of her worry that she could relax. She asked if she should have had a signed letter and wondered if it was too late to write one. She said that she should have set it up with the credit card company ahead of time and wondered if she could call them now. She felt she should find out what the legal implications could be and try to fix them now. Courtney was worrying as severely *as if she had done something wrong*. She had many ideas about the consequences of doing something illegal but could not see that they did not apply here. Courtney was similar in this way to many bright people with GAD. They have tremendous imagination about what can go wrong, and they can only trust an answer about their worries if they are *certain* they have been correctly and exactly understood.

Reassurance does not work. There is rarely a time when a really good worrier like Courtney will be able to identify and address every concern. A worried brain just generates another permutation of the problem. Getting at irrational, ruminative worry that needs constant reassurance is the hardest part of GAD treatment.

Seeking Reassurance Through Researching

People with GAD also may try to seek reassurance by getting information. The age of the Internet has made this approach significantly easier—and significantly more damaging. Internet research is likely to trigger more anxiety and rarely provides reassurance. People researching their symptoms on the Internet will always find diseases that might cause them, which heightens anxiety. Even if they are researching anxiety, they will always find something that generates new worry. Research on side effects of medications starts new anxiety over every little physical twinge. It is best for clients not to read anything at all about side effects. If a noticeable physical change occurs within a short time of starting the drug, they can consult their physician.

Similarly, many books and tapes are available for treating one's own anxiety. Most have useful and accurate information. However, we have noted a common problem among people who use these treatment tools without guidance. They tend to get anxious reading about all the possible symptoms of anxiety they could have.

Research tends to make GAD worse for people by expanding the field of worry. Because they do not know how to interpret the symptom description, they may start to worry about their worry. They feel a need to figure out how bad their anxiety is, but they become scared if they decide they have too many symptoms. Most clients do not have enough experience to know whether they should worry about their symptoms. They tend to have trouble correctly applying treatments, and if the method does not work as well as they think it should, they feel like failures and wonder if their anxiety is incurable. Getting help from a therapist for anxiety treatment provides needed support for clients' efforts and helps them be appropriately patient with their progress. Additionally, treatment can be modified to meet clients' individual needs.

Plan Instead of Worrying

One good way to get out of the reassurance trap is to utilize the fundamentals of planning. This is a simple but often-overlooked skill that can make a big difference to calming a ruminative mind. Developing planning skills will help clients replace worrying with planning.

For most situations, a good plan will include:

1. Concretely identifying what the problem is.
2. Listing the options to solve the problem, including timeframes that work for each.

3. Picking an option, including when each step of the option could be completed.
4. Writing out a plan to complete the option. Putting it in writing is an important step that makes thought-stopping work (by later saying, "Stop! I have a plan," and then using thought-replacing).
5. Pick a specific time and method to evaluate the option.

It is helpful to write out a plan on paper, with specifics about each part of the solution to the problem.

It is important to remember, however, that all plans include action steps, and if the situation does not lend itself to action steps, "planning instead of worrying" may not be the best strategy. In these cases, a version of "worry well and only once" (discussed later in this chapter) is a more appropriate thought-management strategy. For example, look at Courtney's dilemma. She *could* develop action steps such as calling the credit card company, but such an action would give her worry a weight it does not deserve. It would be best for her to make a plan only if a problem emerges—for example, if her sister tells her the credit card company has called about it. At that point Courtney could formulate and write down an action plan. But until that happens she is to put all thoughts of this out of her mind. This approach would make more sense than planning because Courtney's worry is irrational and asking questions of the credit card company may cause more trouble than good. Just imagine the conversation she might have with a customer service representative! Her anxiety would certainly skyrocket if she heard a representative say she really should not have done that.

But planning might work very well in the case of a man who has an irrational fear that his wife will leave him because she does not demonstrate enough caring for him, despite no evidence that she wants to leave. The man's constant seeking of reassurance from his wife creates a bigger problem than he already faces in having an irrational worry. In this case, the planning method would involve:

1. Identifying the problem: "I fear my wife is going to leave me because she does not behave in a caring manner. My problem is managing my fear." Note that he might identify a relationship problem or want to identify the problem as her lack of concern for him, but his real problem is the anxiety he suffers. The other problem is imagined (that she does not care for him).
2. Listing the options to solve the problem. He might develop some ideas about what could help him feel less worried. For example, perhaps he would worry less if they had a weekly date, or he might feel better if she would agree to tell him she loves him at least once a week when he has not asked her if she loves him. Note that these options rely on

his wife to cooperate. She might do so or she might not. Therefore, although he can certainly ask his wife to help him, ultimately, he needs to choose an option that is in his control. For example, he could plan to do some thought-replacing when the worry about her leaving comes to his mind, telling himself, "Unless she tells me she is unhappy, I am just going to be the best husband I can be. If she leaves me anyway, then I will have done the best I could." And then he should distract himself.

3. Then he will pick his option for handling it. For example, he may choose to have only one conversation with her in which he tells her that he is having trouble with controlling worry and there are some ways that she could help him feel reassured. He would then ask her if she is willing to do those things. Regardless of her answer, he also needs an option that he totally controls, such as telling himself he is doing his best and then distracting himself from worry.

4. He will need to select a time limit to revisit the plan and see if it is working. This is the evaluation of the plan. He may write into his calendar to check in with his worry in 3 months and see if he has worried less. (For a *very* ruminative person, this may be paced, as in first having a daily check-in and then a weekly and then monthly or quarterly evaluation of his option to solve his problem.)

Many people do not know the difference between planning and worrying, so they must clarify those differences on a practical level. The biggest difference between planning and worrying is that a good plan has action steps. If you follow the steps, the problems will be handled and the worry will cease. The second big difference is that a plan does not need constant review. An anxious brain, however, may replan the plan; this should be identified as worry disguising itself as planning and stopped.

Cognitive-Behavioral Therapy:
The Major Tool for Worry Elimination

The many techniques of cognitive-behavioral therapy (CBT) are the best methods for eliminating worry. These techniques use the thinking brain (the prefrontal cortex) to control the anxiety-generating anterior cingulate gyrus (ACG), the basal ganglia (BG), and the limbic system. Cognitive-behavioral therapy is a style of therapy that focuses on changing thoughts and does not look for insight into the problem before change occurs. It also focuses on changing behaviors that might reinforce symptoms rather than on eliminating them.

How does CBT work? Cognitive-behavioral therapy utilizes the executive functions of the prefrontal cortex (PFC)—analysis, intentional action, decision making—to change ruminating worry on a neurochemical level. The PFC is the target of CBT. Therapy teaches clients with GAD to consciously direct their thoughts and to concentrate on thought-replacement. How does this change the brain? Conscious thought and concentration are PFC activities that affect the operation of the subcortical brain—the ACG—where rumination occurs. When someone deliberately changes a thought, the PFC overrides the ACG.

The left PFC has the ability to control all other parts of the brain (Figure 7.1). It can also cool off the "hot" overactive limbic system, where negativity is generated (Schwartz, 1998). Cognitive-behavioral therapy guides people to deliberately focus on neutral or positive thoughts that will modulate or replace fearful thoughts. The more often the fearful tone is diminished, the calmer the limbic activity gets. Cognitive-behavioral therapy targets the BG as well, because the PFC can intentionally channel the energy of the BG toward positive activity and use its high tone for necessary persistence and consistency in making effective interventions on worried cognitions.

Cognitive-behavioral therapy works with children and adolescents as well (Flannery-Schroeder, Choudhury, & Kendall, 2005). The key is to teach them planning, problem-solving, and resource identification at each age. As they go through school, their minds mature and the types of prob-

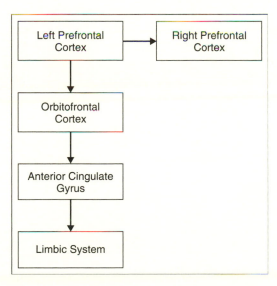

FIGURE 7.1. The left prefrontal cortex controls all other parts of the brain.

lems they have change. Young people do not generalize information from one experience to another, so teaching, reteaching, modeling problem-solving, and planning at home and in school effective CBT techniques for children. Including parents and teachers in treatment is necessary to accomplish this goal.

Thought-Stopping and Thought-Replacement Techniques

Mike was one of the most ruminative clients ever to walk into my office. He was bright, with a high idea-generating mind. He was successful by external standards, but not by his own. As with most GAD clients, he did not want wealth for its own sake but rather because he believed that accumulating wealth would allow him to relax his efforts. With enough money in the bank, he could stop being anxious about whether he was good enough or whether he had tried enough.

Mike constantly worried about what could go wrong at his job, irritating his wife with his fretting. He made life at home tense—when he actually did come home from work. He frustrated coworkers with his negativity, which he perceived as reasonable caution to be sure "all the bases were covered." They saw him as discouraging and controlling. He began to worry about his partners' kicking him out because of the tension.

Mike found it hard to let go of any mistake he ever made, and he ruminated about problems so constantly that he felt he could not escape from his own brain no matter how hard he tried. If he could have let go of the worry, his attitude and behavior at work and at home would have been much more reasonable. Thought-stopping and thought-replacing became a key to his treatment.

Thought-stopping. Stop ruminating. Easier said than done. When people brush off worriers, saying, "Oh, just don't worry" without telling them how they should go about that, they are not giving them enough. If they could stop, they would stop. Yet thought-stopping is the easiest method of all to teach clients—if you can show them the next part, thought-replacement. It goes like this: When he has a negative thought, the client says to himself, "Mike! Stop it!" (People can do this silently so as not to embarrass themselves in public.) This simple action literally stops the negative chain of thought from getting started and going down the old familiar neural pathway. However, thought-stopping alone is insufficient to break the rumination. The next step completes the method by replacing the negative thought with a new thought.

Thought-replacing. The hard part of this method is to immediately re-place the negative thought. This requires making a plan for how to replace the thought. Following are some thought-replacement ideas:

- Use a positive repetitive thought, such as an affirmation, a poem, or a prayer. If the GAD rumination is incredibly obsessive, the replacement may need to be just as obsessive. Better to ruminate on a positive than on a negative. Although this is not the ultimate goal, it can be a good interim measure to calming the brain.

- Sing or talk out loud. This competes with the ruminative thought.
- Watch television, play a video game, read—do anything to distract attention. The idea is not be become obsessive with electronics, but they can be diverting.
- Change locations and distract oneself. For example, take a walk with the intention to notice everything in the neighborhood. See how many plants you can name or pretend that something wonderful and important is about to happen and that you are going to be called on to provide an eye-witness account of what everything looked like the moment before the event.
- Refocus on the work or task you were doing when the thought overpowered you. Pay conscious attention to what you are doing. This may be the most effective thing to do when at work, where singing or going for a walk may be out of the question.
- Turn on music and start to draw what you hear, dance to it, or otherwise immerse yourself in it. For kids and teens, making a CD of their favorite songs or compiling songs they want to share has the double benefit of cheering them with music and distracting them.
- Lots of people use the computer for distraction: games, email, instant messaging, chat rooms, blogging, and so on. Keep an eye on this to be sure it does not become obsessive, and make you are not searching for information as a way to reassure yourself.

Figure 7.2 shows how thought-stopping uses the brain's cognitive control to weaken the tendency to worry.

Thought-replacement techniques can also be nonverbal. These work particularly well with children. Have clients draw pictures of symbols that

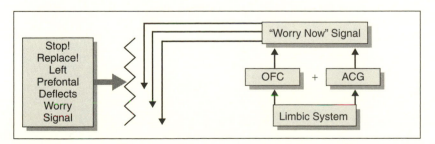

FIGURE 7.2. Thought-stopping and thought-replacing weaken the "worry now" signal.

stand for the thought-replacement they are going to try. Plan these out while in a therapy session, and then draw in a notebook or on a set of index cards that can be put into a photo-album holder. When clients want to replace a thought, they can flip through their replacement ideas until they find a good one. Kids can draw pictures of a book to remind them to read the book, or a picture of a favorite doll to remind them to play, or a symbol that reminds them of their favorite computer game.

Many athletic persons enjoy recalling a sporting event, play by play, as a distraction. For example, mentally replaying a game of golf, stroke by stroke, or a weekend football game would be excellent thought replacements.

Another thought-replacement idea is to use daily activities as a focus. Simply bring conscious attention to the task at hand to redirect worry thoughts. This works well for students and people who have a variety of things to do on any day. It may seem like a mundane replacement idea, but it works surprisingly well.

Another very important but simple technique is the Daily "Two P" Thought-Replacement List. It provides a constantly varying and relevant list of ideas about what to think about other than the worry.

THE DAILY "TWO P" THOUGHT-REPLACEMENT LIST

1. Every morning take 60 seconds to identify things that could be thought about during the day—what books to take out at the library, what homework to do first, what order to run errands, what phone calls to return first, what Hawaiian island to visit first on vacation, whether you'd rather buy a Mercedes or a BMW if you had the money, and so on. Only things that can be considered Pleasant or Productive can go on the list. List these things on a sticky note or an index card. Each thought should be identified via *one* reminder word on the list.
2. Place this list in a visible or readily accessible spot—on your phone, car dashboard, computer monitor, or in your wallet or a pocket.
3. As soon as you stop the rumination with thought-stopping, consult this list.
4. Repeat this process daily until rumination is no longer a problem. Calming rumination takes time, and this simple tool will help you stay effective without generating new ruminative thoughts.

Persistence is key. The key to making thought-stopping techniques work is to focus on how persistent the thoughts are and how the ACG actually creates persistence. What is rumination, after all, but a very persistent thought? Teaching clients about this persistence helps them use it to their advantage. When people start to practice thought-stopping, worry can act in a downright Pavlovian way, responding with *increased* persistence if it is intermittently given into. The anxious brain is persistent in creating rumination, and there is a direct correlation between consistently applying this method and succeeding in decreasing the overactivity in the anterior cingulate gyrus (ACG) that is experienced as negative rumination.

Persistence was a vital part of treatment for Debbie, introduced earlier in this chapter. Debbie was a self-described "worry wart" before her anxiety snowballed out of control. Although her cancer treatment years before was successful, she developed constant, racing thoughts about whether her cancer would recur. Fortunately she was a hard worker in therapy, particularly in her use of thought-stopping. She told me that the key to making it work was being ready for the incredible persistence it required: "When you told me I would have to thought-stop every time, even if it was a thousand times a day, I thought you were kidding. If you hadn't warned me, I would have given up in despair after about 100 times, thinking it would never work for me. Since you said 1000, I figured I had better keep trying. After a couple of days, though, it got much better."

Worrying About Not Worrying

Worry about not worrying may spring up as people stop what they believe to be legitimate concerns, even if they are not certain their worry will come true. For example, what if a person is worried that their cancer test will come back positive or that their loved one due to come home soon really is dead on the highway?

- The worrier *must* develop a deep belief that worrying is useless.
- The worrier must believe that any problem life brings can be responded to helpfully without worry, and that when a problem does come up, a solution or plan can be identified in a timely fashion.
- The worrier must learn that he or she can reliably identify problems when they occur and that being on the lookout for problems is unnecessary and a waste of time. (We are not talking here about reasonable preparation for predictable events.)

For example, suppose the GAD worrier starts to worry, "What if I am refusing to worry about something that really is happening?" The worrying about not worrying must be stopped. Worriers must replace that thought with: "If and when a real problem occurs, I am able to recognize and respond to it. That will be soon enough." I sometimes joke with clients about their ability to recognize a problem: "Have you ever failed to notice a splitting headache?" *A problem that needs a response will make itself known to you.* We may have to clarify how that works in more subtle circumstances, but the point is that the time to worry is when the test result comes in or the call comes that an accident occurred. I try to remind them of the maxim, "95% of the things you worry about never happen," and I ask, "How much time do you want to waste worrying?"

Other CBT-Style Worry-Management Techniques

Several other cognitive tools are available to help diminish worry opportunities.

Do the Worst First
One little method can help a lot to get worry off the mind: Get it over with. If you are going to worry all day about what you have to do (like make a phone call you do not want to make or pay the bills) just do it first and save yourself the worry. What a relief!

Worry Well and Only Once (Stop! I Already Worried!)
Some worries just have to be faced head on, and worrying about them the right way can help eliminate secondary, unnecessary worrying.

WORRY WELL AND ONLY ONCE

1. Set aside 10 minutes to worry about whatever your concern is.
2. Worry through all the issues involved in the situation. Try to cover every aspect.
3. Formulate an action plan to take if *and only if* the problem being worried about does indeed come up. For example, Courtney, who was worried about using her sister's credit card, could plan to write a letter to the credit card company explaining the situation and have it signed by both her sister and her. She could also get a recommendation for a good lawyer and write down the lawyer's phone number in her daybook. However, she would not actually write the letter or call the lawyer unless the credit card company did indeed contact her sister about Courtney's using the card.
4. Set a time when it will be necessary to think about the worry again.

---

5. Write that time in a calendar so you really know that you won't forget to think about it.
6. Then, whenever the worry pops up again, say, "Stop! I already worried!" and divert your concentration as quickly as possible to another activity. You must have a plan for what you will replace the worry with.

The "worry well and only once" method worked well for Debbie, who was out of control with worry about whether her cancer would recur. Although her cancer had shown no signs of recurrence, Debbie's worry flared up again as her annual checkup approached. We decided to try the "worry well and only once" method, setting a 10-minute time limit on the worry and then thinking through all the possible ramifications. She covered things such as "Will the doctor tell me I need another biopsy?" and "Do I need to get a friend to go along to the doctor help me stay calm?" She worried once about what she would do if the biopsy was positive, making plans like "I will use the same surgeon as before"; "My mom can watch my children while I am in the hospital"; and "I can get people to cover my car-pool responsibilities." We covered everything from the mundane to the serious but unlikely "What if I die while in surgery?" It is critical to this method to cover all the bases, but 10 minutes is a surprisingly adequate amount of time to do that.

When Debbie said she had no other worries that were related to the surgery, we set a timeline for when she thought she would need to think about this problem again. We agreed that the next time she should let the possibility of cancer recurring cross her mind was in 2 weeks when she had her checkup. Until that moment any further thought was counterproductive. She wrote in her electronic calendar that she could worry again, if she needed to, after the doctor's appointment.

Having worried well, we moved to the "only once" part of the method. Debbie practiced telling herself, "Stop, Debbie! You already worried!" This part of the method, illustrated in Figure 7.3, may sound simplistic, but it works. Because she had already worried, *her brain believed her,* and this made it easier to worry only once. Once we made a list of distractions she could carry with her and look at for ideas to replace the urge to worry, she had completed "worry well and only once."

The "worry well and only once" method is similar to the "plan instead of worrying" discussed earlier in this chapter in that both methods involve planning. However, the critical difference between the two is that "plan instead of worrying" involves formulating a plan to *resolve* the problem being worried about whereas "worry well and only once" involves making a plan

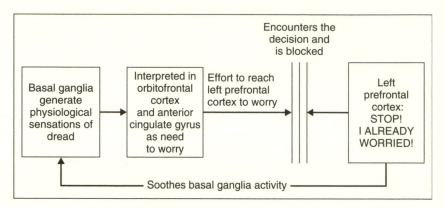

FIGURE 7.3. "Stop! I already worried!"

to worry. In the "plan instead of worrying" method, clients create a plan of action and then follow through on that plan (for example, by having a conversation with the spouse and using the thought-replacement "I have been the best husband I can be"). In the "worry well and only once" method, clients create a plan of action to take if *and only if* the problem does indeed arise ("I will contact the surgeon I used before *if* the biopsy is positive"). Both methods ultimately help to reduce or eliminate unnecessary worrying.

"Plan instead of worrying" works best with situations that can be resolved, like completing schoolwork for the weekend, getting ready for a meeting at work, or finishing tasks that need to be done to prepare for guests. For situations that are not so easily resolved (like Courtney's worry about credit card fraud) or that can not be resolved until later (like Debbie's medical checkup), "worry well and only once" is the best option.

In some cases it can be difficult to decide whether to "plan instead of worry" or to "worry well and only once." When this happens, I use a rule I call the "Two-Dollar Mayonnaise" rule. Let's say you have a small worry such as, "Oh darn, I cannot tell if the new mayonnaise jar was sealed. What if it is spoiled?" If you try to overcome worry with "worry well and only once" and serve the mayonnaise anyway, are you going to worry yourself sick for days afterward about whether you food-poisoned people? If so, throw out the jar. Two dollars is a small price to pay to avoid days of worry. However, if the worry is: "I am afraid I have a brain tumor because I have a headache, so I think I will go get a $1,000 CT scan just to stop worrying," the better method to use *would* be "worry well and only once." In other words, if the cost of eliminating the worry is small, it is worth paying the price. If it isn't, the worrier should focus on reducing the worry rather than on solving the problem. (Of course, "cost" involves more than just monetary cost; it can be cost in time, stress, inconvenience, and so on.) Whatever the type of cost, keeping it low is important. The theory here is that worrying for days is far more likely to irritate an anxious brain and generate more anxiety than dumping the worry immediately and completely from your mind. And it obviously does not apply if you are obsessively throwing out every jar you open.

Regardless of whether they are devising an action plan that they will carry out (as with "plan instead of worrying") or devising an action plan to carry out only if a problem arises (as with "worry well and only once"), worriers can review their plan as a way to get rid of anxiety about whether they can accomplish it. In this case, having a plan becomes part of the thought-stopping statement: Worriers can simply say, "Stop! I have a complete plan!"

Clearing the Mind of Worry

Sometimes you just need to get everything off your mind. Tools from focusing therapy can help the ruminative mind put thoughts to rest (Gendlin, 1981, 1996). The complete process of focusing is an excellent therapeutic method for becoming aware of all the implications of an issue. It is especially powerful with anxious clients whose physical symptoms cloud their thinking. Gendlin's method uses the body's response to *clarify* issues. Learning to read the body relieves much anxiety on a permanent basis. Clients learn to listen nonjudgmentally to the body's message and do not misinterpret sensations as anxiety. Ann Weiser Cornell's book *The Power of Focusing* (1996) is an excellent resource for those who want to use this method in therapy.

The "clear your mind" technique is modified from the focusing method. It works to turn off and quiet the ruminative mind.

CLEAR YOUR MIND

1. Sit quietly with your eyes closed and imagine an open container in front of you.
2. Ask yourself, "What is going on in my life today?"
3. As each thing comes to mind, see and name it but don't think about the issue, situation, person, or decision, etc.
4. Imagine putting each thing into the container.
5. When no more issues are coming to mind, put a lid on the container and mentally put the container away.
6. Once you have cleared your mind, you can invite the most important thing you need to focus on to come to your attention. That might be the work in front of you or a problem you want to think about without confusion. If you have used this technique just before sleep, however, invite a peaceful thought into your mind.

For clients who do not like or appreciate using imagery, you can modify this method so that it does not use the image of a container. Clients might instead write down thoughts in the form of a list. The list should then go into a drawer or briefcase or otherwise be literally put out of sight (and out of mind). A variation of this tangible technique is an idea you might hear at an Al-Anon meeting: using a "God Box." The client writes down worrisome issues on slips of paper and then puts them in the box, thus turning the worry over to God.

Another variation comes from a school counselor I know. She asks children to write or draw a picture of their worry and put it in a backpack they keep in her office. Once a week, when she visits with them, she has them open the backpack. The children then see which of the worrisome things actually happened. The counselor has them throw away their unnecessary worries as a practical and concrete way of showing them that most of the things we worry about never happen and that most worries are just a waste of thought and time. Regardless of the method used, the goal of "turning it off" is to give the ruminative mind a chance to rest and calm down the hot activity in the brain.

Dispensing With Irrational Guilt

Guilt is a big burden for GAD clients. You can see this in excessive apologies and explanations. They never want to be misunderstood. If they make a mistake, they want to make sure you know exactly how it happened. They are serious about this because they cannot bear the anxiety of guilt. They hate being teased, because teasing implies they did something wrong. People with GAD do not easily brush off mistakes and do not readily feel forgiven. You will never catch them shrugging and saying, "So it goes!" Their lives become a constant struggle to avoid the anxiety of being wrong. They end up appearing, and being, humorless.

Guilt is a spiritual issue, but no religious practice will remove it. This is because the guilt is irrational (not reasonable or logical) and is not responsive to logic. It is not responsive to spiritual tools either. Prayer, preaching, cleansing, confession—none take away GAD guilt. There are three types of guilt generated by the anxious brain:

- Guilt about being anxious
- Guilt about real mistakes (legitimate guilt)
- Guilt about imagined mistakes (illegitimate guilt)

All of these are spiritual in nature. What do we do about them?

Guilt about being anxious. Regardless of their religious or spiritual discipline, people often believe their worry is a failure of their spiritual discipline. Thus, they not only feel disconnected from the peace of having a vibrant spiritual life but also feel guilt for not doing it well enough. Beliefs they may hold about forgiveness have little impact on their worrying. Discussing their spiritual beliefs about anxiety and its relief will be informative about how to correct this irrational thought. Consultation with a spiritual leader from their own faith may be great consolation for the anxious person.

Legitimate guilt. Everybody makes mistakes, and those with GAD wish they were exempt from this. People with GAD typically feel they do not measure up to their values. When they do not perfectly measure up, the negativity of the anxious brain exaggerates actual guilt. More perfectionism always fails to provide relief. In this case, guilt becomes a cognitive therapy issue—when do they know they have permission to stop worrying about what they did?

Illegitimate guilt. The overactive limbic system and anterior cingulate gyrus (ACG) together generate negative mood and negative sensation that cannot be easily dismissed. The feeling of dread they bring up is misinterpreted as guilt. The cortex of an anxious brain may have too little energy to override all that overactivity. So the guilty feeling needs an explanation and GAD worriers will eventually find something they did (or didn't do) that might be a reason for the guilt.

The method to interrupt legitimate and illegitimate guilt is the same. It involves clarifying which kind of guilt it is.

1. First, explain to clients that their brain generates negative, self-diminishing thoughts and guilt.
2. Ask clients to determine whether the situation about which they feel guilty has been resolved. The Serenity Prayer is a tool for this:
   Grant me the serenity to accept the things I cannot change, the courage to change the things I can, and the wisdom to know the difference.

   Have clients identify which aspects of their guilt fit into things they can change and which aspects fit into things they cannot change. If there is a legitimate guilt, there will be a situation that needs or needed action. Clients might need to make an apology or fix a problem they created. If they have already done those things, they need to accept what they cannot change.
3. Thought-stopping and thought-replacing are the next step. Whenever the old guilty thoughts come up, apply this cognitive method of interrupting them.

Bob was typical of the perfectionistic, explanatory, rigid personality that goes with guilt-ridden GAD rumination. He simply could not be wrong about anything, from how he disciplined his children to how he handled an argument with his wife to how he corrected an employee.

One example of his unnecessary guilt stemmed from a situation that had occurred a decade ago when he had "hurt his daughter." It was something he could not forget and could not forgive himself for. His 5-year-old daughter had been playing in a tree in the yard, and Bob had instructed her to come down. When she refused, Bob walked away from her. Moments later, she fell and hit her head. She was not seriously hurt and did not require medical care, and there was no evidence all these years later that she had any repercussions from the incident.

When Bob's guilt kicked in he would begin ruminating on the "what ifs": "What if she injured her brain back then? Any time now she could have an aneurysm or something because of it. What if she hurt her brain and she would have been smarter if she hadn't fallen?"

Bob needed to learn why he was so plagued by thoughts of that minor accident and how to stop his rumination. His therapist began by explaining to Bob that dread is just dread. It may not have *any cause at all* except that his brain was firing when it ought to be quiet. He had thought of the guilt for so long that he had worn a rut in his brain, so when it had no specific path to be on and he felt dread, he fell into this rut of neuronal firing. Understanding this helped Bob see that his response to this situation was out of proportion. In neurobiological terms, he used his prefrontal cortex (PFC) to override his anterior cingulate gyrus (ACG) rumination and limbic negativity.

Bob also had to determine the difference between *potential guilt for something that might have happened* and *legitimate guilt for something that is over with*. Many GAD sufferers take a small legitimate guilt and worry it into a horrific act for which no forgiveness is possible. They thus feel guilt for something that actually did not happen. Yes, Bob's daughter did fall out of a tree, but she suffered no ill effects. He took his small legitimate guilt for walking away and built it into guilt for damaging her brain (which did not happen).

Bob applied the Serenity Prayer to his situation. He had to accept that he had walked away from his daughter and she fell. That was something he could not change. Although he wanted to take her in for a brain scan, there was no medical reason then or now to do so. He had to use his wisdom to know that it was in the past and there was nothing to be done. And he had to remind himself that, in fact, there was nothing wrong, and that the reason he couldn't forget the incident was that when his brain generated a feeling of dread, he ruminatively went back to the scene to explain the dread he felt. Once Bob was able to use the Serenity Prayer as a reminder to stop bashing himself, he then used thought-stopping and thought-replacement to interrupt the guilty feelings.

Calming Anger and Irritability

Aggressiveness is a byproduct of anxiety for many people. Edginess and irritability are endemic to those with anxiety, but for some that translates into flying off the handle too easily. Conversely, anxiety is a byproduct of anger for many with GAD. "Fight or flight" means that people under stress may need to fight back.

Whether a person shows feelings of aggression depends on his or her previous experiences with anger. For some clients anger can be so anxiety-provoking that they have no idea they are angry. People with GAD may have an undetected fear of being angry. As long as anger stays unidentified, the anxious client's symptoms will stay in place.

Some clients face genuine risks if they show they are angry—they may be hurt or abused, emotionally rejected, or lose a job. Any real risk must be addressed directly before open expression of anger is encouraged.

Knowing, Not Showing, Anger

This is a symptom-control technique intended to decrease tension while raising conscious awareness of anger. Any anger discovered is dealt with in psychotherapy before it is shown to anyone. Chronic anxiety often diminishes if clients are simply able to say they are angry in session and are allowed to gradually work on safe expression of that anger. Assuring clients that "to know you are angry does not require you to *show* you are angry" usually helps.

The technique is simple:

1. The next time you feel strong anxiety, immediately sit down and answer this *specific* question: "If I were angry, what might I be angry about?" Write as long a list as possible, using single words or brief phrases to identify all the things you might be angry about. The hypothetical nature of this question is a key feature. You do not have to feel committed to being angry about anything once it is on the list—you are only being speculative about it.
2. You then may destroy the list or discuss it in therapy.

Asking clients to discuss their reactions to writing this list helps them gain insight into the connection between anger and anxiety. This opens the door to deeper levels of psychotherapy to resolve psychological problems with being angry.

Learning How to Be Angry

Once clients know they are angry, therapists should make sure they know *how* to be angry. Skill-building for expressing anger (and also how to apologize) is necessary. Knowing how to diffuse anger with a reasonable apology not only reduces fear of confrontation but also diminishes legitimate guilt by providing a way to make an amend. Any good anger-management program will have the skill-building tools needed.

CONCLUSION

The GAD watchword is *persistence*. The symptoms are persistent, and the treatment only works when it is applied persistently. Therapists working with clients who have GAD must cover ground over and over to pick up on all the subtleties of the client's thought process and to reinforce the calming techniques.

Treatment for GAD can begin quickly with a focus on physically calming down, much as it does with PD. However, unlike with PD, cognitive changes to eliminate worry take time and practice. The good news is that the high energy of the anxious brain can be tapped for energizing therapy.

Clients often benefit from the therapist's deep sympathy for the pain of worry. You can talk to clients about how anxiety ruins their quality of life, drains them of energy, and robs them of joy—about how it is uninterruptible when clients don't have the proper tools to stop it. This can eliminate some of their guilt and shame for seeking help and debunk the myth that they should "just get over it." Accustomed as they are to overseeing and directing things, these clients feel profound relief when they can turn over their problem to a therapist who unequivocally offers comfort and has ideas about how to change things.

Therapy for GAD involves helping clients figure out what stops them from stopping their worry. It teaches them that their anxious brains are generating the worry and that this is a physical problem, which further diminishes their guilt. Clients learn specific techniques to relax, change their lifestyle, and control their anxious brain. When therapy starts, the therapist is the expert. By the time it ends, the clients are the experts in self-control. It is a satisfying exchange of roles.

CHAPTER EIGHT

MEDICATING FOR GENERALIZED ANXIETY DISORDER

Generalized anxiety disorder is defined as excessive worry about normal life events to the extent that worrying interferes with a person's ability to function well socially, at work, or in relationships. Unlike panic or social anxiety, GAD does not involve worrying about feeling or appearing anxious; rather, the main feature of GAD worry is its ruminative quality. The typical GAD patient will say, "I cannot shut off my brain" from worrying about things. The excessive worry often leads to physical symptoms, which are of concern in the treatment. Medications target the cognitive and physical symptoms of GAD by (1) diminishing rumination, (2) decreasing hyperarousal, and (3) ameliorating some of the physical consequences of the neurobiological state. Among the physical concerns that medication may target are:

- Tension and the physical problems that are created and maintained by tension, such as headaches
- Sleep disturbance, particularly difficulty staying asleep or getting refreshment from sleep
- Fatigue and difficulty with concentration and attention resulting from the stress of worry and from the interrupted sleep

GAD affects about 3% of the population over the age of 18 (National Institutes of Health, 2006). In the general population, it affects women slightly more than men; in clinical settings, women represent about two-thirds of those seeking treatment (American Psychiatric Association, 2000).

173

RISKS ASSOCIATED WITH GENERALIZED ANXIETY DISORDER

It is an irony of GAD that people who have the high neurobiological arousal contributing to the disorder often have a high drive that is positive in other ways. They may be go-getters with energy to take on and success-fully accomplish a variety of tasks. However, with that high drive, they are less likely to create the emotional well-being and physical relaxation that would help them to balance their stress level. The worry of GAD creates stress from the high tone of the stress response system and the hypervigi-lant attention to problems that GAD sufferers apply to ward off errors. The impact of GAD in people's lives includes risks of:

- Higher incidence of headache from the tension levels and stress associated with GAD.
- Higher incidence of depression. There is a 50% comorbidity between depression and GAD, which is in part related to the neurobiological underpinnings that both disorders share. Additionally, most people who have had GAD for some time will say they feel depressed about whether they will always suffer the constant worry.
- Stress-related symptoms, such as high blood pressure.
- Higher incidence of irritable bowel syndrome (IBS). When people have IBS, the chronic arousal of the GAD tends to trigger episodes of the IBS.
- Higher incidence of sleep disturbance. Many people with GAD suffer from restless sleep, which then enhances the fatigue. Fatigue and lost renewal during sleep time makes it harder to manage stress and the emotional symptoms of GAD.

THE ETIOLOGY OF GENERALIZED ANXIETY DISORDER

Although much still needs to be learned about why and how people develop GAD, there is no question that neurotransmitter dysregulation and neuroanatomical functions play a role for most people in developing this disorder. The kinds of neurotransmitter imbalances and dysregulated function that contribute to panic disorder are also seen in GAD. This is one reason for the high rates of comorbidity of the various anxiety disorders. But differences in symptom expression occur even when similar neurobiology exists. One important reason that different kinds of anxiety disorders develop is the psychological impact of life experience and developmental events. Positive and negative experiences shape later development of anxiety because they affect personality and coping styles, as well as cognitive and emotional functioning. At the neurobiological level, even though there are similarities among all the anxiety disorders, important differences exist in the severity of the neurotransmitter dysfunction and in neuroanatomic structure. It is not yet possible to quantify differences in ways that will predict symptom severity or medication choice, but they can be seen in the kind of symptoms that develop. Medicating for GAD involves use of similar drugs but aims at the specific symptom expression of this type of anxiety.

The Neurobiological Causes of Generalized Anxiety Disorder

Neurotransmitters and neuroanatomy affect the development of GAD in several ways. The functions of serotonin (SE), norepinephrine (NE), and dopamine (DA) are all relevant to GAD, and of these three monoamine neurotransmitters, it is SE and NE that are most often the target for medication treatment. Chapter 5 includes a discussion about how these two neurotransmitters affect production of each other and why dysregulated function may create symptoms of panic. Those factors are also relevant in the discussion of GAD. However, particular features of NE and SE function on neuroanatomical structures affect the development of GAD symptoms. A look at how these neurotransmitters create tension, stress, and worry will enhance the understanding of why medications improve the GAD symptom picture.

The neurotransmitter gamma aminobutyric acid (GABA) also plays a significant role in generating anxiety symptoms, and it has effects in several anatomical regions of the brain that could either modulate or diminish excessive neural activity. This chapter looks at the role all these neurotransmitters have in generating the symptoms of GAD.

Serotonin

Serotonin (SE) is the neurotransmitter most likely to contribute to GAD because of its overall impact on the regulation of mood and cognition. Serotonin neurons are densely found in the dorsal raphe and they project to many important structures in the brain that control negativity, cognitive clarity, and the ability to shift mental attention from one topic to another. The major areas of the brain affected by low levels of SE and that therefore contribute to symptom development of GAD are:

- *The limbic system.* The limbic system includes parts of the brain that recognize emotional templates and coordinate emotional responses to events and situations. An overactive limbic system is on the lookout for trouble. When SE is dysregulated, the limbic system is more active and less able to modulate its activity. The result is an increase in negativity, making people increasingly likely to find things to worry about and less able to find positives in any situation.

- *The prefrontal cortex.* In the prefrontal cortex (PFC), activity to solve problems occurs. It takes some energy to look for good solutions and evaluate their chance of working. When SE levels are low, the PFC has lower energy and interrupted concentration, making it harder to ward off anxiety. Low SE levels in the PFC also make it harder to see positive outcomes, as there is less energy to modulate the negativity of the limbic system.
- *The anterior cingulate gyrus.* The anterior cingulate gyrus (ACG) plays a major role in shifting attention from one topic to another. Lower levels of SE appear to cause less flexibility in the ACG, which contributes to rumination, as the brain cannot easily switch from the worry to another thought.

Additionally, The SE/NE feedback loop is part of the problem, just as it is in PD. Lower levels of SE interact with NE, and in people with GAD the neurotransmitter system may have difficulty re-regulating itself. When SE is low and NE cannot stimulate the SE neurons to produce more SE, NE may continue to rise in an attempt to get the production re-regulated. Higher NE leads to sensations of negative arousal, as seen in the GAD symptoms of hypervigilance, tension, and irritability.

Norepinephrine
Heightened NE activity leads to anxiety symptoms. Many physiological systems are affected by NE because of its impact on several neuroanatomical structures and systems.

- NE release can be dysregulated, so that excessive NE in the synapse affects major systems in the brain.
- High levels of NE cause high arousal throughout the stress response system. A hair-trigger stress response then exists, causing a person to overreact to minor stress in both their physiological and emotional states. High stress response in the brain equates to a person's believing that the event causing the stress is objectively too much, and all the physical manifestations of stress are experienced more often and more intensely.
- Cardiovascular activity is affected by NE. Norepinephrine is directly connected to blood pressure levels, so heightened NE may affect blood pressure. Additionally, the heightened level of NE can cause tachycardia (elevated heart rate). When this is severe, it may be experienced as panic, but when it is milder, it leads to the unpleasant feeling of being under stress.

- The basal ganglia (BG) is the brain region that associates muscle activity with emotional responses. When high levels of NE chronically keep BG tone too high, tension and overreactivity to stress result.
- The peripheral nervous system (PNS) can also be affected by high NE. Norepinephrine acts on the nerves that affect physical functioning outside of the brain, and its impact on the muscles is relevant in GAD. Norepinephrine causes the muscular tension that marks GAD, and in acute anxiety, as adrenalin also rises, muscle tension increases and feelings of weakness or shakiness can occur. Acute anxiety is a strongly aversive sensation of something being very wrong, and it may go on at length, creating eventual exhaustion and fatigue from the stress that such anxiety creates in the body. Beta-blocker drugs have their biggest impact on the peripheral neurons that affect heart rate, muscle nerves, sweating, and so on.

Gamma Aminobutyric Acid (GABA)

A third neurotransmitter involved in the cause of GAD is the neural chemical GABA. There are two primary ways that problems with GABA functioning might lead to the increased worry and tension found in GAD.

GABA and the benzodiazepine receptors. GABA is a ubiquitous neurochemical, active in all regions of the brain. Its function is to slow chains of neuronal firing. GABA may specifically cause problems in several brain regions related to GAD:

- *The anterior cingulate gyrus.* When GABA is not working well there may be a tendency to increase rumination. This is because of the failure to slow activity in the ACG, where the brain does considerable work shifting from one idea to another. Thus, rumination may be the result of inefficient GABA-A functioning.
- *The limbic system.* Slow, inefficient GABA may also contribute to overactivity in the limbic system, where negativity is stirred.
- *The prefrontal cortex* needs GABA to help slow and stop deliberate cognitions of worry. When it is low on GABA, it will be unable to suppress worry in any part of the brain effectively.

Two aspects of GABA functioning are targets of medication:

- The ability of GABA to function relies on its relationship to the benzodiazepines. When those receptors are not able to assist efficient GABA activity, problems with suppressing neuronal activity may occur. (See Chapter 5 for a discussion on benzodiazepine receptor functioning.)
- A GABA neuron has two GABA receptor sites: GABA-A and GABA-B. If activated, the GABA-A receptor site modulates the amount of chloride

that is transmitted through the neuron. An increased chloride flow has an overall relaxing effect on the cell and subsequently on the nervous system. So, if GABA-A is not working efficiently, anxiety and tension are heightened.

MEDICATIONS USED IN TREATING
GENERALIZED ANXIETY DISORDER

By identifying symptoms and noting the triggers for the symptoms, physicians and their patients can identify the medications that are most likely to have a positive impact on decreasing panic and GAD. Table 8.1 summarizes the neurotransmitter and neuroanatomical contributions to GAD and the medications used to treat those problems.

Medication choices depend on which symptoms seem to predominate the GAD symptom picture (Vasile, Bruce, Goisman, Pagano, & Keller, 2005). When intense rumination dominates, a different medication will be tried first than if severe tension and heart rate concerns top the symptom chart. However, serotonin (SE) has a wide-ranging impact on several systems and neuroanatomical regions of the brain where SE is most active for controlling anxiety and mood. Therefore, the first medication choice for GAD typically is one of the selective serotonin reuptake inhibitors (Dahl et al., 2005; Goodman, Bose, & Wang, 2005; Maron et al., 2004). Improving SE levels can have the broadest possible positive impact on GAD symptoms.

Medications to Raise Serotonin

There are several types of serotonergic medications that have been observed to lower anxiety. Of these, BuSpar (buspirone) and the SSRIs are the most frequently used in treating GAD. The tricyclic and MAOI antidepressants may also be used, but generally they are considered second-line medications.

BuSpar (buspirone)

BuSpar (buspirone) is a serotonin-1A partial agonist. (An agonist *stimulates* the release of a neurotransmitter.) BuSpar's impact on SE is as follows: BuSpar affects the presynaptic receptor area of a SE nerve cell, which means it works on the neuron that is releasing SE into the synapse. An auto-receptor receives the same neurotransmitter that the cell has released. When a medication occupies the auto-receptor site, there is a temporary decrease of the flow of SE. This then allows SE to accumulate in the vesicles (storage containers located at the end of the nerve cell) at a larger rate. Eventually, these

TABLE 8.1   Etiologies of GAD and Medication Choices

Etiology of GAD	Symptoms	Medications
Increased NE at peripheral nerve receptors	Tremor, increased heart rate; most seen when GAD and SAD are comorbid	Beta-blockers: Inderal (propranolol), Tenormin (atenolol)
Increased release of NE from presynaptic nerve cell	Increased anxiety, dread, increased heart rate, impact on peripheral nervous system: tension, shakiness, and sensation of weakness	Alpha-2 auto-receptor agonists: Catapres (clonidine hydrochloride)
Dysregulation of effects of GABA	Increased acute anxiety, increased heart rate, increased tension	Benzodiazepines: Xanax (alprazolam) Klonopin (clonazepam) Ativan (lorazepam) Serax (oxazepam) Valium (diazepam)
Overactive anterior cingulate gyrus	Rumination	BuSpar (buspirone) SSRIs: Prozac (fluoxetine) Zoloft (sertraline) Paxil (paroxetine) Luvox (fluvoxamine) Celexa (citalopram) Lexapro (escitalopram)
Underactive prefrontal cortex	Low mental energy, poor concentration, poor attention, loss of problem-solving skills from unsuppressed negativity	SSRIs (see above)
Deficient chloride channel transmission (GABA malfunction)	Increased tension, increased feeling of anxiety	Benzodiazepines (see above)
Overactive basal ganglia	Increased motivation/drive, increased tension, hypervigilance	No known medication that absolutely works on this area
Comorbid depression	Difficulty suppressing negativity, increased GAD symptoms	SSRIs, SSNRIs, and atypical SSRIs (see Table 5.3), tricyclics (see Table 5.4), MAOIs (see Table 5.5)

vesicles will release a larger amount of SE between the presynaptic nerve cell and the postsynaptic nerve cell.

BuSpar stimulates the release of SE by causing the neuron to temporarily slow release of SE, so that there is plenty of SE in the vesicles to be released into the synapse. When the vesicle is later stimulated to release SE, there is more of it to release. It is now believed that this process eventually normalizes SE regulation. Because of its action, its side effect profile is minimal. Table 8.2 demonstrates the effects and the dosage of BuSpar (buspirone) for GAD.

SSRIs, SSNRIs, and Atypical SSRIs

These medications have also been used for treating GAD. SSRIs block the reuptake of SE molecules into the neuron that released them, thereby making more SE available in the synapse and also causing the presynaptic (releasing) neuron to increase production of SE in the neuron. SSNRIs and atypical SSRIs work slightly differently, but their main effect, like the SSRIs, is to increase serotonin and regulate serotonin transmission in the neuron. The most frequent side effects for this category of medications include gastrointestinal discomfort, headache, weight gain, loss of libido (anorgasmia), and possible drowsiness. (The mechanisms of these medications were discussed in Chapter 5.)

Tricyclics

Although not the first choice for GAD, the tricyclic antidepressants may be helpful when the response to an SSRI has been limited or ineffective. Tricyclics affect both SE and NE, creating balance in the system that regulates these neurotransmitters by increasing NE levels, which helps to increase SE levels. The most important concern with tricyclics is the heightened side effect profile, which often includes lightheadedness or dizziness (as a result

TABLE 8.2 BuSpar			
Drug Name	**Dose Range and Duration**	**Considerations For Use**	**Withdrawal Pattern**
BuSpar (buspirone)	5mg 3 times per day for first week; may increase 5mg every 5 days to a target dose of 15–60mg/day	Initial effects occur in 1–2 weeks; long-term effects occur in 4–6 weeks; results in lowered sensation of anxiety and nervousness or tension	Very mild

of a change in blood pressure between sitting and standing) and weight gain. Other side effects include gastrointestinal difficulties such as constipation, dry mouth, and dryness of mucous membranes. See Table 5.4 for suggested dosage and considerations for use of tricyclics. The dosages in treating GAD are the same as in treating PD and social anxiety.

MAOIs

As noted in Chapter 5, monoamine oxidase inhibitors (MAOIs) are often considered a second- or third-line medication because they have an even greater side effect profile than the tricyclics, including lightheadedness and dizziness, weight gain, decreased libido, decreased sexual performance, and significant dietary restrictions. Foods that contain tyramine (such as aged meats and cheeses, pickled foods, smoked foods, and alcoholic beverages, especially red wine) must be avoided. Over-the-counter medications that have a decongestant must also be avoided, as the combination of the decongestant and the MAOI may cause seriously elevated blood pressure (in some cases stroke has been reported). Hence, MAOIs must be used with caution. See Table 5.5 for a review of the MAOIs. Dosages for treating GAD are similar to those for treating PD and social anxiety.

Medications to Decrease Release of Norepinephrine

Medications to slow the release of norepinephrine (NE) target the alpha-2 NE auto-receptor (located on a presynaptic nerve cell). Alpha-2 agonists activate this auto-receptor to slow its release of NE neurotransmitters. The anxiolytics (anxiety-lowering medications that affect NE) stimulate the alpha-2 auto-receptor and decrease the release of NE.

Another way of blocking the effects of NE is to use a beta-blocker. If a beta-1 receptor on a peripheral postsynaptic neuron is activated (i.e., if it receives NE), symptoms of anxiety are heightened, such as tachycardia, dilated pupils, tremors, and sweating. A beta-blocker such as Tenormin (atenolol) has a direct blocking effect on the postsynaptic beta-1 receptor. If medication blocks the beta postsynaptic receptor, there will be less activation of anxiety symptoms. Because these medications affect the heart, side effects of slowed heart rate must be noted.

The medications most often used for GAD to block the beta-1 receptor are listed in Table 11.2, because they are most often used for the peripheral nervous system effects that are the hallmark of social anxiety.

Medications to Enhance GABA and Chloride Conductance: Benzodiazepines

Benzodiazepines such as Xanax (alprazolam) and Klonopin (clonazepam) are medications that positively enhance the neural chemical GABA. They work on a benzodiazepine receptor site near the GABA-A receptor site. When the benzodiazepines bind to their receptor sites, they make the GABA-A sites work more effectively. When the GABA-A receptor site works more effectively, it results in an increased flow of chloride and a heightened sense of relaxation. Main effects of the benzodiazepines include lowering anxiety, increasing sedation, antiseizure effects, and muscle-relaxant qualities.

When GAD symptoms include chronic acute anxiety, the benzodiazepines are most likely to be used for reducing high degrees of worry and nervousness or agitation. It is not typical for the benzodiazepines to be prescribed on an as-needed (PRN) basis for GAD, as they may be for panic or social anxiety. Rather, their use is intended to lower the heightened anxiety over a period of time, usually about 4 weeks and possibly longer with good supervision. That allows time for other medications, such as the SSRIs, to take effect and for psychotherapeutic methods for controlling thoughts to be taught and practiced.

The benzodiazepines also have potential side effects, including amnesia, dependence, and withdrawal phenomenon. Prolonged use of these agents has potential risks including drug dependency and withdrawal. They should be used with extreme caution in people who have been addicted to alcohol, due to the higher risk of addiction to this medication. See Table 5.6 for a list of benzodiazepines and their dosages, which are the same for treating GAD.

INSOMNIA AND GENERALIZED ANXIETY DISORDER

Insomnia deserves special attention in the treatment of GAD, as it is a common feature of this disorder. There are several different types of insomnia:

- Difficulty initiating sleep
- Difficulty remaining asleep, with frequent waking episodes
- Poor quality of sleep

Insomnia can be classified in several different ways:

- Primary insomnia with actual sleep pathophysiology. This is often detected through sleep studies.
- Insomnia secondary to either a psychiatric disorder or a general medical condition.
- Insomnia secondary to medication or substance abuse.
- Insomnia due to circadian rhythm disruptions. This, for instance, may involve having jet lag.

- Insomnia caused by other conditions such as restless leg syndrome or a periodic limb-movement disorder.

It is necessary to identify the type of insomnia affecting the GAD client and treat the underlying cause for the insomnia. For example, if a medical condition such as pain syndrome is associated with the insomnia, the etiology of the pain syndrome must be treated. If there is a circadian rhythm disturbance, it is necessary to re-regulate the circadian rhythm. When a patient is suffering insomnia due to a psychiatric disorder such as depression, the underlying depression must be treated. When patients have GAD, the etiology of the insomnia may be related to the overall heightened arousal of the nervous system rather than one of the other causes. In these cases, if the insomnia does not improve with the treatment of the GAD symptoms, pursuing pharmacologic treatments might be necessary.

Pharmacology of Insomnia

Pharmacologic treatment for insomnia is a somewhat controversial area. There is still some belief that using a pharmacologic intervention for treating insomnia may cause dependence on and tolerance to the sedative/ hypnotics, but research indicates that Lunesta (eszopicione) can be used long-term (studied up to 6 months) without significant addiction.

All of the following sleeping aids should be given approximately 20 to 30 minutes before one wishes to fall asleep. Patients should be ready for bed prior to taking these medications, because when they do take effect they work quickly.

Nonbenzodiazepine Hypnotics

Nonbenzodiazepine short-acting hypnotics are currently the sleeping medications of choice. These medications include Ambien (zolpidem tartrate), Sonata (zaleplon), and Lunesta (eszopiclone). These medications act selectively on a specific benzodiazepine receptor area (omega-1), causing sedation without affecting cognition, memory, and motor functioning. (As selective for the omega-1 benzodiazepine receptor, they do *not* act on an omega-2 area, which would cause cognitive and motor sedation.) These agents are good hypnotics because they are rapid in onset and short in duration. They also do not cause the significant withdrawal or dependence that are problems with benzodiazepine-type medications.

Ambien. Ambien (zolpidem tartrate) was the first omega-1 selective non-benzodiazepine sedative/hypnotic to be introduced. It has a half-life of 1.5–3 hours. (Half-life is the amount of time it takes for half of the concentration of the medication to be metabolized out of one's body. It takes five half-life durations for a medication to be eliminated from the body.) Ambien usually requires 7–8 hours to be eliminated from the body; thus a person must allow at least that many hours of sleep when taking Ambien. "Hangover" symptoms may be experienced if one awakens before the medication is out of the body. Although each person has an individualized metabolism for medication, this is an important guideline to be aware of. A controlled-release formula of Ambien is available for patients who get 5 hours or less of sleep on regular Ambien.

The dose range for Ambien is 5–10mg (6.25–12.5mg of the controlled-released formula). Reports of dosing patterns in other countries are reported to go as high as 20mg, but most people respond well to 10mg, which is the recommended US dosage limit (12.5mg of the controlled-release formula).

Sonata. Sonata (zaleplon) was the second omega-1 nonbenzodiazepine sedative/hypnotic released in the United States. It has a half-life of approximately 1 hour and stays in the nervous system for approximately 5 hours. Thus you must allow a 5-hour time frame to sleep when taking Sonata. As with the Ambien, if people awaken in under 5 hours, they will probably feel somewhat drowsy. The very short half-life of Sonata makes it an attractive medication for those who awaken in the middle of the night but still have 5 hours to sleep. This medication may also be helpful for jet lag.

The dose range for Sonata is 5–20mg. In my experience most people need at least 10mg and often up to 20mg for this medication to be effective.

Lunesta. Lunesta (eszopicione) is a newer nonbenzodiazepine sedative/hypnotic released in the United States. It has been studied for long-term use with insomnia, and 6-month data on the use of Lunesta shows it can be used consistently without significant withdrawal. This has made Lunesta a unique medication for insomnia.

Lunesta has a half-life of approximately 6 hours, which is longer-acting than Ambien and Sonata. However, the majority of people, after experiencing a good 8 hours of sleep, do not feel hung over. Because of its longer half-life, however, there is a possibility of drowsiness in the morning.

Lunesta comes in a 1mg-, 2mg-, and 3mg-strength size. The typical maintenance dose is 3mg.

Melatonin Agonists

Rozerem (ramelteon), the most recently introduced a sleeping aid, is unique in that does not work on the GABA receptor area. It is a melatonin receptor agonist, working on the same receptor area that melatonin works on. Activating the melatonin receptors induces sleep.

People who do not tolerate the nonbenzodiazepine sleep medications may do well with Rozerem because it has a nonaddictive profile and affects a completely different neurochemical system.

The half-life of Rozerem is approximately 1–2.6 hours. The typical dose is 8mg.

Improving Sleep

Even if using medication, it is also important to examine one's sleep habits to ensure quality sleep. For example, caffeine, especially if used 6 hours before bedtime, can interfere with sleep onset. Life factors like regular exercise and awakening at the same hour each morning can improve sleep quality and regularity.

MEDICATION OF GENERALIZED ANXIETY IN CHILDREN AND ELDERLY POPULATIONS

The role of medications in the child and adolescent population is currently being investigated. Few research studies are completed, but the early indications are that the same medications used to treat adults with GAD will also be effective in treating children and adolescents (Clark et al., 2005; Gothelf et al., 2005). At this time many medications are being used for children with good effect, but they are being prescribed off label (prescribed for conditions other than what they were originally indicated for).

The benzodiazepines are rarely used with children (Witek, Rojas, Alonso, Minami, & Silva, 2005), but may be utilized with adolescents who are finished with puberty. The SSRIs seem to be effective in children without excessive risk, although, as with all medications in children, watching for side effects requires special caution. Unusual side effects may occur and must be immediately evaluated by the physician. Children metabolize medications at different rates than adults and the doses are therefore individualized to the child's weight and age.

In each category of medication there are specific distinctions for how the drugs might be safely used in children and adolescent populations. For these reasons, and because child psychiatrists have the most experience in seeing how their patients respond to these medications, it is best to utilize the expertise of a child psychiatrist when considering medication treatment for this special population.

Treatment of GAD in the geriatric population is similar to that in the adult population, but several factors regarding medication must be taken into consideration. Geriatric patients are often on several other medications for a variety of different medical conditions. Thus, physicians must communicate carefully in assessing potential drug interactions. The metabolism of the older patient is slower than the younger adult, so it is likely that a lower dose of medication will be used. The SSRIs may be very beneficial in this population. In the very elderly, caution with benzodiazepines should be exercised, as these medications have sedating effects and may also cause confused cognitive states. Their action may complicate assessment for dementia, and their withdrawal effects may take longer to diminish.

PEARLS ABOUT MEDICATING FOR GENERALIZED ANXIETY DISORDER

Important ideas to take away regarding the use of medication with GAD include:

- The SSRIs are considered to be first-line treatment for GAD.
- Benzodiazepine-type medications are often thought as second-line treatments or augmenters for GAD.
- BuSpar (buspirone) has been thought to be a helpful antianxiety agent in treating GAD. It is especially helpful when treating those who have an addiction to alcohol, as the benzodiazepines must be used with extreme caution with recovering alcoholics due to the risk of addiction.
- SSNRIs, such as Effexor (venlafaxine), which increase norepinephrine (NE) and serotonin (SE), have been proven to be helpful in treating GAD. Cymbalta (duloxetine) has not been FDA-approved for GAD.
- Tricyclic antidepressants and atypical SSRIs, such as Serzone (nefazodone) and Remeron (mirtazepine), may also be effective in treating GAD.
- In the past, other agents have been used to treat GAD, among them barbiturates. They reduced anxiety more by causing sedation than by changing the cause of the anxiety symptoms. Barbiturates are very sedating, significantly addicting, and are currently not a favorable choice in treating GAD or other anxiety disorders.

Debbie, introduced in Chapter 7, was an excellent candidate for medication therapy. She was referred to me by her therapist after being treated for a month. She had constant worry about all aspects of her life (children, health, future, and finances). She could not shut her brain off about the worrying. She not only was frustrated about her life, but also was feeling exhausted and had many physical symptoms (upset stomach, headache, and body aches). A good medical workup revealed no medical basis for her complaints. Although she did have a normal thyroid blood level, her thyroid stimulating hormone (TSH) was at the high normal range. I discussed with Debbie the possibility of putting her on a low dose of the thyroid medication Cytomel. Although it may have relieved some of her fatigue and helped her to enhance the effects of other medications used to treat GAD,

Debbie decided not to go with this option. This reluctance to use medication is typical of people who have GAD. She agreed to revisit this option later in treatment.

After reviewing the medication options and the course of treatment, Debbie agreed to try a course of medication that I felt would reduce her anxiety. I immediately started her on Effexor XR (venlafaxine), an SSNRI antidepressant that increases serotonin (SE) and norepinephrine (NE). (XR indicates extended release, a means of delivering the drug over a period of time in the body without having to take additional doses.) Effexor XR is an FDA-approved medication for GAD. The increased SE could help to relieve Debbie's overall anxiety. The increased NE could both enhance the SE and mildly increase Debbie's energy to help her deal with her exhaustion from constant worrying. I started her at a low dose (37.5mg) and targeted a dose of 150–225mg.

I also informed Debbie that these medications take time to be effective, and even if she started to feel improvement within weeks, the regulating effects of the medication on the serotonergic system would need considerably more time than that. If she did well on the medication, she would remain on it for 6–12 months before we would consider tapering it. Making sure that she understood the way the drugs work was important to gaining her compliance in using them. Like many GAD patients, she was reluctant to try medication, and I wanted to prevent any attempt to hurry off it.

I also needed to help Debbie with immediate relief of her anxiety. I put her on a low dose (0.5mg twice a day) of the benzodiazepine Klonopin (clonazepam). Debbie remained on the Klonopin for 3 weeks and experienced immediate relief from her anxiety. At 3 weeks the Effexor XR started to work and she did not need the Klonopin. I also prescribed 10mg of the quick-acting sleeping pill Ambien for 3 weeks. Ambien was a reasonable choice because Debbie had 7 hours of available sleep; if she had not had this amount of time to remain asleep, I would have considered Sonata, which has shorter duration of action.

The immediate benefits of lowering anxiety and improving sleep were dramatic. As Debbie felt less overwhelmed and more energetic, she was able to utilize her psychotherapy more effectively. She found it easier to concentrate and block out worry, and she felt less irritable as she became less tired and anxious.

Over the course of the year Debbie did quite well. For some time, her tendency to ruminate was intense, and she needed to go up to 225mg of the Effexor XR. However, after 6 months I reduced her dose to a maintenance of 112.5mg/day. She began to do very well in mastering relaxation, and as she resumed normal activities, she kept a somewhat slower pace of activity at home to diminish some tension. She also mastered thought-replacing so that she felt some control over her worrying. After a year she was able to wean off the medication, and her anxiety remained in remission.

CONCLUSION

Generalized anxiety disorder (GAD) involves persistent worry that disrupts concentration, interferes with daily life, and creates distress for those who cannot dampen their continuous anxiety. Often GAD will precede depression and intervening into its negative effects may help to avoid the depressed mood that can accompany this disorder. The causes of GAD may include disruption in the level of norepinephrine resulting in hypervigilance to problems and overemphasis on negativity. There may also be failures to suppress negativity due to low levels of serotonin affecting several aspects of brain function, such as overactivity in the anterior cingulate gyrus and heightened tone in the basal ganglia leading to mental and physical tension.

Pharmacological interventions target the neurotransmitters that can ameliorate these problems. Utilizing selective serotonin reuptake inhibitors (SSRIs) to raise levels of serotonin can modulate activity in the prefrontal cortex, creating more energy to suppress worried thinking, and may also regulate the activity of the anterior cingulate gyrus and the limbic system. The medications with combined effects on serotonin and norepinephrine (SNRIs) seem especially effective with this type of anxiety. The anxiolytic effects of BuSpar (buspirone) occur as the result of increasing the serotonin level and thus make it effective with GAD. Many with GAD can benefit from the MAOIs or tricyclic antidepressants when they do not respond well to the SSRI's. Other anti-anxiety medications are used sparingly, as the intensity of anxiety warrants, because the major need with GAD is to relieve tension and rumination.

It is likely that without intervention a person with GAD could also develop depression in addition to the lifestyle and relationship problems that emerge with these symptoms. It is therefore necessary to integrate treatment for GAD with medication and psychotherapy and effectively plan for lifelong management of this disorder. Stressful situations can trigger relapse, but those who are prepared to manage stress and identify signs of relapse can get control of the reemergence of the disorder with a plan to promptly reinstitute medication and/or psychotherapeutic interventions as needed.

CHAPTER NINE

SOCIAL ANXIETY DISORDER: FEAR OF EXPOSURE

If PD can be characterized as mindless terror and GAD as worry without reason, social anxiety disorder (SAD) is fear of exposure. SAD is the most common of the anxiety disorders. Without other people present (or the anticipation of others' being present) the person with SAD may feel little anxiety. In the company of others, however, people with SAD experience physiological responses associated with embarrassment, shame, or humiliation. This disorder is different from PD in that sufferers do not necessarily fear for their physical safety.

Social anxiety disorder has equal rates of occurrence between men and women in clinical treatment settings, but epidemiologically there is a higher incidence in women (American Psychiatric Association, 2000). This chronic condition affects 3–13% of people in the United States at some time during their lives (National Institute of Mental Health, 2006). There are two peaks of incidence:

- 11–15 years of age
- 18–25 years of age

It is likely that the changes that occur physically, socially, and educationally at these ages are part of the etiology of the disorder. Between the ages of 11 and 15, individuals experience profound physical changes and must negotiate stunningly complex social changes in relations between boys and girls. From 18 to 25, individuals are expected to take on unprecedented levels of independence and decision-making and navigate changes in social environment from home to school or independent living.

It is speculated that when people are affected by SAD at younger ages, they hold themselves back from achieving in social and academic ways because they avoid putting themselves in positions where others might observe them and they might fail (Eisen, Kearney, & Schaefer, 1995; Eisen & Schaefer, 2005). Indeed, about 66% of socially phobic individuals are unwed and their social and educational levels are lower than average (American Psychiatric Association, 2000). This suggests the extreme importance of identifying and diagnosing children and adolescents with SAD so that they can achieve their potential socially, educationally, and professionally.

People with SAD are often slow to seek help because it is relatively easy for them to avoid being in places where they feel the symptoms of their anxiety—thus their anxiety is easier to live with. As long as people with SAD can avoid the kind of exposure they fear, they do not feel their symptoms. It is when the symptoms prevent sufferers from doing important or necessary tasks that they finally seek psychotherapy.

When they do seek treatment, the symptom management is more difficult than for PD or GAD. It is difficult to diminish the visible evidence of anxiety without medication. Also, avoidance works so well to get rid of anxiety that reexposure to anxiety-producing situations must occur in very small steps. And, as will be discussed later, the impairment of SAD, if it starts in childhood, also affects social and vocational skills, so therapy must typically focus on skills-training during treatment (Herbert et al., 2005).

DIAGNOSTIC CRITERIA

The *DSM-IV-TR* (American Psychiatric Association, 2000) describes two basic types of social anxiety. The first type, referred to as *specific social phobia,* is the one most people recognize as some version of stage fright or fear of public speaking. This "performance anxiety" is limited to situations in which the performance of a specific task is going to be observed and evaluated. The second type of SAD, *generalized social phobia,* occurs in a wide variety of social settings. People with generalized SAD feel the same fearful sensations as those with specific social phobia; however, their fear is prompted by such varied circumstances as signing their name in public, meeting an individual, eating in a restaurant, or sitting in the center of a room such as an auditorium. The symptoms are those of powerful fear, all of which are associated with the output of norepinephrine (NE) to the various regions of the brain that activate the viscera.

Three Clusters of Symptoms

Both types of social anxiety are marked by physiological, cognitive, and behavioral indicators:

- Intense physiological arousal that is unpleasant and visible to others
- Cognitive fear of being observed when looking frightened or embarrassed
- Behavioral avoidance of anything that triggers the arousal

Physiological Symptoms

People with SAD experience arousal that is similar to and equally as unpleasant as that of the panic attack, although it might not become as severe. The arousal, however, is always due to an identifiable cause: the presence of another person who could be judging them. The physiological symptoms of the autonomic nervous system arousal marking social anxiety include:

- Rapid heart rate
- Sweating
- Flushing
- Gastrointestinal disturbance (nausea, frequency of urination, diarrhea)
- Tremors of muscles and voice

The physical symptoms are fear responses. They are the biological outcome of the amygdala sending signals of alarm to the autonomic nervous system and the overly active norepinephrine (NE) system stimulating the physical signs of alarm through too much NE affecting the peripheral nervous system. For those who suffer from specific social phobia (performance anxiety), the fear of experiencing performance-related fear becomes a problem. Unless the reward of performance is good enough, they will avoid feeling such fear. It has been said that celebrity Johnny Carson felt this kind of stage fright before every performance, feeling nauseated and shaky before walking out and beginning his famous monologues. Many actors, speakers, musicians, and other performers feel this kind of fear, but they get so much reward from the outcome of performing that they will endure it. But many who feel this fear from simply giving a report at a staff meeting, saying their name in a community gathering, taking a test, or giving a speech in a school will forever avoid any occasion that might demand the "performance" of speaking up when strangers are in the room.

People with generalized social anxiety fear common, daily situations in which they might be scrutinized, such as writing a check at a store, asking for help from a clerk, or getting too close to others riding in an elevator.

Their physical symptoms may feel like exceptional shyness or a full blown panic.

There are several theories about why these particular physiological signs are so marked with social anxiety. One theory comes from evolutionary biology and has to do with this being part of a vestigial pattern of defense. The flushing and avoidance of eye contact, often accompanied by a small smile or nervous laugh, are like the signs of submission that animals make when confronted with an aggressive, stronger animal. It makes sense socially: If you are facing someone of greater power and fearing a negative evaluation, you might respond by placating that person and submitting to his or her power. The visible signs of submission may look slightly different from one person to another, but all involve SAD physiology. This may be caused by postsynaptic hypersensitivity of the serotonin system (Schneier, 2005).

Another theory is that SAD flushing is an exaggerated version of shame. If you are expecting someone to judge you negatively, your innate response is that of being exposed. The shame response is exactly that. The red face of shame is due to being caught at something you did not want the person to notice you doing, and defensive reddening and averting of eyes can also be seen as a submission to the person observing. Vascular flushing in SAD is shame without cause, but the SAD person's cognitions play a major role in triggering the physical responses.

Cognitive Symptoms

Probably as a result of both temperament and life experience, people with SAD expect to be evaluated and judged as lacking. Their cognitions include:

- Being certain that others are observing and rejecting them.
- Expecting to be humiliated (if you are laughing, it is at them).
- Expecting to be embarrassed because others will see their shaking hands, wobbly knees, quivering voice, or red face.

The fear of looking afraid. The fear of being evaluated explodes into the fear of being seen as afraid. Signs of embarrassment, like flustered speech and an urge to get away, quickly become added to list of symptoms. In this disorder, people have the physiology and the temperament of shyness first (Lonegan & Phillips, 2001; Rapee, 2002; Winston, Strange, O'Doherty & Dolan, 2002). The origin of the cognitive pattern of SAD is similar to that of the other anxiety disorders. In this case, the person is in a situation that others would deem innocuous, but the SAD sufferer feels afraid, decides there must be a reason for that fear, and hence attributes the fear to something in the situation (Easter et al., 2005; Gazzaniga, 2005; Grillon, 2002). Thus, the cognitive pattern is set in motion by a false belief.

Negative expectations. Once the initial cognition of expecting judgment, rejection, and humiliation has taken root, it leads to the *constant* expectation that someone else is observing and evaluating them. This leads SAD sufferers to feel afraid when being evaluated and expect negative outcomes. What we look for, we find. And thus the vicious circle of social anxiety develops: The cognition triggers a physiological fear response, which reinforces the cognition that there was indeed something to fear.

People with SAD are not necessarily worriers, and they do not feel out of control like those with PD. Rather, they believe that if they can just stay out of the limelight, they will feel fine. Life, however, does not always make that avoidance easy, and thus behavioral symptoms appear.

Behavioral Symptoms

The behavioral signs of SAD are obvious and simple. People with SAD avoid social encounters that they have connected with feeling fear. Most generalize those quite broadly, except in the case of performance anxiety, which may be linked to only one type of performance, such as taking a test or public speaking. When SAD sufferers can successfully avoid such situations and still live the kind of life that fulfills them, the disorder is not crippling. However, most will, at some point in their lives, be confronted with a situation that requires them to deal with their disorder. Many people with SAD enter therapy in midlife when they must overcome their SAD or lose an important promotion or job opportunity.

Freezing. A particularly devastating feature of the behavioral symptoms of this disorder is "freezing" during a SAD attack. This occurs on both a cognitive and behavioral level. People often describe this response as their mind "going blank." They intensely avoid eye contact and feel urgency to escape from the situation but cannot think of a way to do so. This is probably a function of the interaction of the noradrenergic system and basal ganglia (BG) functioning. Too much norepinephrine (NE) can momentarily freeze smooth and flexible functioning in response to a startling or frightening situation (Jhou, 2005). For people with SAD, who are likely to have excessive firing of NE throughout their nervous system, the sensation of being frozen just adds to their embarrassment and intensifies their fear of future embarrassment in similar circumstances.

Avoidance. Because the arousal of fear is too rapid and intense to be controlled, avoiding every possible situation that could trigger the reaction becomes the primary method of symptom management. Many people hold themselves back from stellar performance at work or school, avoid dating situations, and refuse to interview for jobs. They won't risk being in the spotlight for good grades or professional achievement, and they may avoid any academic or professional progress that would require them to be tested or publicly demonstrate what they can do. Unlike the high-functioning, high-energy GAD client, a person with SAD will hold back from displays of competence. Of course, this takes a serious toll on developing competence, and the magnitude of lost opportunity for SAD sufferers is heartbreaking and immeasurable.

THE ANXIOUS BRAIN AND SOCIAL ANXIETY DISORDER

The activation of fear circuitry and heightened NE release in the brain are the keys to understanding the responses of SAD. The amygdala is causal both to the creation of fear responses and to unlearning the fear response.

The Task of the Amygdala: Learning to Be Afraid

Brain imaging, especially fMRI, has led to important discoveries about how the brain operates under different kinds of emotional conditions. Remember that the thalamus takes in sensory information, among its various complex tasks. (See Figure 1.9, which shows the path of thalamic connections.) It relays that information directly to the amygdala for fast response. In that way the amygdala is the early warning system of the brain. The thalamus also relays the information to the left prefrontal cortex (PFC). The left PFC integrates the sensory information with information from the hippocampus about the details or context of the current sensory data, compares all of this with long-term memory of former situations, and then decides whether action is called for.

Is it necessary to be afraid or not? The PFC answers that question and then sends information through the anterior cingulate gyrus (ACG) to the amygdala to help it learn whether a stimulus is currently a cause for alarm or not. This is learning at a very practical level. For example, the amygdala may detect smoke in the air, a new stimulus from the environment and usually a reason to take action, but fear may not be the appropriate response. Via the pathway from the cortex through the ACG, the amygdala learns that the smoke from a piece of burned toast is cause for action but not fear, so it does not trigger fight or flight. On the other hand, the acrid smell of smoke from an electrical fire in a wall is probably unusual enough that the amygdala will signal "danger!" and initiate fight or flight activity.

The various parts of the amygdala receive signals of alarm from the thalamus and from olfactory sensation, and they relay those signals to parts of the brain that will turn on fear reactions. Some fear reactions are necessary and inborn. All people have an acoustic startle—when loud, sudden noises occur, the amygdala instantaneously causes body reaction. Everyone reacts with fear to loud, sudden changes in the environment or to certain things such as snakes, darkness, or unexpected events that have components associated with the things we innately fear. The amygdala is prepared to handle the things that are frightening by stimulating fear circuitry. It connects to the hypothalamus to set the stress response system in action. It also connects to the locus coeruleus to get NE pumping to start fear responses, which may be submission signs but also include the cardiovascular symptoms of SAD. This flurry of activity all occurs without mediation from the PFC. It is an instantaneous response, and all of it begins before the PFC can receive the sensory information the amygdala is responding to.

The Amygdala of SAD Has an "Unlearning" Disorder

People *learn to react* with fear to situations that are associated with pain. A child who touches the flame of a candle and gets burned may react to all candles with fear, unless, over time, she learns that candles are not always associated with burning. The child may, in the meantime, associate fear of candle flame to all flames, and thus may need to learn which flames are to be feared and which are not. So the child learns the fear of a candle, and then unlearns it. She accurately learns candles are only to be feared if you are touching the flame. This learning and unlearning of fear is the process of the PFC modulating the amygdala (Bouton, 2002). In those with strong phobic responses, however, the amygdala seems to have an unlearning disorder.

These unlearning disorders may have a genetic basis. A deficit of the serotonin (SE) transporter gene, affecting the transportation of SE, causes poor connectivity from the anterior cingulate gyrus (ACG) to the amygdala (Maron et al, 2004). This has been found in people with anxiety and depression disorders. This gene has two versions—long alleles and short alleles—and people get one version from each parent. Being genetically endowed with two short alleles on the gene impairs transmission of signals from the ACG to the amygdala, inhibiting learning from the PFC to calm the activity in the amygdala. This means there is more experience of fear even in situations that have previously not caused harm. The constant stress of feeling afraid can lead to anxiety and ultimately to depression, because it is hard for the amygdala to unlearn reactions to fear cues. It is why a person cannot just decide not to be afraid. The amygdala continues to generate fear until it learns not to.

Why do people develop fear of performing? First of all, they learn to be afraid. Performance anxiety may just be the result of having felt strong fear responses when being evaluated publicly—that stomach-grabbing, knee-knocking, hand-trembling response to suddenly being in the spotlight. In subsequent similar situations the amygdala responds to the anticipation of a replay. The amygdala learns *very quickly* that fear goes with public speaking. It then produces the fear response in all similar situations of performance. These are typically very specific situations and are easy to avoid. When not in the performance mode, this person may feel no other kind of anxiety.

FACTORS IN THE DEVELOPMENT
OF GENERALIZED SOCIAL ANXIETY DISORDER

Whereas specific social anxiety may develop via the amygdala's learned response to a specific situation (such as public speaking), generalized social anxiety may stem from other causes.

Temperament

One important factor in developing SAD is an inborn shy temperament. Not all shy children grow up to have social anxiety, but all with generalized social anxiety suffered from shyness as a child (Eisen & Schaefer, 2005; Reiss, Silverman, & Weems, 2001; Winston, Strange, O'Doherty, & Dolan, 2002). Discussing all the brain factors that create temperament is beyond the scope of this book, but they are genetically endowed, inherited, inborn traits that are identifiable in infancy and consistent over time.

Temperament is the result of combinations of these inborn traits. Traits range in strength and affect temperamental style by the way they interact with each other. Temperamental style is a significant contributor to the way people experience the events of their lives. For example, what is exciting to a bold child may be overwhelmingly frightening to a child of a sensitive nature. Thomas and Chess (Thomas, 1977; Chess & Thomas, 1986), who first studied temperament in a large longitudinal study, identified nine traits of temperament in children. They described the temperament of the shy child as:

- Slow to warm up
- Resistant to change
- Solemn, without much smiling
- Not averse to others, but needing time to know them and not necessarily wanting the stimulation of many people at one time

Several others have described shy temperament somewhat differently, but they concur that temperament is an etiological factor in SAD (Gladstone, Parker, Mitchell, Wilhelm, & Malhi; 2005; Lonegan & Phillips, 2001). Add to this list a biological sensitivity (overreactivity) to stimulation, and one can see how SAD children would find stimulation from social experiences very tiring and trying.

Children with shy temperaments can successfully adjust to social settings, but they must be given time to observe the setting until they can understand the rules of engagement. These children may need the same amount of observation time every time they enter a different environment, even when those environments are similar, because they are slow to warm up to new situations. Shy children may also enjoy the company of others, but generally not too many others and not all at one time. Enjoying socializing does not translate into enjoying a party, a big classroom, or a group game. Instead, they prefer to interact exclusively with a few close and meaningful friends.

The shy child's desire for quietness in friendship is driven by traits that are genetic and hereditary. Shy children are usually born that way, and they need enough time to formulate thoughts and feelings without pressure. The challenge of adapting to a stimulating environment with many people and activities is more than they care to take on. They tend to feel overwhelmed when there is a lot going in the environment, and if they are pushed to participate before they are ready, they feel aversively high levels of tension and anxiety. If children with shy temperaments are given the right kind of encouragement to try new things with support and the flexibility to pull back when they feel overwhelmed, they can learn to operate socially without any fear. But shy children who are pushed or who have many aversive experiences may develop SAD (Hofmann, 2005; Lonegan & Phillips, 2001).

The Sensitive Amygdala

Recent research from brain imaging studies gives insight into the anxious brain. There is evidence that SAD clients may have an enlarged amygdala that is very sensitive to social cues (Phan, Fitzgerald, Nathan, & Tancer, 2006). The amygdala is normally very active in recognizing facial expression (Bremner et al., 1999; Lobaugh, Gibson, & Taylor, 2006). The infant from birth is noticing, registering, and memorizing the facial expressions of its caregivers, because the face contains information about how the caregiver is going to interact with the infant. The infant also memorizes the internal state he or she experiences in conjunction with the caregiver's face. Thus, the amygdala learns which emotional tone goes with the facial expression. If the loving face of a mother is associated with feeling warm, well fed, and calm, the loving face will evoke those feelings whenever the infant sees it (or later remembers it). If the infant is cold, hungry, or upset, he or she will immediately calm down at the sight of the mother, even before the diaper is changed or the bottle is presented. When the caregiver's face is hostile and the interchange with the infant results in the child's feeling pain or fear, the infant memorizes the expression in concert with the feeling experienced. Later, seeing a hostile expression on someone's face will evoke the feelings of fear and pain.

The enlarged right side of the SAD client's amygdala creates a hypersensitivity to negative faces (Easter et al., 2005). The hypersensitive amygdala is easily triggered to perceive a negative facial impression as a threat. And it creates a low threshold for what is threatening. People with SAD react instantly to the slightest possibility that someone's facial expression represents a negative response. The remote likelihood that someone is laughing at them or irritated with them immediately sends them into the shame response. Because the amygdala does not need the intervention of conscious thought to trigger physiological reactions to threat, and because it takes only milliseconds for facial flushing to begin, these reactions are nearly impossible to stop in the moment. Thus, treatment for SAD focuses on teaching the amygdala to stop reacting to the environment as if it is threatened.

Shame as Traumatic Stress

Some generalized SAD develops from experiences of shame akin to traumatic stress. Shame can become like trauma when shame experiences build until one experience functions as the straw that breaks the camel's back. The child with a shy temperament feels as if each painful "exposure" is like a small trauma. When shy children go through life experiencing one small humiliation after another, their brains become primed to feel shame, with all the physiological sensations that accompany it—a moment of feeling frozen quickly followed by a blanching and then a flushing, heart rate increase, and stomach-dropping sensation.

The shy child may start to have many of these shame experiences, especially when being raised by parents who push too hard or who are insensitive or cruel. Then one day this child, primed by a history of shame, is put into a situation that may be no more severe than the previous situations but nevertheless is too much for the child to handle. This traumalike experience creates cues that thereafter trigger shame, just as in PTSD. One client, Jorge, reported that when he was a seventh grader, he was forced to stand in front of the class and do a math problem on the board. He was struggling because he knew he did not have it right, and the teacher turned to the class and joked, "Well, I guess we can see who did not do his homework last night!" Jorge turned bright red as the class laughed loudly and long. But the degree of shame he felt was intense to the point of trauma. Jorge's amygdala learned to regard the possibility of humiliation as dangerous, in the exact way traumatic events are learned.

As a consequence of trauma, generalization to the cues of trauma becomes widespread, and the emotional responses to these cues become stronger and harder to control (see Figure 3.3). Furthermore, the generalization is not particularly *consciously* connected to the situations in which the social anxiety is intense. Adults may have no idea why they cannot calm down in situations they *know* are not threatening.

Many people who enter treatment for SAD as adults discover during therapy that their current inability to desensitize is due to the subtle cuing from a particular event in their youth that appears to bear no similarity to the current situation. Therapy can help these clients uncover the symbolic connections between these seemingly dissimilar situations. EMDR (described in Chapters 4 and 10) is one of the most effective ways to desensitize the brain to this kind of SAD etiology.

The Interaction of Social Development, Hormones, and the Brain

Many SAD clients in treatment have reported one particular incident in their junior high school years that stays with them. These experiences are often linked to social embarrassment. These anecdotes are convincing examples of the power of embarrassment to shape future experiences. It is amazing how often one embarrassing incident with a teacher or in front of peers is used years later to sum up their sense of being incompetent or ineffective. Most people have such experiences: feeling humiliated in a classroom for saying something stupid, being humiliated by dropping a tray in the lunchroom in front of the boy you wanted to impress, or being laughed at in gym class for failing to climb the rope or make the free throw. Those unpleasant memories are dim or forgotten for many people, but in the minds of those with SAD, they remain formative.

Why is this age such a potent time for social anxiety? The potential for social embarrassment to shape personality at this age is stronger than at other ages because several factors combine powerfully:

- Brain changes occurring during this time create vulnerability. During early puberty the brain is rapidly pruning off unnecessary dendritic connections and forging more efficient connections between networks of cells. The brain is different, literally day to day, as this stage of development goes forward, so the mind of the teen at this age is in turmoil.

- Socially, pressure peaks during these years as the demand to function in dating relationships begins to affect all individuals rather than just the precocious ones.
- Puberty adds additional stress, making teens feel alien to their own bodies. The bodies they see in the mirror not only look different, but also experience urges they are not yet equipped to understand and respond to.
- Physically, teens must suffer through a feeling of odd coordination as they grow too fast. Comfort and ease with the patterns of physical action (like ball-playing or running) has to be re-established in a taller, longer body.
- Academic work begins to heat up in junior high school, and it is at this age that students are asked to get to know several different teachers and adapt to their teaching styles.

Most children at this age feel awkward at least some of the time. Throwing the shy child at this stage into a terrifying new situation without enough time to adjust practically guarantees a rough social experience that will be hard to forget. The embarrassment, fear of rejection, and actual or imagined humiliation are a potent mix that create life-shaping memories.

CONCLUSION

Social anxiety disorder is one of the most debilitating forms of anxiety when it involves lost potential and withdrawal from life. SAD sufferers handle the discomfort of anxiety by avoiding situations that stimulate it. The lack of distress a person feels when successfully avoiding situations reinforces the temperamental preference for withdrawal.

All people with anxiety have their individual history and temperament, and good therapy will always take into account life experiences that need clarifying or resolution. In order to control anxiety symptoms for people with SAD, it is likely that working with temperament and history will be necessary to achieve symptom control. The development of their behavioral patterns is like an intricately woven tapestry: Life experiences interact with temperament to create the warp and weft of the weave that shows the current picture of behavior and emotion. Doing therapy with clients who have SAD requires the equivalent of reweaving, pulling out one damaged thread at a time and creating a new image of how the client can respond to experiences in stronger, more confident, and more effective ways.

CHAPTER TEN

TREATING SOCIAL ANXIETY DISORDER

Jeremy's problem was that he was bald. He said if he were not bald, flushing in social settings would not be such a big problem for him. "But how can people not notice when my whole head turns red and sweats?" When Jeremy had to speak in a meeting at work, or when he was in a restaurant talking with the server, he would flush and sweat, and the more he felt his flush was noticed, the redder he got. He felt like he was like a light bulb, burning brightly whenever someone looked at him.

Jeremy described having symptoms of SAD all of his life, but he had been able to tolerate his condition and find ways of getting around the worst of it. What finally brought him to therapy was what brings many clients into treatment for SAD: a recent life change that made the symptoms much more of an interference. Jeremy had recently lost a promotion to a peer, and he wanted to interview for a new job. He knew he could not get a good job if he was noticed sweating during an interview—who would fail to notice his "bald head turning blotchy red and dripping sweat?" Jeremy was good at his work as an engineer, and he thought he could get a better job without too much trouble, but he definitely could not interview with these symptoms.

Jeremy was typical of clients with SAD in many ways. As he told me his history, he noted that he had been a shy child. He was the only son of a couple who had him late in life. His father had not known what to do with this boy who shied away from sports and did not want to stray too far from home. Jeremy was good at school and had one or two good friends but not many acquaintances. He did not feel as if he needed them. He reported that his mother worried about his shyness and decided it would be beneficial for him to go to summer camp after the sixth grade. At this age, many boys like to go to camp to hike, make campfires, and learn to use a bow and arrow. But it is also the age when boys can torture each other for being different. Jeremy was in hell for 3 weeks: stammering, turning red, and never for a moment being ignored when he blushed, which he did constantly because he did not know anyone at the camp. Any encounter with a new person was an occasion to turn red. He escaped finally by faking sickness and made a lifelong vow to never put himself in that kind of situation again.

Regrettably, the same type of situation struck in his freshman year of high school, when he was required to take a speech class. Although he had a few friends in the class, when he stood in front of everyone to speak, he felt frozen. His legs trembled, his voice shook, and he worked his way through the required 3-minute speech in only 45 seconds, barely getting back to his seat on his wobbly legs. He could not look at anyone for fear of seeing them jeer at him.

Although it may not seem as if anything terrible happened in his life, Jeremy felt traumatized, and the prospect of being looked at while he was showing signs of his shyness was terrifying to him. Jeremy's brain treated the worst occasions of shyness as if they were real terror, and he never wanted to feel that feeling again. As he got older, the shyness was a stumbling block to dating. The force of hormones helped him to overcome that, but he did not meet new women readily. Although he had been married, he was now divorced, and he was again in a dating mode. However, even going to a restaurant was a big challenge. He not only feared the server's noticing his discomfiture, but also worried about whether his date would notice and dismiss him for it. He was essentially cuing terror when he thought of turning red in public, albeit at a lower intensity than a severe trauma victim would.

Jeremy had two important goals for therapy: to be able to go on a job interview without turning red and sweating and to be able to take a woman to a restaurant without embarrassing himself by looking embarrassed.

Jeremy's treatment took the shape of that for most clients with SAD. It would be necessary for him to find ways to relax about his symptoms, as eliminating flushing altogether is very hard to do early in treatment, and some clients never manage do it.

Unlike with PD and GAD, the first step of treatment for SAD is to address the cognitive aspects of the disorder. Clients benefit, of course, from learning about why they have this disorder, but the main goal of cognitive change is to help clients feel less concerned about the severity of flushing.

Physiology is addressed next. Retraining the SAD brain involves teaching the prefrontal cortex (PFC) to control and ultimately modulate the activity of the amygdala. The underlying neurobiology of this disorder is harder to change, because consciously controlling the amygdala's alert takes constant effort, and changing the sensitivity level of the amygdala to threat is slow going. More than with any other anxiety disorder, the treatment for SAD involves practicing in real-life situations. Such *in vivo exposure* begins with many small experiences of learning that social situations are not threatening.

Treatment addresses behavior after a person is able to control physiology well enough to calm anxiety while practicing new behavior. The powerful drive to avoid anxiety has held the SAD sufferer back from new experiences. To develop the willingness and ability to practice in vivo exposure, cognition and physiology have to be under control.

Step 1. Address Cognitions. Whereas other anxiety disorder treatment starts with physiology, SAD treatment starts with thoughts. This involves:

- Psychoeducation about shy temperament (the biology of the shame response and the hypersensitivity of the amygdala to social cues).
- Identifying and correcting cognitive errors.
- Identifying and changing false beliefs.

Step 2. Address Physiology. Eliminating or reducing reactivity to the environment, especially to the faces of other people, is the next step. This involves:

- Controlling the rapid heart rate and excessive stress response.
- Learning relaxation for in vivo exposure.

Step 3. Address Behavior. This is the last step because it won't be successful unless a person with SAD is able to reduce symptoms sufficiently to start doing things that could trigger anxiety. It involves:

- Identifying avoidance behaviors and eliminating them.
- Practicing for situations in therapy sessions before in vivo exposure.
- Learning social skills of all types.
- In vivo exposure.

STEP 1. ADDRESS COGNITIONS

As noted earlier, not all shy people develop social anxiety, but nearly all social phobic clients were shy as children. Although few people are aware of it, the connection between temperament and the development of paralyzing fear is strong. As shy children, SAD clients felt socially incompetent and ashamed because of their blushing and embarrassed reactions in front of others.

Psychoeducation: The Necessary Precursor to Change

Psychoeducation is an important part of establishing clients' compliance with treatment. Understanding the biological basis for their sensitivity and physical symptoms goes a long way toward making them feel less helpless. Such knowledge makes clients feel less incompetent and more ready to practice the therapy skills we suggest. If medication is part of the treatment plan, psychoeducation can help clients understand why they are being referred to a psychiatrist.

What do people need to learn about the flushing, sweating, weak-kneed, heart-palpitating, and trembling reaction to being in public?

- First, they must understand this is not happening because there is any real risk of danger.
- Second, this reaction is not specifically a fear of danger but rather a fear of exposure. It is the autonomic response to being exposed with a risk of humiliation. The biological response is one of submission, leading to averting the eyes and backing away.
- All of these sensations can be explained as extraordinary embarrassment or shame.

Using the expression "fear of exposure" is meaningful. (It does not matter that the particular exposure is imaginary.) Why does one client feel comfortable when speaking in front of a crowd but have trembling hands when signing her name in front of someone? How can one person be so nervous about making an error that he will not eat in a restaurant but be able to shop without fear, and another person be unable to shop for fear that a clerk will ask if he needs help? It is the *imagined outcome* that causes the fear. What SAD individuals imagine others will think or do and what they imagine they will look like govern their choices. They believe that what they fear will really happen. Thus, it is not the situation itself but their belief about how they will look that makes them start to fear new situations. And it is the heightened fear response that causes the intensity of that fear.

Teach about the role of the amygdala and the heightened norepinephrine (NE) response. As mentioned in Chapter 9, that it is likely that clients with SAD have an enlarged amygdala compared to populations without SAD. The slightest hint of negativity in another's face signals danger, causing the amygdala to initiate a fear response. The NE affecting the peripheral nervous system causes increased heart rate, trembling, and cardiovascular flushing. Norepinephrine is a powerful learning aid. It causes the brain to highlight the specifics of a "danger" situation, so that in future similar situations the amygdala won't miss a cue (see Figure 2.7). It will be hypervigilant to all possible reminders of what caused the tension and emotional arousal. This assures greater reactivity to potentially negative faces.

Teach that fear is unnecessary. People in treatment for SAD need to develop a new belief: that their physiological response, as powerful and uncomfortable as it is, is *unnecessarily* trying to protect them. They need to learn that the therapy process will help them slow or eliminate the fear through a process that involves:

- Learning to tolerate uncomfortable sensations while coming to believe that the sensation is unnecessary.
- Learning to calm the body and take control of the thoughts (false beliefs).
- Acting in direct opposition to the false beliefs.
- Practicing repeatedly so that the amygdala can relearn cues. (The amygdala relearns through multiple experiences of becoming calm and feeling safe in a situation that previously evoked fear.)

It is quite important to get people to buy into this therapy process intellectually. (This is using the executive decision-making power of the left prefrontal cortex to override the emotional demand of the limbic system; see Figure 4.1.) If SAD sufferers believe the therapist's explanation of their overreactivity, they will be more likely to complete uncomfortable practice sessions that allow their brains to learn about what is risky and what is not.

Identifying Cognitive Errors and False Beliefs

Cognitive errors are misperceptions of actual events or situations that have occurred. *Beliefs* are generalized views that people hold about themselves, others, and the world. False beliefs develop out of cognitive errors. For example, suppose a woman is talking to an acquaintance at a party when he suddenly cuts off the conversation to say hello to another person. Instead of assuming that the man was enjoying talking with her but was distracted by the other person, the woman might have the *cognitive error* that he found her boring. This could lead to the *false belief* that all people will find her boring (or that she *is* boring).

There are specific kinds of beliefs that are common to SAD, and they stay in place because they are not challenged by correct cognitive processes. Cognitive errors begin developing during childhood, when understanding of social exchanges is immature. Beliefs about people and themselves are rarely tested against adult, mature wisdom. In fact, they are reinforced by experiences that seem to prove them true. Table 10.1 identifies typical cognitive errors seen in people with SAD and the kinds of false beliefs that may develop from them.

Correcting Cognitive Errors

Treating SAD involves finding which cognitive errors are being used and correcting them so that false beliefs can be eliminated and new erroneous beliefs do not develop. Cognitive errors common in SAD cause people to filter new experiences through a negative lens. They stop seeing the moments when they had a good reaction from someone or succeeded socially. They begin to make inaccurate generalizations about their experiences and do not draw good conclusions. Thus, they begin to see risk in situations where none exists.

This is largely the result of false beliefs revealed in negative self-talk— that internal dialogue of which many are unaware. The impact of beliefs

TABLE 10.1   Cognitive Errors and the False Beliefs that Develop From Them

Cognitive Error	False Belief
People are scrutinizing me.	Whenever I'm in a public situation, I'll be scrutinized.
People are evaluating me.	Whenever I'm in a public situation, people will evaluate me.
People are rejecting me.	I will always be found lacking by others.
People are noticing my embarrassment and responding negatively.	People will always notice my embarrassment and respond negatively.
People are noticing me in public situations because of the way I look or act.	If a group of people bursts out laughing as I pass by, it's because of the way I look or because of something I did.
Past situations have turned out badly.	The worst possible outcome will always occur. (This is known as *catastrophizing*.)
I have no control of what's happening to me.	I am unable to influence whether others accept me and whether I will succeed in social circumstances.

about the self, the world, and other people can be easily seen in the choices people make, and these beliefs are revealed in self-talk. Thus, becoming aware of self-talk is a critical part of identifying the cognitive errors that create or reinforce false beliefs.

Several methods are available to identify self-talk that reveals the false beliefs caused by cognitive errors.

Nonverbal Communication

One way to identify unnoticed self-talk is to watch what a client does while talking during sessions.

- Note excessive explanatory styles, eye contact changes, and other appearances of nervousness that crop up unexpectedly.
- Immediately identify these changes and stop to discuss what has prompted them.
- Ask about what clients sense in their body and ask what thoughts intruded to cause the sudden shift in their feelings.

For example, a client may avert his eyes while telling his therapist about a dating situation that bothers him. Asking him about what caused him to avert his eyes may identify negative self-talk such as "My therapist must think this is laughable."

The Three-Column List

Another way to identify negative self-talk is to make a three-column list with the following headings:

- My goal, action, or intention
- My first thought about this
- The opposite of my first thought

Table 10.2 shows a sample three-column list.

TABLE 10.2   The Three-Column List

Goal, Action, or Intention	First Thought	Opposite of First Thought
I am invited to a party with people at work.	I will make a fool of myself by being too shy to talk to anyone.	I can certainly talk to people I know and will not make a fool of myself.
I did not ask that pretty girl on a date.	Big surprise. I will never ask a girl out.	I can learn to ask a girl out.

If the thought listed in column #2 is negative, you can discuss the impact of such negativity on achieving the goal or intention. Working on the "opposite thought" in column #3 is very useful for creating new self-talk about future situations. It can also be used to help clients recover from a situation they perceived went poorly.

The ABCD Method

Albert Ellis's ABCD Method helps clients identify their inner dialogue. This cognitive tool is exactly what SAD sufferers need in order to analyze how their cognitive errors and false beliefs affect their behavior. Ellis and Dryden (1987, pp. 52–53) described this method thoroughly in their book, *The Practice of Rational Emotive Therapy*. The following is a brief summary of how it works:

THE ABCD METHOD

A is the Activating event. Describe the situation that contributed to your anxiety.
B is the Belief that you hold about:

1. Yourself
2. Others
3. The situation

Try to notice self-talk that starts with "shoulds" and oughts." These are essentially *demands* you make on yourself or those around you.
     Also notice any extremes in appraising a problem, such as:

- "It would be awful if _____."
- 'This is the worst _____."
- "I cannot stand it when _____."

C What were the Consequences of A and B? Describe how you felt and acted.
D Now, look at the Beliefs (Demands) you have about yourself, others, or the situation. Question them, and question your extremes in appraising situations. For example, ask yourself, "How do I know that _____?" "Why must I always _____?" "Why do I think this the worst _____?"

Using the ABCD Method in psychotherapy will give people the necessary practice to use it outside of sessions to question their overreactivity to situations.

Use Cognitive-Behavioral Therapy Techniques

Specialists like Rian McMullin (2000), Aaron Beck (1979), and David Burns (1980), among others, have discussed how to change cognitive errors. Cognitive errors include drawing false conclusions from experience or inaccurately generalizing from one situation to another. A SAD sufferer must watch for errors in self-talk that create anxiety, such as "I was nervous talking to my boss today; I will be nervous whenever I talk to her again." Such cognition must be immediately corrected. For example, a new self-statement would simply be, "Just because I was nervous once does not mean I will feel nervous again." If that change is consistently repeated with a confident statement such as, "I am calmer each day in social conversations," the cognitive error will be corrected.

Changing False Beliefs

Changing false beliefs begins with a simple reframe of the problem. Therapists explain that the origin of the client's problem does not lie in personality deficits or life experience. Rather, it is a gift of nature. A gift? clients with SAD learn to reframe shyness as *sensitivity*. They learn that there are aspects of this sensitivity that are also positive. Sensitivity to the world allows people to be creative: Being sensitive to sound might create a musician, being sensitive to color might create an artist or a designer, being sensitive to emotional nuance might create a good therapist. But, like many talents, their sensitivity is a two-edged sword (Arons, 1996). The downside is excessive focus on the negative, which can overwhelm a person who is not taught how to handle the sensitivity.

How does therapy tackle irrational beliefs? Once the false beliefs are identified, there are many approaches to help undo them.

Learn Alternative Beliefs

Teach clients alternative beliefs and have them practice them as homework. For example, if a person believes that she must perfectly obey a set of social rules in order to be worthwhile or loveable, the alternative belief would be that she is loveable as she is. The homework assignment might be to memorize—or just read—lines from an inspirational work (such as the *Desiderata,* an excellent piece for anxiety, attributed to various authors) and repeat those lines out loud several times a day. Then the person might write about what would be different in a typical day if she believed she was loveable as she is.

Change Negative Inner Dialogue

Most cognitive methods address self-talk as a factor in psychological problems. Regardless of the specific style of working, therapy focuses on how the language people use in normal conversation and in inner dialogue shapes their reality. Ask SAD clients to begin *consistently* changing negative inner dialogue. Ellis and Dryden (1987) suggested that whenever people notice themselves using powerful rating words such as "It would be awful if I had to walk out of the movie because I felt sick" or "I cannot stand it when everyone looks at me in the meeting," it would be more helpful to change the talk to a more realistic phrase such as "I would prefer not to be noticed." This has a powerful impact on the prefrontal cortex (PFC) evaluation process over time.

Search for Situations That Disprove False Beliefs

As homework, ask clients to look for and write down situations in which they did *not* experience rejection, humiliation, and so on. Have them bring this list into therapy for discussion or ask them to write about the situations to enhance awareness of the positives. When describing this assignment, stress the difference between what clients *feel* and what actually happened. For example, when the client attended that work party, did he simply *feel* embarrassed or did others *actually* humiliate him? Do not let clients rationalize by saying that the other person probably was *thinking* negative thoughts. Rather, they can only record spoken words and specific actions; if the other person remained engaged in conversation and stayed pleasant, the situation must be recorded as a positive. Keep up this search for positives as a regular part of therapy. It is like the line from that old song: "Accentuate the positives, eliminate the negatives, don't mess with Mr. In-Between." Unlearning a lifetime of negative filtering takes some time.

Use Affirmations

This involves making a positive statement about oneself and saying it as if it is already true. The idea behind affirmations is that we all manifest the reality we believe. By affirming what we want to be true about our lives, our situations, our character, and our attitudes, we operate on the belief that such truth is becoming manifest, even as we speak. For example, if a client wants to become more comfortable talking at meetings, she can say, "I am confident and competent when I express myself at staff meetings." Affirmations do not differentiate past, present, and future—they are said as if they are true *right now*.

As people challenge false beliefs they begin to change the reactivity of their amygdalas. This is a necessary first step in treatment; if the amygdala remains overreactive, it will be hard to get clients into the situations that provide new learning.

This three-part process of addressing cognitions—(1) psychoeducation, (2) identifying and correcting cognitive errors, and (3) identifying and changing false beliefs—guided the beginning of treatment for the client introduced at the beginning of this chapter. Once Jeremy learned that there was a biological basis for his SAD symptoms, he felt less incompetent and more willing to focus on identifying and changing his false beliefs about why he had SAD symptoms and correcting cognitive errors that maintained his anxiety.

During an early therapy session, Jeremy reported that he grew up believing he was not as able as others to handle social encounters. Although he saw himself as competent at work, he believed he was "socially impaired." A close examination of Jeremy's inner dialogue revealed that he did view himself as worthwhile and loveable, yet he firmly believed he could not order a meal in a restaurant while on a date without blushing. This, however, was *not* the most problematic of his beliefs. What made him unwilling to stick his neck out in public was the crippling belief that his date would notice him turning red, judge him to be socially incompetent, and reject him or laugh at him. He also believed he could not stand it if he were to blush and sweat and be noticed. For Jeremy, staying home was a small price to pay to avoid certain humiliation. In therapy we had to (1) identify these beliefs, (2) ascertain that they were false beliefs, and (3) find ways to change them. Then we had to change his way of talking to himself (i.e., correct his cognitions).

Jeremy did pretty well identifying and changing his beliefs about himself in relation to social anxiety. He quickly noted that he believed he was doomed to have these reactions and that nothing could change them. He had made flushing, sweating, and being embarrassed part of his identity. As he learned the underlying neurobiology of SAD and the impact of early experience, he decided to believe that the SAD symptoms were not his fault and that they could be changed if he took the right steps.

With regard to correcting cognitive errors, however, Jeremy had his work cut out for him. He had spent years incorrectly ascribing negative thoughts to other people and putting himself down whenever he felt anxiety. Finding and correcting the invalid, incorrect, or illogical thoughts that dominated his self-appraisal and his actions would only take place with time and effort. He was willing to do it. A good example of how much work it took to identify and change his thoughts was how he changed his idea that people were paying attention to him and would not be accepting of how he looked. He had to correct that thought by observing himself first. I asked him to note what kinds of things he paid attention to when he was out, such as which people he noticed and what kinds of thoughts he had about them. He was able to see that he was usually thinking about his own business when he was out and noticed other people much less than he would have guessed. Then, he had to start changing his own thoughts (his cognitive errors) when he was out in public. He had to catch himself thinking some version of his normal self-deprecating thoughts like, "I bet I look flustered and stupid, and I bet everyone thinks I am a fool." Then he had to immediately correct the thought to a more accurate one that we worked out in therapy. He chose to say to himself, "I am a competent person and I can be confident in my choices. If I look embarrassed, other people will be sympathetic towards me." We bolstered his ability to believe the corrected thought by using EMDR to resolve his early life trauma and to install positive cognitions.

Another important part of Jeremy's early treatment was pharmacological intervention. Starting Jeremy on medication helped lower his feelings of fear while he began learning how to interpret new situations as not frightening. An SSRI lowered his overall noradrenergic arousal, and the occasional use of a benzodiazepine and beta-blocker made individual, planned relearning experiences work more effectively. (A more detailed description of Jeremy's pharmacological treatment is given in Chapter 11.)

STEP 2. ADDRESS PHYSIOLOGY

Changing the physical SAD fear response is challenging because the signs of social anxiety are mediated without conscious awareness. They are also visible to onlookers, so it is clear that others *will* notice. This fear of being noticed takes over and creates stronger signs of fear. Therefore, work to diminish physiological symptoms of SAD must occur simultaneously with the restructuring of negative cognitions about how others will respond to signs of their fear. That is why therapy usually starts with cognition and moves on to physiology.

Rule Out Physical Causes

This is necessary because certain medical conditions can create or exacerbate SAD symptoms. These must be treated medically before the client can recover from SAD. Table 10.3 details several medical conditions that mimic the symptoms of anxiety. Items to especially watch for in the medical conditions listed in the table are:

TABLE 10.3 Similarities Between Social Anxiety Symptoms and Medical Conditions

Possible Medical Condition	Anxiety Symptom
Heart problems	Tachycardia or palpitations
Thyroid problems	High thyroid creates shaky, nervous feelings
Hormone problems	Can simulate dread, shakiness, nervousness, or negativity
Hypoglycemia	Shakiness and tremors of hands and feelings of apprehension
Hypoadrenocorticism (adrenal fatigue)	Exhausted feelings, weakness

- Tachycardia or palpitations can be caused by a variety of problems, including mitral valve prolapse. The palpitations can be especially frightening, as they may be strong and intense, even though the cause is probably anxiety-generated overactivity in the peripheral nervous system.
- High thyroid or rapidly fluctuating thyroid levels are very likely to cause anxious sensations. Hashimoto's syndrome, an unusual thyroid condition that is overrepresented among people with PD and SAD, results in unpredictable thyroid function. When high, thyroid can simulate anxiety sensations. This condition is frustrating because of the difficulty in diagnosing it.
- Problems with female hormonal function can simulate anxiety, and the best way to diagnose this is to track it over a couple of months or look at recent changes such as postpartum. Evaluate for lifecycle changes, as perimenopause is a time of notoriously volatile emotional shifts for some women and may escape medical notice because the age range of onset is so variable.
- Hypoglycemia is too often ignored in psychotherapy and, sadly, in medical situations, yet it has quite an impact on anxious symptoms. This disorder can mimic a variety of mental health conditions and is not identifiable with the standard fasting blood sugar level. It can only be accurately diagnosed with a glucose tolerance test. The symptoms are likely to include some of the key SAD symptoms, including shakiness, tremors of hands, and feelings of apprehension.

- Hypoadrenocorticism (adrenal fatigue) leads to exhaustion and negativity, which complicate the picture of SAD social function.

Diaphragmatic Breathing and Progressive Muscle Relaxation

Lowering the excessive responsivity of the noradrenergic system in the brain is necessary if people with SAD are going to successfully change their behavior. This requires using the diaphragmatic breathing method discussed in Chapter 4 and the progressive muscle relaxation method discussed in Chapter 7. The goal is not so much to calm a flare-up of anxiety once it starts (as with PD) but rather to remain calm going into situations that could predictably cause anxiety. (The calmer you remain, the less likely you are to feel the norepinephrine surge of SAD.) Figure 10.1 diagrams the changes that occur when a person makes a conscious decision to breathe and think positive thoughts.

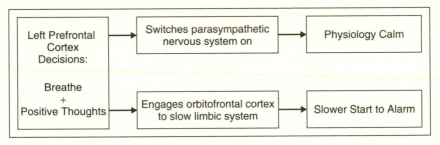

FIGURE 10.1. Social anxiety reaction—stop priming for it.

Mindfulness for Shifting Awareness

Various mindfulness techniques are excellent for stress management and anxiety disorders in general (Kabat-Zinn, 1991; Nhat Hanh, 1989; Samtorelli, 2002; Schwartz, 2005). These are useful with both adults and children (Semple, Reid, & Miller, 2005). Being mindful of current surroundings and internal states helps people ignore the beginning physical symptoms and thus decrease the buildup of those symptoms. A technique I call "Mindfulness for Shifting Awareness" is an excellent way of achieving this. It both calms the body and helps people remember that they can choose where to direct their attention. It provides a nonverbal, experiential lesson on self-control of attention.

MINDFULNESS FOR SHIFTING AWARENESS TECHNIQUE

1. Start by sitting comfortably with your eyes closed, and breathe evenly.
2. Follow the breath into your body as you breathe through your nose.
3. Notice each sensation as breath flows in. Notice the coolness of the air, the pressure of the airflow, and how it feels through your nose, throat, trachea, and lungs.
4. Follow the breath out of your body, exhaling through your mouth. Note the sensations of pressure change, the warmth of the breath, and how it feels through your mouth.
5. Without opening your eyes, become aware of every sound in the environment, paying special attention to location, intensity, and any movement that you can detect. Identify the layers of sounds—the subtle tones under the louder tones.
6. Focus on a sound that may fade away, such as a plane or car passing by, and use that focus to draw awareness back inside. Follow the breath back into the body.
7. Expand awareness of the body each time you return to it. Feel your heart beating or feel the blood flowing through the arteries and veins.
8. Again, follow the breath out of your body, noting the sensations of pressure change, the warmth of the breath, and how it feels exhaling through your mouth.
9. Repeat these steps several times.

Mindfulness exercises of all types are excellent for all age groups. They work with children and the elderly in particular because the technique does not require specific abstract cognitive processes. Distractibility is irrelevant, as when people feel distracted while doing this, they simply redirect their attention again.

Energy Therapies

Another method for managing physiological arousal is energy therapy, which goes by several names and comes in several versions: Energy Tapping, Thought Field Therapy, Emotional Self-Management, and Emotional Freedom Technique. These are all variations on tapping on acupressure points to reduce the energetic arousal of negative emotional states (Lambrou & Pratt, 2000; Gallo & Vincenzi, 2000). Tapping (with the fingers) on points that affect the meridians of energy that run through the body can decrease negative arousal rapidly. Some systems teach tapping in specific patterns to enhance the effect for specific types of arousal. Often within minutes of beginning the tapping, the body calms down. When physiology is calm, anxiety that was aroused by the thought is gone, and people can view the experience without seeing it as anxiety-producing. This is fear elimination at an energetic level, and although it is very useful for all types of anxiety, it is especially helpful for SAD, which is invariably triggered by specific thoughts.

Another benefit of the energy therapies is that they work for all age groups. Energy tapping is a terrific tool for children and adolescents because it allows them to manage their own arousal when they are not in the therapy office. Two excellent resources on this method are *Energy Tapping* by Fred Gallo and Harry Vincenzi (2000) and *Instant Emotional Healing* by Peter Lambrou and George Pratt (2000).

Three Deep Breaths and Good Preparation

This is a simple technique—a reminder for people to stay calm and focused when they go into settings that may cause social anxiety, such as giving a report at a work meeting or having to tell their supervisor they want to change their work schedule. "Three deep breaths and good preparation" is the tag phrase to remind people how to remain calm. The first part, "three deep breaths," presumes that the client will have been working on calming down panic symptoms by using diaphragmatic breathing and progressive muscle relaxation, as described in Chapters 4 and 7. Calming the body with a few breaths, as described for generalized anxiety, is the goal. The idea of "good preparation" is obvious, but it will remind clients to check in with themselves ahead of time: "Have I done what I need to do to be ready and do I have the skills I need to do it?" This would mean, for example, writing out notes for a report that they can easily read so they won't lose their train of thought, or practicing out loud several times the exact way they want to tell their boss they need a specific day off. If they are not ready, they must do more preparation. If they *are* ready, they can do thought-stopping with the statement, "Stop! I am prepared!" Then, going into the anxiety-producing situation, the person can repeat "three deep breaths and good preparation" as a reminder to breathe and believe in their preparation.

STEP 3. ADDRESS BEHAVIORS

In vivo social exposure is the primary means of addressing SAD behavior, but EMDR is also successful in the treatment of SAD, and this technique can be used in addition to in vivo exposure. Virtual reality therapy as a replacement for in vivo exposure is also promising. In addition to these techniques, long-term psychological treatment is often necessary to help clients recover from a lifetime's worth of negative experiences.

Preparing for In Vivo Exposure

Preparing clients for in vivo exposure is a critical first step. It involves:

- Assessing for social skills deficits
- Social skills training, including assertiveness training, conflict management, and anger management
- Systematic desensitization and/or EMDR

Assessing for Social Skills Deficits

Many SAD clients have very real social skills deficits, and these must be assessed before any significant progress can be made. To assess clients for social skills deficits, note their ability and willingness to:

- Ask others to go out socially. This applies to dating and friendships. This can crop up unexpectedly and therapists should be alert for surprising pockets of insecurity about social events.
- Do the social interactions of conducting personal business (e.g., writing checks; talking with retail personnel; purchasing, returning, or exchanging goods; questioning bills received).
- Conduct the business of their job (e.g., consulting a supervisor, talking with a coworker on break, talking with a coworker about a work situation).
- Assert their needs.
- Confront others when necessary, especially when their needs are being ignored.

Social Skills Training

In order for SAD clients to succeed at any level, they must have the necessary skills. Speaking up at a meeting or talking to a stranger requires social skill. In preparation for in vivo success, therapists must ensure that their clients are not only confident but also competent to carry out their plan. Why is this such an issue for people with SAD? For many, early childhood involved avoiding the very social experiences that would have taught these skills. I have treated many clients who are successful in their work but do not know how to go through a reception line at a wedding or balk at the thought of returning an item at a retail store. Sue Ellen was a case in point.

A midlevel manager at work, Sue Ellen had a family of her own and got along well with neighbors. However, she had been invited to a wedding and was feeling overwhelmed by her ignorance regarding how to conduct herself. Besieged with doubt about her ability to handle the situation without embarrassment, she had endless questions about what to wear, what to spend on a gift, where to put the gift, and what to say in the reception line. Her own wedding had been very small, she had never attended a friend's wedding, and she did not believe in her ability to figure out what to do. Her anxiety was greatly reduced and her confidence strengthened by getting clear information about social behavior. Successfully avoiding SAD symptoms at the wedding did wonders for her belief that she could cope in future social settings.

Many people with SAD are seriously impaired in their social and vocational achievement. This population is the least likely to be married or to rise to their full potential. Building social skills takes time and practice, but each small step brings clients closer to the minor social freedoms that improve their quality of life.

Social skills training improves success rates of in vivo exposure (Herbert et al, 2005; Vasey & Dadds, 2001). The training should be tailored to the individual client's needs. If clients are fearful of dating situations, they can be taught basic conversation skills and given tips on starting conversations with strangers and flirting. If interpersonal skills are an issue in the workplace, clients can be taught better ways of communicating with supervisors or coworkers. Job interviewing skills can be taught to clients seeking employment. Basic social skills training can be done in the therapy room, but community resources can also be put to valuable use. Community colleges, for example, often have classes for adults that fit various social skills needs such as job interviewing.

Assertiveness training. Learning that fear is not a necessary component of asking for what you want is important new information for the SAD brain. Assertiveness is an attitude that people with SAD must cultivate. Assertiveness means you believe your needs and wants count as much as those of everyone else and should be taken into consideration as much as others. When clients begin to value themselves equally to others in their life, they put themselves on an equal footing with their peers and family. On a personal level, they become more willing to take care of themselves: When people are assertive they are more likely to get the exercise, leisure, fun, and rest they need. As consumers, they are more likely to protect their rights when it comes to good service, returning products that are defective, or questioning inaccurate bills.

Clients with SAD tend to be unassertive because assertiveness puts them in the public eye. They will be noticed if they demand something. The unassertive attitude carries over to family life as well, because their shy temperaments lead them to avoid conflict. Unassertiveness causes a person to feel the stress of unmet needs plus the stress of undesired conflict. Improving assertiveness reduces stress and also helps SAD clients be less reactive to challenges.

So how does the SAD client develop this assertiveness? It usually takes some work to find the areas in which clients need to become more assertive, because they are often self-effacing enough that they have not or do not put demands on family or colleagues. They might be urged to look at whether they:

- Limit work each day to predictable, reasonable hours.
- Keep time for their personal needs, such as exercise, meditation, and healthful meals.
- Can say "no" to someone who makes a request when it would be inconvenient or difficult to give that person what was asked for.

Therapists looking for an in-depth discussion of assertiveness training can choose from the many books written on this subject. A few basic guidelines are provided here.

To build assertiveness at work, clients can:

- Ask about the time frame for work projects, so unreasonable expectations about job completion can be identified. Regardless of whether the unreasonable expectation is your own or someone else's, you need to know it so you can make a plan to resolve it. One style of asking another person to change their expectations is to say, "I have a problem and I need your help." Then describe what you perceive as the problem and ask the person how he or she wants you to resolve it. For example: "Boss, I have a problem and I need your help. You asked me to put all this stock back on the shelves immediately, but I am also supposed to help out with pricing right now. Which task do you want me to do first?" In this way the statement is not a complaint but rather a specific request. This approach also immediately puts both people on the same side of the problem: desiring to solve it.
- Learn to speak about obstacles to getting work done or about conflicts in work schedules. This ultimately leads to more reasonable workloads. Practicing the skills to ask questions and raise objections politely will help a great deal.
- Learn that asking for information is not objectionable to other people. In fact, it usually makes the entire communication process easier.
- Solve problems by making lists of pros and cons. When you feel convinced you have made a good choice, you will speak up for your point of view more cogently and with less fear.
- Always evaluate the result of the assertive action. When you see that your needs were met and that no one rejected you or stopped liking you, you will feel more comfortable in the future and your brain will be less likely to trigger fear.

Building assertiveness at home and taking care of personal needs pretty much start and end with mastering this concept: "Just because they ask does not mean you must say yes." Becoming more assertive—learning to say no—with family is tough. There is a simple action step to get around that problem. When the time comes to be more assertive and start saying no, don't start with "no." Rather, practice saying, "I'll think that over," or "let me get back to you," or "give me a minute to think about that." Do this for *every single* request someone makes of you, regardless of whether you want to say yes or not.

Ideas to help clients become more assertive can be found in *The Assertive Woman* (Phelps & Austin, 1975) and in *The Relaxation and Stress Reduction Workbook* (Davis, Eschelman, & McKay, 1998).

Conflict management. Already lacking in assertiveness, clients with SAD resist getting into conflict because they have no idea how to diffuse it without just giving in and being scared. Learning to apologize appropriately is very helpful. A good conflict-management technique is the "customer service apology."

When people call the phone company to complain about their bill or their service, the customer service agent does not tell them, "You have no right to be upset" or "We have a good reason for this." Instead, he or she starts out by saying, "I am so sorry you are having this problem. Let's see what we can do to make it right." This response helps to diffuse anger and foster cooperation in solving the problem. It is by no means an admission of guilt but rather a statement that the person wants to hear you out and work with you to solve the problem.

Good conflict management involves the following:

- Identifying the actions or inactions for which you are responsible—for example, "It is true that I was late and I did not call to let you know."
- Describing how the other person has been affected, including how the person feels as well as what practical issues occurred—"I know you missed sleep waiting up for me, and you were worrying about me while I was out, which was a rotten way to spend 2 hours."
- Explaining how this will not happen again—"I forgot my cell phone at my friend's house, and I didn't want to ask him to drive all the way back to get it. In the future I will double-check that I have my phone or will use someone else's to call if I will be late. Also, I will pay more attention to the time, and I will set my phone alarm to go off when it is time to leave for home."
- Asking for forgiveness and, if necessary, for help—"Will you forgive me for causing this problem for you?"

The acronym for this model is I.D.E.A., and it is a good idea for everyone to learn.

Anger management. There are many good models for handling anger. One that is particularly helpful for showing legitimate anger is D.E.S.K.:

D – Describe the behavior that angered you—for example, "You came home 2 hours after curfew last night and you did not call."

E – Express how you feel about it—"I am angry with you for being so inconsiderate as to not call, and angry because I was kept awake wondering if you were safe."

S – State what you want to happen or what you will do—"You will be punished for breaking the rules by not being allowed to go out Saturday night."

K – Know what will happen if you do not get what you want—"If you cause any trouble about curfew in the future, we will reconsider whether you can still drive the car for your social activities."

Systematic Desensitization

Systematic desensitization is an important part of preparing for successful in vivo exposure (Wolpe, 1990). A behavioral therapy technique, this method involves listing every feared aspect of a situation and rating how upsetting each is on a scale of 0–100. This creates a hierarchy from least disturbing to most disturbing. While imaging the least disturbing aspect of the feared situation, the client relaxes the body, breathes, and calms the mind until the body is totally relaxed. Then the next disturbing situation is brought up, and the client calms down to a 0 rating again. This continues until the client can imagine being in the most frightening aspect of the situation and remain totally calm, at which point the client is ready for in vivo exposure. (For a thorough description of the process of systematic desensitization, see Wolpe's *The Practice of Behavior Therapy,* 1990.)

The level and type of preparation for in vivo exposure will, of course, depend on the individual client's needs. Preparation for Joe, described in the following case study, involved learning relaxation techniques, social skills training, and systematic desensitization.

Joe's social skills were seriously impaired, and this had badly affected his life. His social anxiety was pervasive, and he especially hated being taken by surprise. Like many with SAD, it didn't take much to surprise him. He could hardly tolerate being in a store where a clerk might approach to ask if he needed help. He froze whenever he was taken unaware like this. Therefore, he tended to window shop and to frequent stores where such intrusions were unlikely.

Joe was well liked at work, but he had always kept a low profile job as a maintenance man who could work alone and only encounter people when they asked him to fulfill a work order. He was proud of the quality of his work, but he would never consider taking a position that offered more compensation because it would mean more exposure to others. He believed that coworkers did not reject him, but he had only one friend with whom he spent occasional social time, and he had never dated. With all those impairments, it might have seemed that Joe had bigger problems than going to the mall to shop. However, that was his social outing every weekend. He wanted to be among people, but in a way he could control.

Joe did all of the preparatory steps of breathing, relaxation, and cognitive restructuring to prepare for the in vivo outing, but social skills training was a vital part of getting him ready for a successful experience. He practiced in therapy all the skills of talking with clerks, thanking them for their help, declining their help, asking for information, and so on. This kind of practice made him more confident that he would be able to use these skills in a real-life situation.

After Joe had practiced these skills, we began systematic desensitization. Once he was able to completely relax while imagining that he was talking with a clerk in a store, he began exposure to the real thing. He started by just window shopping—calming himself as he stood outside imagining that he was talking to a clerk he could see. Then he took charge by entering the store, walking up to the clerk to ask a brief question, and then leaving. Eventually he was able to browse in the store without worrying if he would be "surprised" by an offer of help.

In Vivo Social Exposure

The left side of the amygdala needs many opportunities to learn that social exposure is not dangerous. To help the emotional brain learn, real-life exposure to feeling the fear and overcoming it is necessary (Herbert, 2005). To that end, SAD treatment includes planned, rehearsed, and orchestrated experiences of trying social behaviors in the real setting that the client fears. This exposure to the feared situation should be made in small steps after the client has undergone the proper preparation. It should also be timed to gradually increase the length or depth of exposure. For example, if the exposure goal is to be seated in a movie theater without fear, the client initially goes for as long as can be tolerated and then leaves, perhaps sitting first in the back and gradually increasing exposure to sitting in the middle.

As the following case description shows, in vivo exposure includes the following:

- Cognitive restructuring from above
- Calming physiology with breathing and relaxation
- Calming the mind with thought-stopping and thought-replacement
- Attention to positive outcomes
- Possible use of as-needed medication

Therapy for Jeremy, introduced at the beginning of the chapter, began with identifying some of his false beliefs. He was especially stuck on the idea that if people observed him sweating, they would judge him as undesirable and he would lose their respect. He further believed that if people looked at him he would turn red. To challenge these beliefs, he applied several of the cognitive methods described earlier. The one that helped most was searching for situations that disprove false beliefs. He began to note that at work coworkers came to him for advice, and that when they sought him in his office, he was calm and did not turn red. He then began to notice other examples of times when he did not feel the fear of talking. For example, if he was the first one in a meeting room, he could tolerate others' coming in after him and be calmer about having to speak. He also noted that the longer he had to wait to speak, the worse his fear became. After noticing these situations, Jeremy began to believe that he was often calm and could remain calm talking with others if he practiced his techniques.

Four aspects of the in vivo plan emerged from these observations:

- Thought-stopping and thought-replacement while in the presence of others, to assist in keeping the focus on the activity and not on the buildup of fear.
- Elimination of cognitive distortions and taking small steps to increase tolerance of anxiety. Jeremy was instructed to note that feelings are just feelings. He also was instructed to pay attention to his successes.
- Following the "three deep breaths and good preparation" model for handling speaking in front of others. This requires knowing and practicing diaphragmatic breathing and progressive muscle relaxation. It also involves preparing notes and practicing giving reports or speaking in group settings.
- Judicious use of medication on an as-needed basis to keep fear at a tolerable level while learning to calm down in the present moment.

In the first part of the plan, the goal was not to speak more effectively, but to reduce anticipatory anxiety when Jeremy was in the meeting itself. To manage that, Jeremy used thought-stopping and thought-replacement (see Chapter 7) to stop his fearful thoughts when he was in a meeting. He practiced this in conversations when coworkers came into his office, focusing attention instead on what others were saying to him. Then he tried it in meetings. He took notes on what others said, thought about the implications of what others were doing, and generally dragged his attention from his fear of speaking to the content of the meeting. This was not only distracting but also practical, as it made his own contributions more effective. When he felt that he was getting better at thought-stopping, he rated the degree of fear he felt when it was his turn to present information. He noted his fear had decreased just by virtue of having little anticipatory anxiety.

The second part of the in vivo plan involved learning to tolerate being observed. Jeremy was accustomed to going into a meeting room before others arrived. He felt much calmer when he was seated before others got there. To identify his negative thoughts about what others might think when he walked in, Jeremy tried the ABCD technique. This helped him realize that he believed that his coworkers were waiting to see if he was going to sweat. He then asked himself, "How do I know that my coworkers are watching me to see if I sweat?" When he thought about this question, he realized that there was no evidence that this was indeed what his coworkers were doing.

This gave him the courage to practice going into the room when a few people were already present, and then go in even a little later. He was able to accomplish this by observing that most people were absorbed in their own thoughts and their own agenda for the meeting and were not too concerned about how he looked. Remembering that his feeling was just a feeling also helped. He was gradually able to enter a room for a meeting when most people had arrived without turning red. These successes were given due attention, and Jeremy made a conscious effort to remember them whenever he started to feel nervous.

The third part of the plan involved learning to speak more effectively without nervousness. Most of the time Jeremy was not called on spontaneously in meetings. Although he attended many meetings every week, he usually knew ahead of time what he would be expected to comment on. This was the time to learn relaxation and breathing. He learned diaphragmatic breathing and how to breathe with no one noticing. He practiced his breathing when others were present to be sure he could do it without feeling observed. As he became comfortable with breathing, he also practiced muscle relaxation. Although tension was not his problem, being able to relax his body helped eliminate flushing, because the fear response was calmed more quickly.

Using the "three deep breaths and good preparation" technique, Jeremy was able to induce relaxation during meetings. He wrote up brief reminder notes that he could glance at comfortably to keep his contribution in the meeting succinct and to the point. He observed that many people referred to notes when they gave reports, and that observation made him feel calmer as well. Now he was ready. He learned to use three slow, deep breaths in the space of time just before he was to talk. This calmed his tremulous voice, slowed his heart rate, and reduced the degree of flushing. As he spoke, he knew that he was ready and thus did not spend time fretting over what he would say. Every time his report went more smoothly and with less embarrassment, he felt better and better.

Jeremy deliberately noticed his feelings and the group response, and he consciously remembered these positive experiences whenever he faced situations that made him nervous. He was filtering for positives, and he was using the learning technique of mentally noticing what went right, not what went wrong.

When he was finally asked to begin leading his team meetings, Jeremy became nervous all over again, but he had the skills to cope. He agreed to use beta-blockers in addition to his other relaxation methods for the first two times of leading meetings. When he "soloed" after that, he was successful enough at controlling his fear response that he was able to lead meetings without any anticipatory anxiety.

These successes increased Jeremy's confidence and his willingness to venture into new settings. He was ready to work on his two original goals: dating and job interviewing, which he accomplished with more ease than he ever hoped for.

As-Needed Medication

Jeremy's is the type of situation in which using medication on an as-needed basis may be effective, but it is one of the very few situations in psychotherapy where this is the case. Psychotherapy's goal is to give people control of symptoms, and using medication only when anxious is generally unwise. It communicates that drugs, not a person's effort, are solving the anxiety. But occasionally as-needed medication helps. After assuring that the steps are small and likely to be successful, clients may take medication about an hour before going into the in vivo exposure situation. (For obvious reasons, this should not be the first time they try the medication.) Although the antianxiety medication will tone down the anxiety reaction, some nervousness will show up in anticipation or in execution of the plan. This nervousness can be dealt with using the nonpharmacological methods discussed earlier. The fact of feeling less nervous because of medication does not interfere with the amygdala's learning that the situation was okay and there was no need to feel scared. To avoid clients' coming to believe that medication is always necessary, limit the use to once or twice before going into the in vivo situation without medication.

Virtual Reality Therapy

There has recently been research into using virtual reality therapies for desensitization and calming anxieties, including airplane phobia (Botella, 2004). (Airplane phobia is either a specific phobia or SAD problem, depending on the reasons for the phobic response.) Virtual therapy has also been used to desensitize people to traumatic experience (combat) and for exposure-related treatments, as in SAD (Klinger et al., 2005). This method is promising as a replacement for in vivo, because it is easier to guide timed exposures and because it allows the therapist to be present during the exposure. The drawback to this therapy is availability of equipment, software, and therapists who know how to utilize the tools and the method appropriately. As this method becomes more well known and the equipment more readily available, it may become a highly effective replacement for many types of in vivo exposure.

EMDR

EMDR, a treatment method that relieves the impact of traumatic experience, can lead to rapid recovery when the client is ready to progress but is held back by factors that do not respond to talk therapy. Developed by psychologist Francine Shapiro (Shapiro, 2001), this amazingly versatile treatment is primarily utilized for resolving the trauma of PTSD, but it can also diminish anxiety, depression, OCD symptoms, and pain. It can also assist in relapse problems with various addictions and be used to enhance performance. It is successful with all age groups and has remarkable applications for use with children and for traumas that occurred in early childhood, even when those traumas are not addressed in therapy until later in life. Research studies convincingly demonstrate the effectiveness of EMDR for reprocessing experience, desensitizing reactions to cues of trauma, and causing new learning about past experience (Bergman, 1998; Shapiro, 2001). Figure 10.2 illustrates how this works.

Led by an experienced practioner, the method involves creating a target image of a trauma and all the associated sensory experiences and cognitions that were present at the time of the trauma. A subjective units of dis-

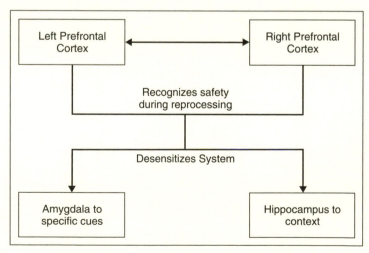

FIGURE 10.2. EMDR opens communication.

tress (SUDS) rating is taken and monitored throughout the process. The client receives bilateral stimulation of the brain via sight, sound, or touch, using one of several different mechanisms, such as a light bar that is followed by the eyes, a tapping mechanism, or headphones with tones in alternate earpieces. Changes in the memory of the trauma occur, as this method stimulates processing of the experience at a neurological level. The result is new learning about the event and consequential relief of the traumatizing fear and subsequent anxiety. There are different theories of how this occurs, but certain studies suggest that brain activity, stimulated while reconstructing and safely reexperiencing the trauma, changes the stress response and the sensitized amygdala reaction.

In the treatment of SAD, EMDR is the best method to handle two types of problems: eliminating anticipatory anxiety and letting go of "shame trauma." The target image is the feared situation. The EMDR process then proceeds as follows:

1. The client selects the moment that epitomizes the anticipated anxiety.
2. The client identifies all of the sensations that accompany it.
3. The client to identifies the negative cognitions.
4. Get the SUD rating.
5. Begin the EMDR technique.
6. At an appropriate time in the process, ask the client to go to the earliest memory of having the feeling—not to the circumstances but rather to the emotion of the event that is anticipated.
7. Process those emotions with the EMDR method.
8. Install positive images of acting without anxiety in the feared situation, and install the new positive cognition (VOC).

EMDR is unparalleled for getting at underlying connections to earlier life experiences that block recovery. What happens almost invariably is that the client recalls the earliest traumatic memory of shame related to the anticipated situation. By desensitizing and reprocessing that shame experience, the client's amygdala sensitivity to future cues of the trauma is greatly reduced or completely eliminated.

When there is anticipatory anxiety due to experiences that are not particularly traumatic, the EMDR method works exceptionally well to increase feelings of competence and confidence, enhancing clients' self-image of successfully performing in the feared situation. Practitioners of EMDR know how to install positive thoughts after desensitizing past experience, and this aspect of the technique is useful for all with SAD.

Robert was a good example of a SAD client who responded rapidly to EMDR. He was about 40 years old when he came in for psychotherapy. He had no interest in psychotherapy in general because he believed he got along fine in the world. He could always get out of things he did not want to do due to his general shyness and wish to avoid the spotlight. He was married with kids and had a good job in a manufacturing plant. His wife handled all phone calls at home and all of the shopping.

Then Robert got a promotion. At first the increased visibility as a manager was not so bad for him, because he knew the men he was supervising at the plant. What finally got to him was that his new boss was coming into town and wanted to have dinner with him. Robert did not go out to dinner. Never. When he did, he feared being observed while eating, and his hands would shake. He feared dropping food in his lap and being the object of scorn. His heart raced at the mere thought of having to eat with his boss, and he was thinking of quitting before he had to face the horror of the meal. In short, his SAD symptoms were finally demanding that he get some outside help.

He went to work fast in therapy, learning and utilizing energy tapping to great advantage and learning to breathe to calm himself down. However, the dinner with his boss was not far off, and although he was doing better, he had anticipatory anxiety about embarrassing himself with shaking hands and dropping food. It took only one EMDR session to reveal that Robert had been the victim of shame trauma when he tried out for the basketball team in eighth grade. He missed shots that other boys were making, and the coach encouraged the whole group to laugh when he tried to do a layup and failed three times in a row. With EMDR Robert was able to re-view this scene and learn for the first time that the coach was wrong and most of his classmates felt forced to laugh out of coercion. He was sur-prised that events from his early adolescence were reverberating into his adult relationships, causing him to fear being the one who was noticed and to be humiliated if he was. EMDR was so successful for Robert that he found it hard to believe that the rapid changes would actually stick. But the dinner with his boss went off without a hitch, and Robert saw improvement of his symptoms in other areas of his life as well.

Long-Term Psychological Treatment

Therapy must address other complications of SAD and life experience to prepare a client for complete recovery. Many forms of long-term psychotherapy are appropriate to ameliorate the impact of negative life experience, and the type of therapy is adjusted to the degree of psycholog-ical damage the SAD client has suffered. Social anxiety disorder shapes life experience and the client with SAD will typically be less resilient to trau-matic experience due to the strong tendency to withdraw in the face of anxiety. Selecting the treatment for the life trauma is complex, and the in-terweaving of symptom management with long-term treatment is best left to the experienced clinician.

DEALING WITH ADDICTION
IN SOCIAL ANXIETY DISORDER CLIENTS

Many people with SAD self-medicate, often with alcohol, to diminish anxiety when in social settings. Drinking before a social function is often an indicator of using alcohol to smooth the social pathway. When clients use alcohol or other drugs (including prescription medication) addictively, the addiction recovery must be part of the long-term treatment plan for SAD (Kushner et al., 2005).

Although the effective treatment of alcoholism is beyond the scope of this discussion, aspects of alcoholism treatment are exceedingly helpful for SAD. In particular, participation in a 12-step self-help group or other recovery group provides guided interactions with others and allows for gradual increasing of participation without a lot of demand. Also, an intentional side effect of the meetings is to build a supportive group outside of the meeting time, which allows people with SAD to practice social skills like conversation and thus build success in interacting with others. Those same benefits accrue to SAD clients who attend meetings for family members of addicted persons, such as Al-Anon.

DEALING WITH RELAPSE TO ANXIETY AFTER GOOD PROGRESS

All anxiety clients fear their progress is only temporary. If they ever experience a bad day, they know for certain they will never be able to function without anxiety again. Clients with SAD are worse than panic sufferers with this fear because they generally are, by temperament, not very resilient and prone to having low expectations of their abilities. As they practice life skills, desensitization, and in vivo exposure, they must be assured that relapses are inevitable. When dealing with relapse, it is helpful to:

- Explore clients' cognitions about what it means to relapse and reframe those experience as:
  - Learning
  - Opportunities to practice
  - Opportunities to use new applications of their methods
- Reduce shame over relapse by utilizing psychoeducational explanations of how unexpected changes in situations spike anxiety on a biological level.
- Redefine success as going forward again after a misstep, armed with new learning about surviving the experience.

TREATMENT OF CHILDREN WITH SOCIAL ANXIETY DISORDER

Social anxiety disorder is the most likely of all anxiety disorders to begin early in childhood. Specific considerations in treating children should be taken into account. The first is that their symptoms and ability to respond to treatment will vary considerably with age (Eisen, Kearney, & Schaefer, 1995; Eisen & Schaefer, 2005; Lyneham & Rapee, 2005). In addition to noting how the child's symptoms change in different contexts (school versus home), therapists must assess the child's:

- Cognitive ability with regard to age and developmental level
- Comprehension of his or her emotions
- Understanding of the circumstances that elicit anxiety
- Capacity to express him- or herself

Early on, it is possible for parents, teachers, and counselors to see the temperamental indications that anxiety might become a problem. Children with SAD in the works tend to:

- Show excessive shyness
- Worry about calamity befalling parents
- Have a morbid fear of being sick, kidnapped, or killed
- Have problems sleeping alone
- "Shadow" the parents or cling
- Have physical symptoms like nausea and visit the school nurse often
- Develop school resistance or avoidance
- Be slow to warm up to new people or appear withdrawn
- Become easily embarrassed or humiliated
- Have solemn demeanor
- Seek reassurance often
- Be socially competent with one or two good friends but have few acquaintances and little interest in group activities like parties (although they may enjoy sports teams)

The signs of avoidance are quite obvious. They want to:

- Skip school (may develop into school phobia)
- See the nurse
- Stay close to home or a parent (separation anxiety)
- Avoid all anxiety-arousing situations

Children with SAD may become quite aggressive or oppositional when pushed to do things that make them anxious, especially as they may be too young to know or explain the nature of their fear. Even very articulate children of 8, 9, or 10 years of age, who seem capable of explaining most anything, are still too young to put their experiences of anxiety into words.

They are more likely to feel the somatic arousal of anxiety and complain of stomach ache or headache than to recognize the feelings as fear. This type of somatic arousal was particularly evident with Megan.

Like many anxious children, Megan was sweet and quite bright. She showed signs of shy temperament from the day she was born. She did not warm easily to strangers, she averted her eyes when visitors tried to chuck her under the chin, and she hid behind her mother's legs whenever a new person came to the house. She managed school with a great deal of tearfulness and demanded that her mother be the first in line to pick her up. She begged her mother not to leave the area when Megan had practice for soccer or choir.

In the third grade, Megan started throwing up whenever she was apart from her mother. Although she was okay if she was at home with her father, her mother was the only one who could soothe her. If Megan went to a girlfriend's house for an overnight, she would be on the phone by 11 P.M. asking for a ride home. She would throw up if her mother and father went out for the evening, thus requiring them to come home early because she was "sick." Megan could say that she was afraid her mother would never return or would die, but she didn't recognize her nausea as a symptom of anxiety.

Although therapists can help educate and guide parents of children with SAD, actual treatment of the disorder is largely in the parents' hands. This is because children have a hard time recreating anxiety in the office, especially if they are comfortable with their parents there. Children's SAD symptoms are prompted by real-life situations, and doing desensitization and relearning is best when the anxiety is felt. There are many ways to go about teaching children anxiety-coping skills for school-related problems, including giving them age-appropriate ways to talk back to anxiety (Chansky, 2004), finding test-taking strategies, offering alternatives to solo speeches, and teaching social skills (Bernstein, Layne, & Egan, 2005; Dawson & Guare, 2004; Eisen & Schaefer, 2005). The following guidelines are useful for teachers and parents helping children with SAD:

- Do not attempt to make sense of what the child worries about or talk the child out of it. Children are often too young to dispute their irrational fears in a formal way. Rather, redirect children's focus to the times they do well or succeed.
- Do not push shy children into situations that terrify them. They will only learn that the situation really was frightening and that they failed to tolerate it.
- Encourage children to enter new situations, but allow them to warm up slowly. Encourage them by suggesting a short frame of time for the experience, such as "Try it for a few minutes."

- Do not fall into the trap of reassuring them. Reassurance is futile for most anxiety problems. There will be no end to the details that need to be covered if a child can engage parents, teachers, or therapists in a game of "Promise me I will be okay if . . .." It is okay to reassure children that they can cope and have skills, but when reassuring becomes a pattern of interaction, it does not produce a lasting calmness. Rather, redirect children to tell you about how they know they will handle the problem.
- Encourage problem-solving. What would the child like to do? How could the child handle a fear? How long can the child be in a situation without feeling too afraid, and how can the child leave while feeling competent?
- Avoid discussing the child's shyness in front of peers or siblings.
- Avoid threatening punishment. The child would do the activity if he or she were not terrified.
- Work in small steps toward facing the fear, discouraging complete avoidance of feared situations.
- Remind children of what they gain by doing what they fear and ask them what they might lose by *not* doing what they fear.

Although parents are responsible for basic treatment, therapists can use their skills with EMDR and energy tapping to great advantage with children. Using age-appropriate play and rehearsal techniques to teach social understanding and social skills is also helpful. Children can learn all of the techniques for physiological management, and these methods can be used when children feel sick to their stomach and or have anxious thoughts. Children also respond well to physical activity such as dancing or exercise, art-making, and games of all kinds to divert attention and teach them how to feel better. Depending on the child and the cause of the anxiety, these therapeutic techniques can reduce children's anxiety significantly. This was the case with Megan, who responded quickly and dramatically to EMDR.

Megan identified staying overnight at a girlfriend's house as her target situation. Because this had happened recently, she remembered how much she had wanted to go home after a few hours away from her parents. While experiencing her anxiety, she began to think that she knew her girlfriend well and liked her, and she remembered that her parents were only a phone call away. She spontaneously began to say to herself new statements such as "There is no reason to feel scared." She suddenly felt as if she was not scared, and she decided she wanted to try staying overnight with her friend. To everyone's amazement, Megan was soon able to tolerate being away from her parents, and several months after the session I received a report that she was still doing well. Megan would now be able to learn many of the important social skills that she might have missed had she continued to avoid being away from her parents.

Children and Cognitions of Social Anxiety Disorder

Some of the best cognitions to defeat anxiety are mostly learned through life experience. However, like all people with SAD, children develop self-explanatory styles that are socially self-defeating and anxiety-producing (Lonegan & Phillips, 2001). It is highly effective for parents and children to watch for and correct cognitive errors as children tell stories about their social experience (Cartwright-Hatton, McNally, & White, 2005; Rapee, 2001). Parents can learn to identify cognitive errors and reinforce the following cognitive corrections:

- Things happen. Everyone has a bad experience once in a while.
- Bad things happen to good people. Many bad experiences are not your fault. If you actually did something wrong, you can correct it.
- Focus on the positive things that happen to you. Rehashing memories of bad experiences only teaches you how to do things wrong again.

In terms of assertiveness training there are some significant teaching differences between children and adults. Children are more concrete and less able to generalize information. Additionally, with each passing year, their abilities to learn and reflect on life change. So do their social experiences. Therefore, they have to relearn some skills over each year. Until about age 17, it is best to teach children new lessons on social and assertiveness skills.

- Teach conflict-management skills deliberately and repeatedly at each age, because conflict and cognitive skills change. This means that conflict-management styles will also change.
- The same applies to problem-solving skills. Teach these by doing problem-solving in academic, social, and family settings—and by doing it over and over (Dawson & Guare, 2004).

Dealing With the Families of Children with Social Anxiety Disorder

Parents tend to fall into one of two camps: They push too hard or they let the child off the hook altogether. Learning to find the right balance requires monitoring the child's reaction to each situation.

- If children are pushed into something and find the experience too difficult, they will show it by crying, refusing to do it again, and demonstrating signs of fear and distress. If those signs do not *completely* disappear, the experience was negative.
- Negative experiences teach children that their fear came true: The situation was too much and they were too incompetent to handle it. That learning causes the child to refuse future similar activities.

- Letting children completely off the hook is a tacit agreement that they are incompetent, and the children will never strengthen social muscles and self-confidence.

The biggest concern is helping parents not to do everything for the child with SAD—or with any other kind of anxiety disorder. The family often wants to mitigate the suffering, so they will take over chores that seem too hard, speak for the child in social gatherings, excuse the child's withdrawal, and stay home with the child rather than go out. Families may even actively argue with a therapist who wants to push a child or adolescent to do more frightening activities, because they hate to see their loved one suffer. The family needs the same education the therapist might provide to an adult client, which helps boost compliance with treatment goals (Dadds & Roth, 2001).

CONCLUSION

People with SAD present the most complicated problems and require the most complex treatment because so many skills must be learned and interwoven for the best success. Physical calming, handling false beliefs, skill-building, and developing confidence are all necessary before success in social venues may be experienced. In my experience, the reward of seeing someone who felt socially disabled go forward in having a fulfilling social experience is worth all the planning and effort that the therapist and client do together.

I often quote an old Chinese proverb to my SAD clients as we make our way through the therapy journey: "A journey of a thousand miles begins with a single step." Take time to lay out a sketch of what steps you will be following and note what kinds of achievements you expect to see along the way. Every small step of progress is necessary, even if not sufficient for complete recovery, and the sense of accomplishment at mastering those steps is worth noticing. Without the first steps toward social competence, none of the others may follow

CHAPTER ELEVEN

MEDICATING FOR SOCIAL ANXIETY DISORDER

As discussed in Chapter 9, SAD presents in two forms. Specific social phobia is marked by the anticipation of being humiliated or embarrassed in specific situations such as public speaking. Generalized social phobia is marked by a fear of all social situations in which the sufferer might feel scrutinized by other people. Specific social anxiety is not as debilitating as the generalized form, which leads to marked avoidance of all social situations that may be associated with a fear of being humiliated and scrutinized.

The most challenging aspect of treating social anxiety is the behavior of intense avoidance of anxiety-producing circumstances. This is because the trigger for the symptoms is typically identifiable and avoidable. Anticipatory anxiety—fear of humiliation, shame, or embarrassment—causes the symptoms that therapy targets for treatment. Whereas PD patients anticipate with fear another panic attack, the anticipatory anxiety of SAD is focused on becoming visibly embarrassed in social settings. Therefore, the SAD sufferer avoids social settings to avoid the potential of having symptoms that others can observe. Such social avoidance interferes with all the kinds of learning and growth that naturally accrue to new experiences. The cognitive symptoms of anticipatory anxiety, if they are debilitating, are treated with medications that diminish rumination and negativity.

The physiological picture of social anxiety includes most of the same symptoms as PD, but they tend to involve more of the cardiovascular (palpitations and flushing), sweating, and muscle tremor symptoms that are associated with the peripheral nervous system. Thus, medications for the physiology of SAD target the neurobiological causes of the disorder in

235

order to make psychotherapy for anxiety, social deficits, and improving skills as effective as possible.

There are estimates that up to 10% of the population over age 18 may experience SAD, with 6.8% in any given year being diagnosed with this disorder (National Institute of Mental Health, 2006). Like so many other psychiatric illnesses, this disorder has a higher prevalence in females than in males in the general population. However, in clinical samples, men may have a higher prevalence than women in seeking treatment (*American Psychiatric Association,* 2000). As with other anxiety disorders, there is a genetic contribution to SAD, as it has higher incidence between first-degree relatives.

Children who have heightened anxiety when faced with new social situations are at higher risk to develop SAD (Reiss, Silverman, & Weems, 2001). There is a strong correlation between children who have separation anxiety and the development of social anxiety in late adolescence and adulthood (Morris, 2001).

RISKS ASSOCIATED WITH SOCIAL ANXIETY DISORDER

Unfortunately, like many of the other anxiety disorders, SAD is debilitating if not treated. Risks associated with SAD, especially if it begins in childhood or adolescence include:

- Less advanced education, as children may refuse school or hold back from pursuing avocational and academic options that might place them in the limelight at school or in the community. Adults might hold back from applying for grants or scholarships or pursuing higher education because of the need to complete interviews.
- Impairment of social skills, possibly loss of social contact.
- Less rewarding life from avoiding activities that could be enriching, pleasurable, and satisfying.
- Less financial success and career satisfaction from difficulty achieving promotion or maintaining employment. (For example, people may not speak well in meetings or may not bring their work performance to the attention of superiors. Worse, a person with SAD might stay in a job that limits contact with unfamiliar people and thus stay in low-paying employment.)

THE ETIOLOGY OF SOCIAL ANXIETY DISORDER

Social anxiety disorder and PD have some neurobiology in common. For some people, the experience of a panic attack in a social setting triggers fear of the social setting and leads to social avoidance. In these people, the underlying neurobiology is like that of PD but a different cognitive frame-work—the fear of being observed to be panicky—leads to the development of SAD.

The Neurobiological Causes of Social Anxiety Disorder

Chapter 5 explained the neurobiology of PD; the same neurotransmitter and neuroanatomical dysfunctions can explain the physiological symptoms of SAD as well. These include the functions of norepinephrine (NE), sero-tonin (SE), gamma aminobutyric acid (GABA), and the neuroanatomical structures of the basal ganglia (BG) and the peripheral nervous system. However, there are some additional possibilities regarding why a person may develop SAD instead of (or possibly in addition to) PD.

The Behavioral Inhibitory System

One explanation for why some develop social anxiety instead of PD is that these people may have a predisposition for social avoidance due to sensi-tivity in the behavioral inhibitory system (Gray, 1995). A growing body of information about dopamine (DA) and serotonin (SE) and their roles in experiencing pleasure and reward (satisfaction) has made it clear that peo-ple have different degrees of temperamental intensity to seek pleasure. Ad-ditionally, knowledge about the impact of the fear response from the amygdala, the overreactivity in the stress response, and heightened norepi-nephrine (NE) supports the theory that some people are by temperament more inclined than others to pull back from situations that are anxiety-pro-ducing. Overreactivity in the inhibitory system could increase anticipatory anxiety by causing excessive withdrawal in the face of anxiety-producing stimuli. This might explain the oversensitivity to the *feeling* of anxiety that is reported in people with SAD, and which is evident in childhood.

The Norepinephrine Connection

The locus coeruleus (part of the pons above the brainstem, a more primi-tive level of the brain) has a dense concentration of norepinephrine (NE) neurons. This area is implicated when there is an excess of NE. In SAD, more than in panic, the effects from elevated NE affect the peripheral ner-vous system and trigger many of the signs of social anxiety: sweating, blushing, tremors, and elevated heart rate or palpitations. The tremors and blushing are feared visible signs of distress that people with social anxiety anticipate to cause humiliation and rejection.

Dysregulation of Serotonin

Serotonin (SE) dysregulation may cause some of the symptoms seen in SAD. Thus, the first-line medications used to treat social anxiety disorders are the selective serotonin reuptake inhibitors (SSRIs).

A theory of why SE dysregulation may underlie social anxiety is based on the impact of increased SE on cognition, emotion, and physiology. Higher SE levels tend to produce less negativity (a change in the limbic system), less anticipatory anxiety (due to improved anterior cingulate gyrus flexibility), and more energy in the prefrontal cortex to counter negative cognitions.

Research on the impact of the SSRIs and how they may balance the SE distribution in the nervous system has led to those observations of change. Many effects occur on the nerve cells when adding an SSRI. As with NE (see the discussion in Chapter 5 on the receptors for NE), SE neurons that release SE have receptors for SE called auto-receptors. When SE is released from the presynaptic neuron in to the synapse between cells, the neurotransmitters can be taken up by either the presynaptic neuron or the postsynaptic nerve cells. By blocking reuptake on the presynaptic neuron, SSRIs may cause an initial increase in the available SE at the dendrite of the presynaptic nerve. The increase eventually down-regulates the SE auto-receptors (causes a decrease in the number of auto-receptors) and rebalances the SE function in the presynaptic nerve cell. The net effect is to increase the amount of SE flowing down the presynaptic nerve cell into the vesicles. The vesicles then release more SE into the synaptic space, which eventually causes an SE rebalance in the postsynaptic nerve cell.

MEDICATIONS USED IN TREATING SOCIAL ANXIETY DISORDER

The medications for SAD are the same ones used for all anxiety disorders, but the impact of these medications on different systems and neurotransmitters indicates that they will be used somewhat differently, especially when both generalized social anxiety and specific social anxiety are comorbid. It is important in the treatment of social anxiety to allow the brain to "relearn" that specific situations are no longer anxiety-producing. Thus, the practice of using medication on an as-needed basis to block anxious physiological responses while doing in vivo psychotherapy practice is more common with SAD than with other anxiety disorders. Table 11.1 summarizes the neurotransmitter and neuroanatomical contributions to SAD and the medications used to treat those problems.

TABLE 11.1 Etiologies of Social Anxiety and Medication Choices

Etiology of Social Anxiety	Symptoms	Medications
Increased NE at peripheral nerve receptors	Sweating, blushing, increased heart rate, increased tremors	Beta-blockers: Inderal (propranolol) Tenormin (atenolol)
Increased release of NE from presynaptic nerve cell	Increased tension (which heightens anticipatory anxiety), increased heart rate, increased startle	Alpha-2 auto-receptor agonists: Catapres (clonidine hydrochloride)
Dysregulation of GABA receptor area	Increased rumination: anxiety and worry (over expectation of rejection)	Benzodiazepines: Xanax (alprazolam) Klonopin (clonazepam) Ativan (lorazepam) Serax (oxazepam) Valium (diazepam)
Deficient chloride channel transmission	Increased tension, increased heart rate, increased flushing	Benzodiazepines (see above)
Kindling (increased firing of nerve cells)	Increased panic for SAD sufferers who have panic symptoms in social settings, increased heart rate, increased flushing	Anticonvulsants: Neurontin (gabapentin) is the most studied
Dysregulation of basal ganglia	Increased anxiety, irritability, tendency to freeze	No known medication that absolutely works on this area
Amygdala sensitivity to negative facial expressions and reactions in others	Increased fear reaction, increased avoidance reactions	SSRIs: Prozac (fluoxetine) Zoloft (sertraline) Paxil (paroxetine) Luvox (fluvoxamine) Celexa (citalopram) Lexapro (escitalopram)

TABLE 11.1   Etiologies of Social Anxiety and Medication Choices
(continued)

Etiology of Social Anxiety	Symptoms	Medications
Comorbid depression (anxiety is part of the depression)	Increased depression	BuSpar (buspirone; see Table 8.2) SSRIs (see above) Tricyclics (see Table 5.4) MAOIs (see Table 5.5)
	Increased anxiety	SSNRIs: Effexor (venlafaxine) Cymbalta (duloxetine) Atypical SSRIs: Remeron (mirtazepine) Desyrel (trazodone hydrocholoride)

Medications to Decrease Release of Norepinephrine

Slowing the release of or interfering with the action of norepinephrine (NE) is an important function of medication for social anxiety. This can cause relief of the most distressing and visible symptoms of anxiety: tachycardia, flushing, and tremors. Two types of medication are especially effective. Alpha-2 agonists, such as Catapres (clonidine hydrochloride), slow down the release of NE from the presynaptic nerve. This has the effect "of stepping on the brakes" for the release or firing of NE. Medications such as beta-blockers also are often indicated. Beta-blockers are cardiac medications that slow down the effects of NE not only on the heart but also on the peripheral nervous system. Table 11.2 details the use of Catapres and the beta-blockers that are used to treat SAD.

Medications to Raise Serotonin

There are several types of drugs in the category of serotonergic medications that have been observed to lower anxiety. BuSpar (buspirone) and the SSRIs are the most frequently used from this category.

TABLE 11.2 Beta-Blockers and Alpha-2 Auto-Receptor Agonists

Drug Name	Main Effect	Side Effects	Dose Range and Frequency	Considerations for Use	Withdrawal Pattern
Inderal (propranolol)	Blocks NE effects on peripheral nerve receptors	Slowed heart rate, drowsiness	10–80mg	Often used on an as-needed basis 2 hours before an anxiety-provoking experience	None if used on an as-needed basis
Tenormin (atenolol)	Blocks NE effects on peripheral nerve receptors	Slowed heart rate, drowsiness	30–100mg	Often used on an as-needed basis 2 hours before an anxiety-provoking experience	None if used on an as-needed basis
Catapres (clonidine hydrochloride)	Alpha-2 agonist, decreases the release of NE from presynaptic nerve cell	Dry mouth, sedation, constipation, possibly depressed mood	0.2–0.6mg per day in divided dose	Start 0.1mg twice a day, may increase 0.1mg/day per week	If stopped abruptly, increased nervousness, agitation, headache, and tremor

SSRIs

The SSRI Paxil (paroxetine) has been FDA-approved for the treatment of SAD. Research continues for many of the other SSRI medications. The initial dosages of the SSRIs are similar to that of other antidepressants. Start with a typical dose, wait 2–3 weeks, and then assess the drug effects before deciding whether or not to make a further increase in dosage. The maximum dose is slightly higher than that for the treatment of depression and usually similar to the maximum dose prescribed for treating PD. See Table 5.3 for a review of these medications and their effects.

BuSpar

Buspar (buspirone) is not a benzodiazepine, but it is an anxiolytic agent. It is not effective on an as-needed basis because it works by increasing SE. Its benefit is that it is not mood-altering or addictive. Table 8.2 reviews the dosage and use of BuSpar for GAD. The dosage for SAD would be similar.

MAOIs

The monoamine oxidase inhibitors (MAOIs) have also been helpful in the treatment of SAD. Chapter 5 discussed the benefits and drawbacks of these medications. Table 5.5 lists the MAOIs and considerations for their use. They would be used similarly with SAD.

Tricyclics

It appears that the tricyclic antidepressants may also be helpful, but there is not as much hard evidence to support this. Tricyclics may help balance SE dysregulation. They may also relax the person by having an antihistamine effect. Table 5.4 lists the TCAs and considerations for their use. They would be used similarly with SAD.

SSNRIs

The dual-action NE/SE reuptake inhibitors Effexor and Effexor XR (venlafaxine) and Cymbalta (duloxetine) may also be helpful in treating SAD. The mechanisms for these dual-acting medications are similar to the SSRIs, but they also increase NE. One additional theory of why the dual mechanism of increasing both NE and SE works is that the NE may bind to the presynaptic nerve cell, resulting in an additional flow of SE from the presynaptic nerve cell.

Medications to Enhance GABA
and Chloride Conductance: Benzodiazepines

The benzodiazepines, especially Klonopin (clonazepam), are also used to treat SAD. The theory for this involves allowing the relaxing neural chemical gamma amniobutyric acid (GABA) to work more effectively through adjusting chloride channels (see Chapter 5). When GABA works more efficiently, people experience less arousal, have a greater ability to feel calm, and are less easily stimulated. For patients with SAD, this translates into less anxiety and less likelihood of having their fearful reactions triggered.

The benzodiazepines are often used in low doses on an as-needed basis (PRN) prior to an anxiety-producing situation. When used in combination with good psychological treatment, these medications are valuable aids to diminishing the experience of anxiety when someone is first going into previously feared situations. By decreasing anxiety, but not totally eliminating it, the benzodiazepine may help people with SAD to encounter new situations with less negative arousal. With less anxiety, they feel more confidence and develop further willingness to overcome their SAD.

People using benzodiazepines must be extremely careful of the interaction of these drugs with alcohol. Regardless of whether they are used on an as-needed basis or an ongoing basis, when combined with alcohol they have a multiplying effect on the intoxication. It is best not to drink alcohol when using a benzodiazepine. Table 5.6 lists the benzodiazepine medications and considerations for their use. They would be used similarly with SAD as with panic disorder; however, one major difference is that they are often used on an as-needed basis 2 hours before an anxiety-provoking experience to improve psychotherapeutic efforts to change fearful responses to new experiences. Side effects and withdrawal patterns are minimal if used on an as-needed basis.

Medications to Decrease Release of Norepinephrine: Beta-Blockers

Beta-blockers are used to treat the cardiac symptoms of anxiety in SAD and the activation of the peripheral nervous system. They are usually used on an as-needed basis before a social gathering or other situation that produces anxiety. After administration of beta-blockers, the person with SAD feels anxiety but does not experience the flushing and tachycardia that is so distressing. Beta-blockers appear to be more effective for physical symptom reduction than the alpha-2 agonists because they block the peripheral NE receptors throughout the body. Alpha-2 agonists decrease the release of NE, but they do not affect the peripheral nervous system.

Medications to Increase GABA: Anticonvulsants

Anticonvulsant medications are more likely to be used for SAD than they are for the other anxiety conditions. Anticonvulsants work by binding to a subunit of a calcium channel structurally related to GABA. Neurontin (gabapentin) is the most commonly used anticonvulsant; it is generally used as an adjunctive medication for anxiety. Table 11.3 details the use of this medication in treating SAD.

PEARLS ABOUT MEDICATING FOR SOCIAL ANXIETY DISORDER

Important ideas to take away regarding the use of medication with SAD include:

- Use benzodiazepines in low doses on a PRN basis to diminish anxiety before an anxiety-provoking situation.
- Beta-blockers used on a PRN basis reduce the embarrassing flushing and tachycardia while allowing the person to work through the situation.
- It is our observation that SAD patients appear to have a higher tolerance for SSRI's than other anxiety disordered patients. Therefore, we may raise the dosage to a therapeutic level more rapidly in SAD than in GAD.

The case of Jeremy, introduced in Chapter 10, is an excellent example of how SAD can change the life of the person who suffers it and cause significant impairment of a social or career nature. Treatment can create or restore higher levels of functioning.

Jeremy was referred to me by his therapist. Like many SAD patients, he was struggling with performance anxiety, especially at work, where he had to participate in frequent meetings with coworkers. He was fearful of sweating, flushing, and looking foolish.

Given his long history of shyness and past social experiences, it seemed likely that Jeremy had generalized social anxiety. His most acute symptoms occurred when he encountered a totally new person in a high-stress situation, such as a job interview. Although psychotherapy helped him change his cognitive view and learn relaxation, he needed adjustment in his underlying neurobiology.

We discussed several different biochemical treatments. Jeremy agreed to a course of treatment that included the SSRI Paxil (paroxetine) CR (CR indicates controlled release, meaning that the delivery of the medication is sustained over a longer period in the nervous system). I combined the Paxil CR with a dose of the beta-blocker Inderal (propranolol) on an as-needed basis before he had to present information at a meeting. The SSRI seemed

TABLE 11.3 Neurontin

Drug Name	Main Effect	Side Effects	Dose Range and Duration	Considerations for Use	Withdrawal Pattern
Neurontin (gabapentin)	Affects calcium channels, decreasing neuronal activity of GABA	Drowsiness, lightheadness	600–3600mg per day in divided dosage	May not be as effective as other medications	Usually no withdrawal

to help reduce his overall anxiety, and the Inderal reduced his physical re-action to performance (decreasing his sweating and flushing). He chose Paxil CR because it was FDA-approved for SAD. (It is my opinion that all the SSRIs are probably helpful for SAD. They have also been reported to enhance in vivo treatment. I started Jeremy on a dose of 12.5mg and grad-ually increased the dose to 37.5mg over 3 weeks. Paxil CR has a more se-dating quality than some other SSRIs, so he took the medication at night.

At the higher dose of Paxil CR, Jeremy experienced decreased libido, a common side effect of the SSRIs. We reviewed different ways of addressing this concern, including a trial of gingko biloba, adding Wellbutrin XL, and decreasing the dose of the Paxil CR while adding an enhancer. (The last option—a lower dose of the SSRI plus an enhancer such as a low dose of an atypical antipsychotic—may lower the libido side effect while allowing the SSRI to work more effectively.) He decided to try the first option. He began the gingko biloba at a dose of 200mg per day in divided doses. He took half the dose in the morning and half the dose at bedtime. This helped improve his libido.

The Inderal helped reduce Jeremy's fear of appearing embarrassed. He felt that if he could not *look* fearful or embarrassed, he would not mind *feeling* it so much. When he used a 20mg dose of Inderal 2 hours before a meeting, he had very good results—reduced sweating and flushing. With the Inderal and the cognitive methods he learned to calm himself, he gained confidence in his ability to perform without the dreaded terror of embarrassing himself. Consequently he was able to limit use of the Inderal to situations in which he would be highly visible or under special stress.

What seemed to work so well in this case was the combination of low-ering the general activity level of norepinephrine (NE) to eliminate the physiological symptoms of SAD while enhancing the 5HT through Paxil. At the same time, Jeremy was learning psychotherapeutic tools to help him be more confident in social circumstances. He ultimately stayed on the SSRI to balance his serotonin (SE) system, but he needed the beta-blocker only in limited situations. This freed him to engage at work and in social settings with greatly reduced SAD.

CONCLUSION

Social anxiety is a debilitating anxiety disorder that combines features of panic and generalized anxiety with the high physical arousal and anticipa-tory worry about being observed to be anxious. The behavioral feature of social anxiety—the avoidance of situations in which a person may experi-ence anxiety—leads to all the significant impairments of this disorder: isolation from social contact, stymied advancement in academic or career aspirations, and loss of social and emotional skills.

Recovery from this disorder depends on careful intersection of the psychiatric medications and psychotherapeutic methods to allow small, regular steps of progress without intense anxiety. Although some people hope for recovery just by taking a pill, in the case of social anxiety, the likelihood of a recovery without both medication and psychotherapy is limited.

The good news for this disorder is that medications are very effective and are essential components of good treatment.

Suggested Reading

Adson, D. E., Kushner, M. G., & Fahnhorst, T. A. (2005). Treatment of residual anxiety symptoms with adjunctive aripiprazole in depressed patients taking selective serotonin reuptake inhibitors. *Journal of Affective Disorders, 86*(1), 99–104.

Ansseau, M., Fischler, B., Dierick, M., Mignon, A., & Levman, S. (2005). Prevalence and impact of generalized anxiety disorder and major depression in primary care in Belgium and Luxemburg: The GADIS study. *European Psychiatry, 20*(3), 229–235.

Anthony, M. M. (2004). *10 simple solutions to shyness: How to overcome shyness, social anxiety, and fear of public speaking.* Oakland, CA: New Harbinger Publications.

Arrol, B., Macgillivray, S., Ogston, S., Reid, I., Sullivan, F., Williams, B., & Crombie, I. (2005). Efficacy and tolerability of tricyclic antidepressants and SSRIs compared with placebo for treatment of depression in primary care: A meta-analysis. *Annals of Family Medicine, 3*(5), 449–456.

Arturo, J., & Benson, R. (2000). *You do that too? Adolescents and OCD.* Ellsworth, ME: Dilligaf.

Azar, B. (2001). Research pointing to a circuit linking the immune system and brain connects illness, stress, mood, and thought in a whole new way. *Medscape, 32*(11).

Baer, L. (1992). *Getting control: Overcoming your obsessions and compulsions.* New York: Plume.

Ball, S. G., Kuhn, A., Wall, D., Shekhar, A., & Goddard, A. W. (2005). Selective serotonin reuptake inhibitor treatment for generalized anxiety disorder: A double-blind, prospective comparison between paroxetine and sertraline. *Journal of Clinical Psychiatry, 66*(1), 94–99.

Bandelow, B., Behnke, K., Lenoir, S., Hendriks, G. J., & Clary, C. M. (2004). Sertraline versus paroxetine in the treatment of panic disorder: An acute, double-blind noninferiority comparison. *Journal of Clinical Psychiatry, 65,* 405–413.

Bang, L. M., Keating, G. M. (2004). Paroxetine controlled release. *CNS Drugs, 18,* 355–364.

Barlow, D. H., & Cerny, J. A. (1988). *Psychological treatment of panic.* New York: Guilford Press.

Belanger, L., Morin, C. M., Gendron, L., & Blais, F. C. (2005). Presleep cognitive activity and thought control strategies in insomnia. *Journal of Cognitive Psychotherapy, 19*(1), 19–28.

Benson, H., M.D. (1996). *Timeless healing: The power and biology of belief.* New York: Fireside.

Berretta, S. (2005, December). Cortico-amygdala circuits: Role in the conditioned stress response. *Stress, 8*(4), 221–232.

Bezchlibnyk-Butler, K. Z., & Jeffries, J. J. (Eds.) (2002). *Clinical handbook of psychotropic drugs* (12th rev. ed.). Seattle, WA: Hogrefe & Hube.

Bielski, R. J., Bose, A., & Chang, C.-C. (2005, April-June). A double-blind comparison of escitalopram and paroxetine in the long-term treatment of generalized anxiety disorder. *Annals of Clinical Psychiatry, 17*(2), 65–69.

Birkhofer, A., Schmidt, G., & Forstl, H. (2005, April). Heart and Brain: The influence of psychiatric disorders and their therapy on the heart rate variability. *Neurological Psychiatry, 73*(4), 192–205.

Blechman, E. A., & Brownell, K. D. (Eds.) (1998). *Behavioral medicine and women.* New York: Guilford Press.

Bradwejn, J., Ahokas, A., Stein, D. J., Salinas, E., Emilien, G., & Whitaker, T. (2005, October). Venlafaxine extended-release capsules in panic disorder: Flexible-dose, double-blind, placebo-controlled study. *The Journal of Mental Science, 187,* 352–359.

Bruce, S. E., Yonkers, K. A., Otto, M. W., Eisen, J. L., Weisberg, R. B., Pagano, M., et al. (2005, June). Influence of psychiatric comorbidity on recovery and recurrence in generalized anxiety disorder, social phobia, and panic disorder: A 12-year prospective study. *American Journal of Psychiatry, 162*(6), 1179–1187.

Campbell, D. (1997). *The Mozart effect: Tapping the power of music to heal the body, strengthen the mind, and unlock the creative spirit.* New York: Avon Books.

Carlbring, P., Nilsson-Ihrfelt, E., Waara, J., Kollenstam, C., Buhrman, M., & Kaldo, V., et al. (2005, October). Treatment of panic disorder: Live therapy vs. self-help via the Internet. *Behaviour Research and Therapy, 43*(10), 1321–1333.

Chambless, D. L., Baker, M. J., Baucom, D. H., Beutler, L. E., Calhoun, K. S., & Crits-Christoph, P., et al. (1998, winter). Update on empirically validated treatments II. *The Clinical Psychologist, 51*(1), 3–16.

Chouinard, G. (2004) Issues in the clinical use of benzodiazepines: Potency, withdrawal, and rebound. *Journal of Clinical Psychiatry, 65*(5), 7–12.

Comer, R. J., et al. (2002). *PDR drug guide for mental health professionals* (1st ed.). Montvale, NJ: Thomson.

Coppen, A., & Bolander-Gouaille, C. (2005, January). Treatment of depression: Time to consider folic acid and vitamin B12. *Journal of Psychopharmacology, 19*(1), 59–65.

Craske, M. G., Barlow, D. H., & O'Leary, T. (1992). *Mastery of your anxiety and worry*. Albany, NY: Graywind Publications.

Czerner, T. B. (2001). *What makes you tick? The brain in plain english*. New York: John Wiley and Sons.

Damasio, A. R. (1998). *Descartes' error: Emotion, reason, and the human brain*. New York: First Bard Printing.

Davis, M., Myers, K. M., Chatwal, J., & Ressler, K. J. (2006, January). Pharmacological treatments that facilitate extinction of fear: Relevance to psychotherapy. *Neurological Psychiatry, 3*(1), 82–96.

Davis, M., & Nyers, K. (2002). The role of glutamate and gamma-aminobutyric acid in fear extinction: Clinical implications for exposure therapy. *Biological Psychiatry, 52,* 998–1007.

den Heijer, T., Geerlings, M. I., Hoebeek, F. E., Hofman, A., Koudstaal, P. J., & Breteler, M. M. (2006, January). Use of hippocampal and amygdalar volumes on magnetic resonance imaging to predict dementia in cognitively intact elderly people. *Archives of General Psychiatry, 63*(1), 57–62.

DesMaisons, K. (1998). *Potatoes not prozac*. New York: Simon & Schuster.

Dobson, K. S., & Craig, K. D. (1996). *Advances in cognitive-behavioral therapy*. Thousand Oaks, CA: Sage Publications.

dos Santos, L., de Andreade, T. G. C. S., & Zangrossi, H., Jr. (2005, June). Serotonergic neurons in the median raphe nucleus regulate inhibitory avoidance but not escape behavior in the rat elevated T-maze test of anxiety. *Psychopharmacology, 179*(4), 733–741.

Follette, V. M., Ruzek, J. I., & Abueg, F. R. (Eds.) (1998). *Cognitive behavioral therapies for trauma*. New York: Guilford Press.

Foy, D. W. (1992). *Treating PTSD: Cognitive-behavioral strategies*. New York: Guilford Press.

Freeman, S. A. (2004, April). Panic attacks with spontaneous ejaculation successfully treated with citalopram and clonazepam. *Journal of Clinical Psychopharmacology, 24,* 463–464.

Friedman, M. J. (2000). *Post traumatic stress disorder: The latest assessment and treatment strategies*. Kansas City, MO: Compact Clinicals.

Fruehling, J. J. (1997). *Drug treatment of OCD in children and adolescents*. Milford, CT: Obsessive-Compulsive Foundation.

Furmark, T., Appel, L., Michelgard, A., Wahlstedt, K., Ahs, F., & Zancan, S., et al. (2005, July). Cerebral blood flow changes after treatment of social phobia with the neurokinin-1 antagonist GR205171, citalopram, or placebo. *Biological Psychiatry, 58*(2), 132–142.

Gambi, F., De Berardis, D., Campanella, D., Carano, A., Sepede, G., & Salini, G., et al. (2005, September). Mirtazapine treatment of generalized anxiety disorder: A fixed dose, open label study. *Journal of Psychopharmacology, 19*(5), 483–487.

Gazzaniga, M. S. (Ed.) (1999). *Conversations in the cognitive neurosciences*. Cambridge, MA: Massachusetts Institute of Technology.

Gold, M. S. (1990). *The good news about panic anxiety and phobias: Cures, treatments, and solutions in the new age of biopsychiatry*. New York: Bantam.

Gray, H. (1995). *Gray's anatomy*. New York: Barnes & Noble.

Guinness, A. E., et al. (Eds.) (1993). *Family guide to natural medicine*. Pleasantville, NY: Reader's Digest Association.

Gunther, T., Holtkamp, K., Jolles, J., Herpertz-Dahlmann, B., & Konrad, K. (2005, September). The influence of sertraline on attention and verbal memory in children and adolescents with anxiety disorders. *Journal of Child and Adolescent Psychopharmacology, 15*(4), 608–618.

Hafen, B. Q., et al. (1996). *Mind/body health: The effects of attitudes, emotions, and relationships*. Needham Heights, MA: Allyn and Bacon.

Ham, P., Waters, D. B., Oliver, M. N. (2005, February). Treatment of panic disorder. *American Family Physician, 71*(4), 733–739.

Heinzel, A., Bermpohl, F., Niese, R., Pfennig, A., Pascual-Leone, A., Schlaug, G., et al. (2005, September). How do we modulate our emotions? Parametric fMRI reveals cortical midline structures as regions specifically involved in the processing of emotional valences. *Brain Research Cognitive Brain Research, 25*(1), 348–358.

Helmus, T. C., Tancer, M., & Johanson, C. E. (2005, November). Reinforcing effects of diazepam under anxiogenic conditions in individuals with social anxiety. *Experimental and Clinical Psychopharmacology, 13*(4), 348–356.

Hendler, S. S. et al. (Ed.) (2001). *PDR for nutritional supplements*. Montvale, NJ: Medical Economics/Thomson Healthcare.

Hettema, J. M., Prescott, C. A., Myers, J. M., Neale, M. C., & Kendler, K. S. (2005, February). The structure of genetic and environmental risk factors for anxiety disorders in men and women. *Archives of General Psychiatry, 62*(2), 182–189.

Kasper, S., Stein, D. J., Loft, H., & Nil, R. (2005, March). Escitalopram in the treatment of social anxiety disorder: Randomised, placebo-controlled, flexible-dosage study. *British Journal of Psychiatry, 186*(3), 222–226.

Kaufman, K. R. (2005, January). Monotherapy treatment of paruresis with gabapentin. *International Journal of Clinical Psychopharmacology, 20*(1), 53–55.

Kendall, P. C. et al. (1992). *Anxiety disorders in youth: Cognitive-behavioral interventions*. Needham Heights, MA: Allyn and Bacon.

Kinder, M. (1994). *Mastering your moods: How to recognize your emotional style and make it work for you*. New York: Fireside.

Kramer, S. & Akhtar, S. (Eds.) (1992). *When the body speaks: Psychological meanings in kinetic clues*. Northvale, NJ: Aronson.

Liebowitz, M. R., Gelenberg, A. J., & Munjack, D. (2005, February). Venlafaxine extended release vs. placebo and paroxetine in social anxiety disorder. *Archives of General Psychiatry, 62*(2), 190–198.

Liebowitz, M. R., Mangano, R. M., Bradwejn, J., & Asnis, G. (2005, February). A randomized controlled trial of venlafaxine extended release in generalized social anxiety disorder. *Journal of Clinical Psychiatry, 66*(2), 238–247.

Liebowitz, M. R., Ninan, P. T., Schneier, F. R., Blanco, C. (2005, October). Intergrating neurobiology and psychopathology into evidence-based treatment of social anxiety disorder. *CNS Spectrums, 10* (10–13), 1–13.

Mackie, K. (2006). Cannabinoid receptors as therapeutic targets. *Annual Review of Pharmacology and Toxicology, 46,* 101–22.

March, J. S. (1995). *Anxiety disorders in children and adolescents*. New York: Guilford Press.

March, J. S. et al. (2000). Anxiety as a predictor outcome variable in the multimodal treatment study of children with ADHD. *Journal of Abnormal Child Psychology, 28,* 527–541.

Marcus, G. (2004). *The birth of the mind.* New York: Basic Books.

McGaugh, J. L. (2003). *Memory and emotion.* New York: Columbia University Press.

Naukkarinen, H., Raassina, R., Penttinen, J., Ahokas, A., Jokinen, R., & Koponen, H., et al. (2005, December). Deramciclane in the treatment of generalized anxiety disorder: A placebo-controlled, double-blind, dose-finding study. *European Neuropsychopharmacology, 15*(6), 617–623.

Panichelli-Mindel, S. M., Flannery-Schroeder, E., Kendall, P. C., & Angelosante, A. G. (2005). Disclosure of distress among anxiety-disordered youth: Differences in treatment outcome. *Journal of Anxiety Disorders, 19*(4), 403–422.

Panzer, M. J. (2005, January-March). Are SSRIs really more effective for anxious depression? *Annals of Clinical Psychiatry, 17*(1), 23–29.

Panzer, P. E., Regan, T. S., Chiao, E., Sarnes, M. W. (2005, October). Implications of an SSRI generic step therapy pharmacy benefit deisgn: An economic model in anxiety disorders. *American Journal of Managed Care, 11*(12), S370–379.

Parnell, L. (1997). *Transforming trauma: EMDR the revolutionary new therapy for freeing the mind, clearing the body, and opening the heart.* New York: Norton.

Pawlyk, A. C., Jha, S. K., Brennan, F. X., Morrison, A. R., & Ross, R. J. (2005, February). A rodent model of sleep disturbances in posttraumatic stress disorder: The role of context after fear conditioning. *Biological Psychiatry, 57*(3), 268–277.

Payne, J. D., Jackson, E. D., Ryan, L., Hoschedit, S., Jacobs, J. W., & Nadel, L. (2006, January). The impact of stress on neutral and emotional aspects of episodic memory. *Memory, 14*(1), 1–16.

Protopopescu, X., Pan, H., Tuescher, O., Cloitre, M., Goldstein, M., & Engelien, W., et al. (2005, March). Differential time courses and specificity of amygdala activity in posttraumatic stress disorder subjects and normal control subjects. *Biological Psychiatry, 57*(5), 464–473.

Rabiner, E. A., et al. (2001). Pindolol augmentation of SSRI: PET evidence that the

Roozendaal, B., Quirarte, G. L., McGaugh, J. L. (1997). Stress-activated hormonal systems and the regulation of memory storage. In R. Yehuda & A. C. McFarlane (Eds.), *Psychobiology of posttraumatic stress disorder* (pp. 247–258). New York: Annals of the New York Academy of Sciences, 821.

Roth, A., & Fonagy, P. (2005). *What works for whom: A critical review of psychotherapy research.* New York: Guilford Press.

Rowlett, J. K., Cook, J. M., Duke, A. N., Platt, D. M. (2005, January). Selective antagonism of GABAA receptor subtypes: an in vivo approach to exploring the therapeutic and side effects of benzodiazepine-type drugs. *CNS Spectrum, 10*(1), 40–48.

Roy-Byrne, P. P., Bystritsky, A., Russo, J., Craske, M. G., Sherbourne, C. D., & Stein, M. B. (2005, March-April). Use of herbal medicine in primary care patients with mood and anxiety disorders. *Psychosomatics: Journal of Consultation Liaison Psychiatry, 46*(2), 117–122.

Roy-Byrne, P. P., Perera, P., Pitts, C. D., Christi, J. A. (2005, October). Paroxetine response and tolerability among ethnic minority patients with mood or anxiety disorders: a pooled analysis. *Journal of Clinical Psychiatry, 66*(10), 1228–1233.

Rubin, K. H., Burgess, K. B. (2001). Social withdrawal and anxiety. In M. W. Vasey & M. R. Dadds (Eds.), *The developmental psychopathology of anxiety* (pp. 407–434). New York: Oxford.

Saavedra, L. M. (2005). Anxious children who received treatment grown-up: An 8-to-13 year follow-up study. *Dissertation Abstracts International: Section B: The Sciences and Engineering, 66*(3-B), 1734.

Schacter, D. L. (1996). *Searching for memory: The brain, the mind, and the past.* New York: Basic Books.

Schmitt, R., Gazalle, F. K., Lima, M. S., Cunha, A., Souza, J., Kapczinski, F. (2005, March). The efficacy of antidepressants for generalized anxiety disorder: A systematic review and meta-analysis. *Revista Brasileirade Psiquiatria, 27*(1), 18–24,

Schneier, F. R. (2005, October). Neurobiological mechanisms of social anxiety disorder. *CNS Spectrums, 10*(10), 8–9.

Schwartz, T. L., Azhar, N., Husain, J., Nihalani, N., Simionescu, M., & Coovert, D., et al. (2005, July-September). An open-label study of tiagabine as augmentation therapy for anxiety. *Annals of Clinical Psychiatry, 17*(3), 167–172.

Seelke, A. H., et al. (2005). Extra ocular muscle activity, rapid eye movements, and the development of active and quiet sleep. *European Journal of Neuroscience, 22,* 911–920.

Sharma, S. C., Bernstein, G. A., Layne, A. E., Egan, E. A., & Tennison, D. M. (2005, November). School-based interventions for anxious children. *Journal of the American Academy of Child and Adolescent Psychiatry, 44*(11), 1118–1127.

Sheehan, D. V., Burnham, D. B., Lyengar, M. K., Perera, P., Paxil, C. R. (2005, January). Efficacy and tolerability of controlled-release paroxetine in the treatment of panic disorder. *Journal of Clinical Psychiatry, 65,* 34–40.

Shneker, B. F., & McAuley, J. W. (2005, December). Pregabalin: A new neuromodulator with broad therapeutic indications. *Annals of Pharmacotherapy, 39*(12), 2029–2037.

Shioiri, T., Kojima-Maruyama, M., Hosoki, T., Kitamura, H., Tanaka, A., & Yoshizawa, M., et al. (2005, October). Dysfunctional baroreflex regulation of sympathetic nerve activity in remitted patients with panic disorder: A new methodological approach. *European Archives of Psychiatry and Clinical Neuroscience, 255*(5), 293–298.

Silove, D., & Manicavasagar, V. (2001). Early separation anxiety and its relationship to adult anxiety disorders. In M. W. Vasey & M. R. Dadds (Eds.), *The developmental psychopathology of anxiety* (pp. 459–480). New York: Oxford.

Society for NeuroScience. (2002). *Brain facts: A primer on the brain and nervous system* (4th ed.). Washington, DC: Society for Neuroscience.

Speca, M., & Carlson, L. (2002). Mediation decreases distress and anxiety in cancer patients. *Psychosomatic Medicine, 62*(5).

Springer, S. P., & Deutsch, G. (1989). *Left brain, right brain.* New York: W. H. Freeman and Co.

Weil, A. (Compilation of 1997 newsletters). *Dr. Andrew Weil's self-healing, 1997 annual edition.*

Weil, A. (1998). *Natural health, natural medicine: A comprehensive manual for wellness and self care.* New York: Houghton-Mifflin.

Weil, A. (2000). *Eating well for optimal health.* New York: Knopf.

Westenberg, H. G., Stein, D. J., Yang, H. C., Li, D., & Barbato, L. M. (2004, January). A double-blind placebo-controlled study of controlled, release fluvoxamine for the treatment of generalized social anxiety disorder. *Journal of Clinical Psychopharmacology, 24,* 49–55.

Williams, L. M., Kemp, A. H., & Felmingham, K., et al. (2004). Implicit perception of fear signals: An fMRI investigation of PTSD. *Journal of Biological Psychiatry, 5*(1), 137.

Wilson, J. L. (2001). *Adrenal fatigue: The 21st-century stress syndrome.* Petaluma, CA: Smart Publications.

Wilson, R. R. (1987). *Don't panic: Taking control of anxiety attacks.* New York: Harper & Row.

Witkin, J. M., Tzavara, E. T., & Nomikos, G. G. (2005, September). A role for cannabinoid CB-sub-1 receptors in mood and anxiety disorders. *Behavioural Pharmacology, 16*(5–6), 315–331.

Worthington III, J. J., Kinrys, G., Wygant, L. E., & Pollack, M. H. (2005, January). Aripiprazole as an augmentor of selective serotonin reuptake inhibitors in depression and anxiety disorder patients. *International Clinical Psychopharmacology, 20*(1), 9–11.

Yartz, A. R., Zvolensky, M. J., Gregor, K., Feldner, M. T., & Leen-Feldner, E. W. (2005, June). Health perception is a unique predictor of anxiety symptoms in non-clinical participants. *Cognitive Behaviour Therapy, 34*(2), 65–74.

Zanoveli, J. M., Nogueira, R. L., & Zangrossi, H., Jr. (2005, November). Chronic imipramine treatment sensitizes 5-HT-sub(1A) and 5-HT-sub(2A) receptors in the dorsal periaqueductal gray matter: Evidence from the elevated T-maze test of anxiety. *Behavioural Pharmacology, 16*(7), 543–552.

Zwanzger, P., Ruprecht, R. (2005, May). Selective GABAeric treatment for panic? Investigations in experimental panic induction and panic disorder. *Journal of Psychiatry Neuroscience, 30*(3), 167–175.

REFERENCES

Amen, D. G. (1998). *Change your brain, change your life.* New York: Three Rivers Press.

Amen, D. (2003). *Healing anxiety and depression.* New York: Penguin.

American Psychiatric Association. (2000). *Diagnostic and statistical manual of mental disorders* (4th ed. Text Revision). Washington, DC: Author.

Anda, R. F., Croft, J. B., Felitti, V. J., Nordenberg, D., Giles, W. H., Williamson, D. F., & Giovino, G. A. (1999). Aversive childhood experiences and smoking during adolescence and adulthood. *Journal of the American Medical Association, 282,* 1652–1658.

Aron, E. (1996). *The highly sensitive person.* New York: Birch Lane Press.

Ayers, C., Wetherell, J. L., Lenze, E. J., Stanley, M. (March, 2006). Treating late-life anxiety. *Psychiatric Times, 25*(3). Retrieved from *http://www.psychiatrictimes. com/article/showArticle.jhtml?articleId=184400673.*

Babyak, K., & Blumenthal, J. A. (2000). Exercise treatment for major depression: Maintenance of therapeutic benefit at 10 months. *Psychosomatic Medicine, 62,* 633–638.

Beck, A. (1979). *The cognitive therapy of depression.* New York: Guilford Press.

Beckham, J. C., Feldman, M. E., Vrana, S. R., Mozley, S. L., Erkanli, A., Clancy, C. P., et al. (2005, August). Immediate antecedents of cigarette smoking in smokers with and without posttraumatic stress disorder: A preliminary study. *Experimental and Clinical Psychopharmacology, 13*(3), 219–228.

Bergman, U. (1998). Speculations of the neurobiology of EMDR. *Traumatology, 4*(1), article 2. Retrieved November 11, 1998 from *www.fsu.edu/~trauma/art1v4i1.html.*

Berk, L., & Tan, S. (1989). Neuroendocrine influences of mirthful laughter. *The American Journal of the Medical Sciences, 298*(6), 390–396.

255

Bernstein, G. A., Layne, A. E., & Egan, E. A. (2005). School-based interventions for anxious children. *Journal of the American Academy of Child and Adolescent Psychiatry, 44*(11), 1118–1127.

Blumenthal, J. A., Babyak, M. A., Moore, K. A., Craighead, E. W., Herman, S., Khatri, P., Waugh, R., Napolitano, M., Forman, L., Appelbaum, M., Doraiswamy, P., Krishnan, K. (1999). Effects of exercise training on older patients with major depression. *Archives of Internal Medicine, 159,* 2349–2356.

Botella, C. (2004). Treatment of flying phobia using virtual reality: Data from a 1 year follow-up using a multiple baseline design. *Clinical Psychology and Psychotherapy, 11,* 311–323.

Bouton, M. E. (2002). Context, ambiguity and unlearning: Sources of relapse after behavioral extinction. *Biological Psychiatry, 52*(10), 00–00.

Bremner, J. D., Staib, L. H., Kaloupek, D., Southwick, S. M., Soufer, R., & Charney, D. S. (1999). Neural correlates of exposure to traumatic pictures and sound in Vietnam combat veterans with an without posttraumatic stress disorder: A positron emission tomography study. *Biological Psychiatry, 45,* 806–816.

Bremner, J. D. (2005). *Does stress damage the brain.* New York: Norton.

Bremner, J. D. (1995). The neurobiology of traumatic stress: Relevance to posttraumatic stress disorder and the so-called "False memory syndromes." Masters in Psychiatry. Retrieved October 12, 1997, from www.med.yale.edu/psych/org/ypi/trauma/masters.htm.

Bunevicius, R., Velickiene, D., & Prange, A. J., Jr. (2005). Mood and anxiety disorders in women with treated hyperthyroidism and ophthalmopathy caused by Graves' disease. *General Hospital Psychiatry, 27(2),* 133–139.

Burns, D. D. (1980). *Feeling good: The new mood therapy.* New York: Avon Books.

Cartwright-Hatton, S., McNally, D., & White, C. (2005, April). A new cognitive behavioral parenting intervention for families of young anxious children: A pilot study. *Behavioural and Cognitive Psychotherapy, 33*(2), 243–247.

Casey, L. M., Newcombe, P. A., & Oei, T. P. S. (2005, April). Cognitive mediation of panic severity: The role of catastrophic misinterpretation of bodily sensations and panic self-efficacy. *Cognitive therapy and research, 29*(2), 187–200.

Chaffin, M., Silovsky, J. F., & Vaughn, C. (2005). Temporal concordance of anxiety disorders and child sexual abuse: Implications for direct versus artifactual effects of sexual abuse. *Journal of Clinical Child and Adolescent Psychology, 34*(2), 210–222.

Chansky, T. E. (2004). *Freeing your child from anxiety.* New York: Broadway Books.

Chess, S., & Thomas, A. (1986). *Temperament in clinical practice.* New York: Guilford Press.

Childre, D., & Martin, H. (2000). *The heartmath solution.* San Francisco: Harper.

Christakis, D. (2004). TV linked to ADHD. *Pediatrics, 113,* 708–713.

Clark, D. B., Birmaher, B., Axelson, D., Monk, K., Kalas, C., Ehmann, M., Bridge, J., Wood, et al. (2005, December). Fluoxetine for the treatment of childhood anxiety disorders: Open-label, long-term extension to a controlled trial. *Journal of the American Academy of Child & Adolescent Psychiatry, 44*(12), 1263–1270.

Cornell, A. W. (1996). *The power of focusing: A practical guide to emotional self-healing*. Oakland, CA: New Harbinger Publications.

Cortes, A. M., Saltzman, K. M., Weems, C. F., Regnault, H. P., Reiss, A. L., & Carrion, V. G. (2005, August). Development of anxiety disorders in a traumatized pediatric population: A preliminary longitudinal evaluation. *Child Abuse & Neglect, 29*(8), 905–914.

Craske, M. G., Golinelli, D., Stein, M. B., Roy-Byrne, P., Bystritsky, A., &Sherbourne, C. (2005, November). Does the addition of cognitive behavioratherapy improve panic disorder treatment outcome relative to medication alone in the primary-care setting? *Psychological medicine, 35*(11), 1645–1654.

Dadds, M., & Roth, J. (2001). Family processes in the development of anxiety problems. In M. W. Vasey & M. R. Dadds, (Eds.), *The Developmental Psychopathology of Anxiety* (pp. 278–303). New York: Oxford University Press.

Dahl, A. A., Ravindran, A., Allgulander, C., Kutcher, S. P., Austin, C., & Burt, T. (2005, June). Sertraline in generalized anxiety disorder: Efficacy in treating the psychic and somatic anxiety factors. *Acta Psychiatrica Scandinavica, 111*(6), 429–435.

Dahl-Davidson J., Yaryura, J., DuPont, R., Stallings, L., Li, D., et al (2004, February). Fluoxamine-controlled release formulation for the treatment of generalized social anxiety disorder. *Journal of Clinical Psychopharmacology, 24,* 118–125.

Davidson et al. (2004, spring). Posttraumatic stress disorder. *Journal of Neuropsychiatry Clinical Neuroscience, 16*(2).

Davis, M., Eschelman, E. R., & McKay, M. (1998). *The relaxation & stress reduction workbook* (4th ed.). Oakland, CA: New Harbinger.

Dawson, P., & Guare, R. (2004). *Executive skills in children and adolescents: A practical guide to assessment and intervention*. New York: Guilford.

DeAngelis, T. (2002). If you do one thing, make it exercise. *Monitor on Psychology, 33*(7), 49.

DeBellis, M. D., Keshavan, M. S., Shifflett, H., Iyengar, S., Beers, S. R., Hall, J., & Moritz, G. (2002). Brain structures in pediatric maltreatment related posttraumatic stress disorder. *Biological Psychiatry, 1*(52), 1066–1078.

Easter, J., McClure, E. B., Monk, C. S., Dhanani, M., Hodgdon, H., Leibenluft, E., et al. (2005, September). Emotion recognition deficits in pediatric anxiety disorders: Implications for amygdala research. *Journal of Child and Adolescent Psychopharmacology, 15*(4), 563–570.

Eisen, A. R., Kearney, C. A., & Schaefer, C. E. (1995). *Clinical handbook of anxiety disorders in children and adolescents*. Northvale, NJ: Aronson.

Eisen, A. R., & Schaefer, C. E. (2005). *Separation anxiety in children and adolescents: An individualized approach to assessment and treatment*. New York: Guilford.

Elias, M. (2004, April). Short attention span linked to TV children show effects by age 7. *USA Today*.

Ellis, A., & Dryden, W. (1987). *The practice of rational emotive therapy*. New York: Springer.

Felitti, V. J., Anda, R. F., Nordenberg, D., Williamson, D. F., Spitz, A. M., Edwards, V., et al. (1998). Relationship of childhood abuse and household dysfunction to many of the leading causes of death in adults: The adverse childhood experiences (ace) study. *American Journal of Preventive Medicine, 14*(4).

Field, T. (2002). Massage for fibromyalgia. *Journal of Clinical Rheumotology, 8*(2), 72–76.

Flannery-Schroeder, E., Choudhury, M. S., & Kendall, P. C. (2005, April). Group and individual cognitive-behavioral treatments for youth with anxiety disorders: 1-year follow-up. *Cognitive Therapy and Research, 29*(2), 253–259.

Gallo, F. P., & Vincenzi, H. (2000). *Energy tapping: How to rapidly eliminate anxiety, depression, cravings, and more using energy psychology*. Oakland, CA: New Harbinger.

Gazzaniga, M. S. (2005). *The ethical brain*. Washington, DC: Dana Press.

Gendlin, E. T. (1996). *Focusing-oriented psychotherapy: A manual of the experiential method*. New York: Guilford Press.

Gendlin, E. T. (1981). *Focusing*. New York: Bantam.

Gladstone, G. L., Parker, G. B., Mitchell, P. B., Wilhelm, K. A., & Malhi, G. S. (2005). Relationship between self-reported childhood behavioral inhibition and lifetime anxiety disorders in a clinical sample. *Depression and Anxiety, 22*(3), 103–113.

Goodman, W. K., Bose, A., & Wang, Q. (2005). Treatment of generalized anxiety disorder with escitalopram: Pooled results from double-blind, placebo-controlled trials. *Journal of Affective Disorders, 87*(2-3), 161–167.

Goodwin, R. D., Lewinsohn, P. M., & Seeley, J. R. (2005). Cigarette smoking and panic attacks among young adults in the community: The role of parental smoking and anxiety disorders. *Biological Psychiatry, 58*(9), 686–693.

Gothelf, D., Rubinstein, M., Shemesh, E., Miller, O., Farbstein, I., & Klein, A., Weizman, A., Apter, A., Yaniv, A. & Isaac. (2005). Pilot study: Fluvoxamine treatment for depression and anxiety disorders in children and adolescents with cancer. *Journal of the American Academy of Child & Adolescent Psychiatry, 44*(12), 1258–1262.

Gray, J. A. (1995). The contents of consciousness: A neuropsychological conjecture. *Behavioral and Brain Sciences, 18*(4), 659–722.

Grillon, C. (2002). Startle reactivity and anxiety disorders: Aversive conditioning, context and neurobiology. *Biological Psychiatry, 52*, 958–975.

Grover, R. L., Ginsburg, G. S., & Ialongo, N. (2005, winter). Childhood predictors of anxiety symptoms: A longitudinal study. *Child Psychiatry & Human Development, 36*(2), 133–153.

Heim, C., Owens, M. J., Plotsky, P. M., & Nemeroff, C. B. (1997). The role of early adverse life events in the etiology of depression and posttraumatic stress disorder: Focus on corticotropin-releasing factor. In R. Yehuda & A. C. McFarlane (Eds.), *Psychobiology of posttraumatic stress disorder* (pp. 194–207). New York: Annals of the New York Academy of Sciences.

Herbert, J. D., Gaudiano, B. A., Rheingold, A. A., Myers, V. H., Dalrymple, K., & Nolan, E. M. (2005). Social skills training augments the effectiveness of cognitive behavioral group therapy for social anxiety disorder. *Behavior Therapy, 36*(2), 125–138.

Hofmann, S. G. (2005, July). Perception of control over anxiety mediates the relation between catastrophic thinking and social anxiety in social phobia. *Behav Res Ther., 43*(7), 885–95.

Hsu, M., Bhatt, M., Adolphs, R., Tranel, D., & Camerer, C. F. (2005, December). Neural systems responding to degrees of uncertainty in human decision-making. *Science, 310*(5754), 1624–1625.

Jhou, T. (2005). Neural mechanisms of freezing and passive aversive behaviors. *Journal of Comparative Neurology, 493*(1), 111–114.

Kabat-Zinn, J. (1991). *Full catastrophe living: Using the wisdom of your body and mind to face stress, pain and illness*. New York: Dell.

Kent, J. M., Coplan, J. D., Mawlawi, O., Martinez, J. M., Browne, S. T., Slifstein, M., Martinez, D., Abi-Dargham, A., Laruelle, M., & Gorman, J. M. (2005). Prediction of panic response to a respiratory stimulant by reduced orbitofrontal cerebral blood flow in panic disorder. *American Journal of Psychiatry, 162*(7), 1379–1381.

Kent, J., Mathew, S. J., & Gorman, J. M. (2002). Molecular targets in the treatment of anxiety. *Biogical Psychiatry, 52,* 1008–1030.

Kessler, R. C., Chiu, W. T., Demler, M. A., Walters, E. E (June, 2005). Prevalence, severity, and comorbidity of 12-month DSM-IV disorders in the National Comorbidity Survey Replication. *Archives of General Psychiatry, 62,* 617–627.

Klinger, E., Bouchard, S., Legeron, P., Roy, S., Lauer, F., Chemin, I., et al. (2005, February). Virtual reality therapy versus cognitive behavior therapy for social phobia: A preliminary controlled study. *Cyberpsychology & Behavior, 8*(1), 76–88.

Korn, M. & Pollack, R. (2002). *New findings in serotonin: Basic science and clinical aspects*. Retrieved June 2003, from http://www.medscape.com/viewprogram/1973_pnt.

Kosfeld, M., Heinrichs, M., Zak, P. J., Fischbacher, U., & Fehr, E. (2005). Oxytocin increases trust in humans. *Nature, 435*(7042), 673–676.

Kushner, M. G., Abrams, K., Thuras, P., Hanson, K. L., Brekke, M., & Sletten, S. (2005, August). Follow-up study of anxiety disorder and alcohol dependence in comorbid alcoholism treatment patients. *Alcoholism: Clinical and Experimental Research, 29*(8), 1432–1443.

Labar, K. S., & Cabeza, R. (2006). Cognitive neuroscience of emotional memory. *Nature Reviews Neuroscience, 7*(1), 54–64.

Lambrou, P., & Pratt, G. (2000). *Instant emotional healing: Acupressure for the emotions*. New York: Broadway Books.

Lancer, R. (2005). The effect of aerobic exercise on obsessive compulsive disorder, anxiety, and depression. *Dissertation Abstracts International: Section B: The Sciences and Engineering, 66*(1-B), 599.

Leibenluft, E., M.D. (Ed.). (1999). *Gender differences in mood and anxiety disorders: From bench to bedside*. Washington, DC: American Psychiatric Press.

Libby, A. M., Orton, H. D., Novins, D. K., Beals, J., & Manson, S. M. (2005, March). Childhood physical and sexual abuse and subsequent depressive and anxiety disorders for two American Indian tribes. *Psychological Medicine, 35*(3), 329–340.

Lobaugh, N. J., Gibson, E., & Taylor, M. J. (2006). Children recruit distinct neural systems for implicit emotional face processing. *Neuroreport, 17*(2), 215–219.

Lonegan, C., & Phillips, B. (2001). Temperamental influence on the development of anxiety disorders. In M. W. Vasey & M. R. Dadds (Eds.), *The developmental psychopathology of anxiety* (pp. 60–91). New York: Oxford.

Lyneham, H. J., & Rapee, R. M. (2005). Evaluation and treatment of anxiety disorders in the general pediatric population: A clinician's guide. *Child and Adolescent Psychiatric Clinics of North America, 14*(4), 845–861.

Manger, T. A., & Motta, R. W. (2005, winter). The impact of an exercise program on posttraumatic stress disorder, anxiety, and depression. *International Journal of Emergency Mental Health, 7*(1), 49–57.

Maron, E., Kuikka, J., Ulst, K., Tiihonen, J., Vasar, V., & Shilk, J. (2004). SPECT imaging of serotonin transporter binding in patients with generalized anxiety disorder. *World Journal of Biological Psychiatry, 5*(1), 137.

McClernon, J. F., Beckham, J. C., Mozley, S. L., Feldman, M. E., Vrana, S. R., & Rose, J. E. (2005, February). The effects of trauma recall on smoking topography in posttraumatic stress disorder and non-posttraumatic stress disorder trauma survivors. *Addictive behaviors, 30*(2), 247–257.

McEwen, B. S., Olie, J. P. (2005). Neurobiology of mood, anxiety, and emotions as revealed by studies of a unique antidepressant: tianeptine. *Molecular Psychiatry,* 10(6), 525–37

McEwen, B., & Margarinos, A. (1997). Stress effects on morphology and function of the hippocampus. In R. Yehuda & A. C.McFarlane (Eds.), *Psychobiology of posttraumatic stress disorder* (pp. 271–284). New York: Annals of the New York Academy of Sciences.

McMullin, R. (2000). *The new handbook of cognitive therapy techniques.* New York: W. W. Norton.

McNally, R. J. (2002). Anxiety sensitivity and panic disorder. *Biological Psychiatry, 52,* 938–946.

Mellman, T. A. (1997). Psychobiology of sleep disturbances in posttraumatic stress disorder. In R. Yehuda & A. C. McFarlane (Eds.), *Psychobiology of posttraumatic stress disorder* (pp. 142–149). New York: Annals of the New York Academy of Sciences.

Middeldorp, C. M., Cath, D. C., Van Dyck, R., & Boomsma, D. I. (2005). The comorbidity of anxiety and depression in the perspective of genetic epidemiology: A review of twin and family studies. *Psychological Medicine, 35*(5), 611–624.

Millon, T. (2000). *Personality disorders in modern life.* Hoboken, NJ: Wiley.

Morris, T. L. (2001). Social phobia. In M. W. Vasey & M. R. Dadds (Eds.), *The developmental psychopathology of anxiety* (pp. 435–458). New York: Oxford.

Murburg, M. (1997). The psychobiology of posttraumatic stress disorder: An overview. In R. Yehuda & A. C. McFarlane (Eds.), *Psychobiology of posttraumatic stress disorder* (pp. 352–358). New York: Annals of the New York Academy of Sciences.

National Institute of Mental Health. (2006). Facts about anxiety disorders. Retrieved March, 2006, from http://www.nimh.nih.gov/publicat/adfacts.cfm

Nemeroff (1998, June). The neurobiology of depression. *Scientific American.* Retrieved from www.lib.calpoly.edu/infocomp/modules/05_evaluate/WIC2b.html

Nhat Hanh, T. (1975). *The miracle of mindfulness.* Boston, MA: Beacon Press.

Ninan, P. T., Liebowitz, M., Dunlop, B., Feigan, S. (2005, June 30). Taming the anxious mind: How psychotherapy and medications transform the brain. Retrieved July, 2005 from http://www.medscape.com/viewarticle/50608A_1.

Northrup, C. (2001). *The wisdom of menopause*. New York: Bantam.

Papadimitriou, G. N., & Linkowski, P. (2005). Sleep disturbance in anxiety disorders. *International Review of Psychiatry, 17*(4), 229–236.

Pert, C. B. (1997). *Molecules of emotion: The science behind mind-body medicine*. New York: Touchstone.

Phan, K. L., Fitzgerald, D. A., Nathan, P. J., & Tancer, M. E. (2006). Association between amygdala hyperactivity to harsh faces and severity of social anxiety in generalized social phobia. *Biological Psychiatry, 59,* 424–429.

Phelps, S., & Austin, N. (1975). *The assertive woman*. San Luis Obispo, CA: Impact.

Pliszka, S. R. (2003). *Neuroscience for the mental health clinician*. New York: Guilford.

Rapee, R. (2001). The development of generalized anxiety. In M. W. Vasey & M. R. Dadds (Eds.), *The developmental psychopathology of anxiety* (pp. 481–504). New York: Oxford.

Rapee, R. (2002). The development and modification of temperamental risk for anxiety disorders: Prevention of a lifetime of anxiety. *Biological Psychiatry, 52,* 947–957.

Reiss, S., Silverman, W., & Weems, C. (2001). Anxiety sensitivity. In M. W. Vasey & M. R. Dadds (Eds.), *The developmental psychopathology of anxiety* (pp. 92–111). New York: Oxford.

Roffman, J. L., Marci, C. D., Glick, D. M., Dougherty, D. D., & Rauch, S. L. (2005). Neuroimaging and the functional neuroanatomy of psychotherapy. *Psychological Medicine, 35*(10), 1385–1398.

Rossi, E. L. (1993). *The psychobiology of mind-body healing: New concepts of therapeutic hypnosis*. New York: Norton.

Rothschild, B. (2000). *The body remembers: The psychophysiology of trauma and trauma treatment*. New York: Norton.

Rothschild, B. (2003). *The body remembers casebook: Unifying methods and models in the treatment of trauma and PTSD*. New York: Norton.

Ruscio, A. M. (2004). Experience and appraisal of worry among high worriers with and without generalized anxiety disorder. *Behaviour Research and Therapy, 42,* 1469–1482.

Samtorelli, S. (2002, July/August). Mindfulness and meditation. *Journal of Consulting and Clinical Psychology, 70*(2),

Schore, A. N. (2003). *Affect regulation and the repair of the self*. New York: Norton.

Schneier, F. R. (2005, October). Neurobiological mechanisms of social anxiety disorder. *CNS spectrums, 10*(10), 8–9.

Schwartz, J. M., Gulliford, E. Z., Stier, J., & Thienemann, M. (2005). Mindful awareness and self-directed neuroplasticity: Integrating psychospiritual and biological approaches to mental health with a focus on obsessive-compulsive disorder. In S. G. Mijares & G. S. Khalsa (Eds.), *The psychospiritual clinician's handbook: Alternative methods for understanding and treating mental disorders* (pp. 281–300). New York: Haworth Press.

Semple, R. J., Reid, E. F. G., & Miller, L. (2005, winter). Treating anxiety with mindfulness: An open trial of mindfulness training for anxious children. *Journal of Cognitive Psychotherapy, 19*(4), 379–392.

Shapiro, F. (2001). *Eye movement desensitization and reprocessing: Basic principles, protocols, and procedures* (2nd ed.). New York: Guilford Press.

Shekhar, A., Truitt, W., Rainnie, D., & Sajdyk, T. (2005, December). Role of stress, corticotrophin releasing factor (CRF) and amygdala plasticity in chronic anxiety. *Stress, 8*(4), 209–219.

Siegel, D. J. (1999). *The developing mind: Toward a neurobiology of interpersonal experience.* New York: Guilford.

Siegel, D. J., & Hartzell, M. (2003). *Parenting from the inside out: How a deeper self-understanding can help you raise children who thrive.* New York: Penguin Putnam.

Siegman, A. W. & Smith, T. (1994). *Anger, hostility, and the heart.* Hillsdale, NJ: Lawrence Erlbaum Associates.

Sobel, D., & Ornstein, R. (1996). Good humor good health. *Mind/body Newsletter, 6*(1), 3–6.

Southwick, S. M., Morgan III, C. A., Bremner, A. D., Grillon, C. G., Krystal, J. H., Nagy, L. M., & Charney, D. S. (1997). Noradrenergic alternations in posttraumatic stress disorder. In R. Yehuda & A. C. McFarlane (Eds.), *Psychobiology of posttraumatic stress disorder* (pp. 125–141). New York: Annals of the New York Academy of Sciences.

Stanley, M. A., Hopko, D. R., Diefenbach, G. J. et. al. (2003) Cognitive-behavior therapy for late-life generalized anxiety in primary care: Preliminary findings. *American Journal of Geriatric Psychiatry 11*(1): 92–96.

Stein, M. B., Hanna, C., Koverola, C., Torchia, M., & McClarty, B. (1997). Structural brain changes in PTSD: Does trauma alter neurochemistry? In R. Yehuda & A. C. McFarlane (Eds.), *Psychobiology of posttraumatic stress disorder* (pp. 76–82). New York: Annals of the New York Academy of Sciences.

Stickgold, R. (2005). Sleep-dependent memory consolidation. *Nature, 437,* 1272–1278.

Talbott, S. (2002). *The cortisol connection: Why stress makes you fat and ruins your health—and what you can do about it.* Alameda, CA: Hunter House.

Teicher, M. H., Ito, Y., Glod, C. A., Andersen, S. L., Dumont, N., Ackerman, E. (1997). Preliminary evidence for abnormal cortical development in physically and sexually abused children using EEG coherence and MRI. In R. Yehuda & A. C. McFarlane (Eds.), *Psychobiology of posttraumatic stress disorder* (pp. 160–175). New York: Annals of the New York Academy of Sciences.

Thomas, A., M.D. (1977). *Temperament and development.* New York: Brunner Mazel.

van der Kolk, B. A., Burbridge, J. A., & Suzuki, J. (1997). The psychobiology of traumatic memory. Clinical implications of neuroimaging studies. In R. Yehuda & A. C. McFarlane (Eds.), *Psychobiology of posttraumatic stress disorder* (pp. 99–113). New York: Annals of the New York Academy of Sciences.

van der Kolk, B. A., McFarlane, A. C., & Weisaeth, L. (Eds.). (1996). *Traumatic stress: The effects of overwhelming experience on mind, body, and society.* New York: Guilford.

Vasey, M. W., & Dadds, M. R. (Eds.). (2001). *The developmental psychopathology of anxiety.* New York: Oxford.

Vasile, R. G., Bruce, S. E., Goisman, R. M., Pagano, M., & Keller, M. B. (2005). Results of a naturalistic longitudinal study of benzodiazepine and SSRI use in the treatment of generalized anxiety disorder and social phobia. *Depression and Anxiety, 22*(2), 59–67.

Verster, J. C., Volkerts, E. R. (2004, spring). Clinical pharmacology, clinical efficacy, and behavioral toxicity of alprazolam: A review of the literature. *CNS Drug Reiews, 10*(1), 45–76.

Walsh, A. (2004). *Why do they act that way?* New York: Free Press.

Winston, J. S., Strange, B. A., O'Doherty, J., & Dolan, R. J. (2002). Automatic and intentional brain responses during evaluation of trustworthiness of faces. *Nature Neuroscience, 5*(3), 277–283.

Witek, M. W., Rojas, V., Alonso, C., Minami, H., & Silva, R. R. (2005). Review of benzodiazepine use in children and adolescents. *The Psychiatric Quarterly, 76*(3), 283–296.

Yehuda, R. (1997). Sensitization of the hypothalamic-pituitary-adrenal axis in posttraumatic stress disorder. In R. Yehuda & A. C. McFarlane (Eds.), *Psychobiology of posttraumatic stress disorder* (pp. 57–75). New York: Annals of the New York Academy of Sciences.

Zvolensky, M. J., Feldner, M. T., Leen-Feldner, E. W., Gibson, L. E., Abrams, K., & Gregor, K. (2005a, December). Acute nicotine withdrawal symptoms and anxious responding to bodily sensations: A test of incremental predictive validity among young adult regular smokers. *Behaviour Research and Therapy, 43*(12), 1683–1700.

Zvolensky, M. J., Schmidt, N. B., Antony, M. M., McCabe, R. E., Forsyth, J. P., & Feldner, M. T., et al. (2005b). Evaluating the role of panic disorder in emotional sensitivity processes involved with smoking. *Journal of Anxiety Disorders, 1996,* 673–686.

INDEX

265